Nothing **Short** of a Miracle

*A true story of faith, family,
community, and perseverance*

Lisa Short

Nothing Short of a Miracle

Copyright © 2020 by Lisa K. Short
Printed Book ISBN—9781702323352
Printed in the United States of America
First Print Date, April 2020

Cover photo by Jodi Short

All rights reserved. Without limiting the right under copyright reserved above, no part of this publication may be reproduced, stored in or introduced into a retrieval system, or transmitted, in any form, or by any means (electronic, mechanical, photocopying, recording, or otherwise) without the prior written permission of the copyright owner. The only exception is by a reviewer, who may quote short excerpts in a review.

CONTENTS

Acknowledgements v

Zach's Words ix

Foreword.. xi

Prologue xiii

1. This is Us 1
2. October 25th 2014 9
3. The Third Day 33
4. Letting Go 39
5. Amazing Grace! 51
6. Coping with the News 61
7. Moving On 67
8. Signs from God 85
9. Waking Up 95
10. The Hobbit 103
11. Facing Facts 111
12. Believe 121

13. The Emerald City 127

14. Testing Our Patience 137

15. Breaking Down 153

16. Feeling the Love 169

17. One Moment in Time 181

18. Rehab 199

19. Going Home 215

20. Reality Sets In 221

21. Gotta Keep Your Head Up 231

22. Walking On 241

23. Blinded by the Limelight 253

24. Time Helps Heal the Wounds 261

Epilogue 273

News and Publications 274

ACKNOWLEDGEMENTS

It's hard to acknowledge the countless friends, family, and community members who deserve more than we can ever begin to repay for their generous, compassionate hearts. Just the word "Thank you" doesn't even come close to expressing the appreciation that I and my family would like to convey. There were so many people who showed up in big ways to support Zach and his family. Many were people who didn't want recognition, and others we didn't even know. I wish I could list all of those each by name who served, prayed, donated, cared, etc. Every one of you made an impact on our hearts and in our lives.

If it weren't for my friend Shelly, who had printed into a book all of my Facebook posts and comments from the time of Zach's accident through the first year following, I don't know if I could have written this book. It became my detailed journal complete with dates, pictures, and everything I needed to get the story chronologically accurate. Thank you, Shelly, for doing that for me! I didn't know it was even possible.

I want to recognize and thank Lori, Nancy, Sandy, Alex, Jill, Skylar, Shelbey, and Sheree who planned, organized, and carried out extremely successful fund raisers (mentioned in this book) on Zach's behalf. Among them, they spearheaded several different undertakings that required a great deal of time and energy. We will never forget the efforts put into bringing these projects to life. The contributions that people made greatly relieved financial hardship for Zach, his family, and Chris and me, giving us all room to breathe and recover. We can't thank you enough, but we will pay it forward whenever we are able to do so.

Our prayer warrior list could go on for pages. There's one whom I'd call our head cheerleader, though, and that was Connie. She was there as a first responder at the scene of Zach's accident, where she prayed over him and continued throughout our entire journey to hold us up with the strong conviction that Zach was going to heal and walk again. Your positive faith gave us strength, Connie.

Thanks to our friend Joy, who posted and circulated the story to the public, keeping them updated with Zach's progress and all his needs via Facebook. There is no doubt in my mind that because of her efforts to share daily news of our journey, our prayer chain grew rapidly, reaching out to hundreds of people far and wide, and contributed to saving Zach's life.

Wendy's and Jim's Country Style Chicken of Salina eagerly jumped on board to provide fundraising that was over the top. We are forever grateful to these places as well as Chuck's Bar and Grill and Southeast of Saline School, who generously opened their doors to let hundreds of people utilize their facilities for the amazing benefit auctions put on for Zach.

Jim and Sharon are held dearly in our hearts for coming through in our time of need, providing us not only with a place to stay during Zach's hospitalization in Wichita, but also with all the comforts that made It feel like home. The two of you just will never know how much we appreciate what you did for us.

Speaking of making it feel like home, the many caring, talented people who helped make Zach and Jodi's house handicap accessible were a Godsend, with Jim, Matt, Larry, Kenny, Mike, Dale, Matthew, Koffman Electric and the Ambucs at the top of the list. Thank you all for the labor and time added on top of your busy work schedules to make it easier for Zach to maneuver in his own home.

Trinity United Methodist Church supported us with their cards, prayers, gifts, and caring hearts all along the way. It is the best feeling ever to know that they are there for us just like family. The members there don't just talk the talk—they walk the walk.

What would life be for Zach today had it not been for the outstanding work of two surgeons, Dr. Robert Bingaman and Dr. Amy Moore? That thought crosses our minds every time we see Zach successfully living his life. God surely had a hand in leading us to them—we firmly believe that. Everything worked out exactly according to His plan and we thank Him every day for answering our prayers by working through you two! And the nurses and staff of Salina Regional Health Center, St. Francis Via Christi Hospital in Wichita, and Barnes Jewish Hospital in St Louis were blessings as well, always professionally doing their jobs to make sure Zach was well cared for. Some became lifetime friends who are dear to our hearts. The KU Rehab Center in Kansas City was WONDERFUL and had Zach up and moving faster than we ever imagined. The home health nurses who came once Zach was finally able to go home were another Godsend. A huge thank you goes out to Steve Peeples, prosthetist and owner of Peeple's Prosthetics in Wichita; there are just not enough words to express the work this man has done for Zach. He has been a coach, a cheerleader, a doctor, a motivational inspiration, and a friend to Zach. His efforts to get Zach up and walking went far beyond what anyone else could have ever done. Because of Steve, Zach is back doing what he loves: living his life. How can that kind of gift ever be repaid? It is priceless!

Lastly but certainly not least (quite the opposite!), I want to express my gratitude for God. I can barely type out the words because it's hard to see through my tears—my heart is overwhelmed with joy and thankfulness for the fact that He gave back my son. There is no feeling in the world that compares to losing a child and then having him returned to you. There is no greater feeling in the world than knowing the love of God and all He does. Thank you, God! My heart is forever yours.

~Lisa Short

ZACH'S WORDS

This is definitely not how I imagined my future, but there's nothing I can do but to make the best of the whole situation. I may not understand why this happened like it did, but I just have to trust that God always has a plan—He's always in control. My prayers are still being answered. I thank God for letting me live and for all the healing He's provided. I feel very blessed to have the supportive friends and family that I do. They have always been there for me. All the people's kind acts, words and donations have been amazing and helped us get through this journey. I'm definitely thankful for that! I owe so much to my burn nurses, doctors, and others. I would never have overcome what I did without them.

I have sure been through a lot and also learned a lot since the day of my accident. When I'm having a bad day, I look back and think about how much worse things could have been. All of the mental and physical pain I went through has made me a stronger person. I prayed and prayed to God, to help me and to make life easier again—and He answered! Not only that, but I've been blessed with opportunities and experiences that I would never have had prior to my accident.

I've learned that the obstacles in my life are only as big as I let my mind view them. My life has changed forever, but I'm thankful I'm still here. I was on my death bed with horrible chances to survive, but with many answered prayers and more support than anyone could ask for, I pulled through. God is good!

FOREWORD

"Lisa, when this is all said and done and things are back to a relative normal, you need to tell your story to others. You are such an inspiration and your words could bring hope to so many."

"Thank you for sharing and for your ongoing personal witnessing to God's unbounded love for us. Amidst all of this, He has given you a voice to speak to us."

"Thanks for your journals, Lisa. I can see how it helps you and you will never know how it is helping us, your readers."

"I see a book in your future. You write beautifully and we all get captured in every update. What a beautiful illustration of God's love and protection. You are not weak—you are a momma!"

"Wow, Lisa! Your words are beautiful and help all of us, your readers, stay updated and grow in our faith. Thank you!"

These were some of the comments I received on Facebook from friends, family, and my community regarding my posts about my son's horrific farm accident. The journey through miraculous events that followed was a path we all went down together one day at a time. Some days we clung to a thread of hope and others we were rejoicing with happy tears and praises. It was as if God loaded us all up on a boat that sailed into a raging storm, tossing us this way and that, but along the way there were also beautiful rainbows.

So many people wanted me to write the story—and how could I not? It's an amazing story. I want my grandkids to know and understand what their mother and father went through. I want to share it with others too, because it might provide hope to those who have given up in times of despair or lost faith for their futures.

It's a powerful testimony of how present God is in our lives today. Maybe it could even help non-believers discover God in their own lives. The problem I had was making myself do it. To tell the story well, I knew that I would have to revisit the painful memories in order to express what I and my family experienced.

It wasn't until three years later that I felt I was ready. I got the push I needed to get started when I went to visit a counselor who agreed with me that writing the story would require a lot of mental energy and time, but that it would bring healing to me and my readers. As it turned out, she was right. As I reenacted the scenes and conversations of the story in my mind, typed them out and then read what I had written, I gained new perspectives that I hadn't seen before. I had a better understanding of reactions and behaviors within the aftermath of the accident. I developed a compassion and forgiveness that helped me move on.

This journey was powerful enough to change lives. I hope that by sharing it with you, it will make a difference in your life journey as well.

Lisa Short

PROLOGUE

It was a beautiful fall day in Kansas. The milo was headed out in rich colors of rust, orange, and red. The corn fields had already been cut, leaving the dry stalks behind to blow in the wind. It was October 25, 2014, and the day was buzzing with farmers in fields all over the county taking advantage of the perfect weather to bring in the remaining crops of the season. For my family, it was another day to get out and harvest soybeans and plant wheat. The hours of harvest are long, but there is great satisfaction in seeing the results of our labor. That Autumn day will forever be etched in our memories....

1

THIS IS US

Fall is a busy time for my family. It takes every one of us to keep all the balls in the air when things gear up. Most years we'll have fields needing to be worked, wheat to plant, crops to harvest, and hay to bale, all at the same time. Things need to be taken care of in a timely manner when they are ready. One day of bad weather can come in and change the whole outcome, so we race the clock, hope for sunny days, and work like crazy to get it all done.

Each of us has a job that we have become comfortable with and enjoy doing. My oldest son Matthew plants wheat with the no till planter, a piece of equipment that sows seed into ground that hasn't been tilled.

For the fields that do get tilled before planting, I drive a tractor pulling an implement called a field cultivator. It works up the soil to pull out the weeds and break up clods of dirt to prepare the field for planting, which is what my husband Chris does. He plants wheat seed with the conventional drill. As soon as I pull out of a field I've finished cultivating, he pulls in and plants.

The youngest of our three kids is our son Zach. He has had his share of working ground and planting, but most recently had taken on the responsibility of running the crew that harvests milo and soybeans.

I enjoy my job cultivating. Sometimes it can be tiring sitting for long hours bumping up and down, but I have to say, it is awesome getting to drive that tractor! I take along my snacks and books on CDs and go around and around pulling the cultivator that combs the dark soil so smoothly that it makes me feel like I'm frosting a huge cake.

Chris scolds me from time to time for listening to my stories on CDs. He tells me that I'm not going to be able to hear things that are wrong with the tractor if I'm not paying attention to the sounds it's making, but honestly, I wouldn't know what sounds wrong anyway! He has a mechanic's ear for things like that and expects me to hear the same things he would, but I just don't have that capability. I do know, however, that I can always depend on him to fix whatever goes wrong if something does break down. He can repair just about anything.

I love getting to feel like I'm contributing to the farming efforts. It is also very satisfying to be out there with Chris and the boys. What other job would allow a gal to spend time with her family, all working together in the outdoors? I am truly blessed.

Kind of ironic considering I grew up in the suburbs of Denver, Colorado. I was removed from farm life just about as far as I could be, but I did always love the *Little House on the Prairie* stories. Somehow, I think I sort of manifested them into my own life. I fell in love with small town living and farm life after my parents moved back to Kansas to be near their aging parents.

I was a junior in high school when I met Chris—my Michael Landon (a TV actor who played "Pa" on the *Little House on the Prairie*), my strong, good-looking, hardworking farmer. We dated for four years, then were married in 1982. He farmed and I worked in a salon as a hairdresser. We had three kids and enjoyed watching them grow up on the same farm where Chris was raised.

There was always so much to keep them all entertained in the outdoors, although probably more so for the boys than for Kelsey, our oldest. She loved playing with the cats, building tree houses, and swimming in the stock tank or nearby river with her brothers, but she opted out of jumping hills on motorcycles in the cattle pens and going hunting in the pastures. When she became old enough, she drove a tractor when we were short of help. She didn't have the same love of farming in her blood that the boys seemed to be born with. Driving the tractor was more like punishment to her, but it earned her a little spending money, which she liked. Kelsey preferred to stay inside or spend time with her friends, but when it was time to harvest wheat in the summer, even she enjoyed being around for that part of farming.

Wheat harvest was a time of year when everything else—sports, vacations, camping, play time—was put on the back burner. For us, it is a nonstop marathon from start to finish, a time when meals are eaten in the fields. When the kids were young, they rode in the combines and along in the semis to the grain elevators, where they sometimes got to have a coke and candy bar and jump in the grain trailers to play in the freshly cut wheat. Sometimes cousins and friends came to visit and be a part of that busy time. It made for special memories.

When the boys were as young as eight years old, they were already driving equipment, which is not unusual for farm kids. They loved helping in the fields with their dad and all the hired men during wheat harvest. They felt so important chattering on CB radios to keep in communication as they worked together. It was fun to hear the crew banter with each other to pass the hours. At times the playful dialogs got a little too carried away for young ears, as far as their mother was concerned, but after a good scolding to the guys from my radio base in the kitchen, things usually tamed down and became more appropriate.

The crew was sometimes surprised that I had been listening in on their conversations. The constant chatter all day while I prepared the meals didn't usually interest me, but every now and then, my radar picked up on talk that I didn't want my boys to be part of. At that time before cell phones, it was the only way for me to keep in touch with their location so that I could deliver the noon and evening meals.

Serving meals twice a day to twelve ornery males at harvest time had its moments, but I could usually keep up with the best of them. I remember a day when one of the combine drivers decided he wanted to have a little fun while I was packing up from serving lunch. He swung his auger out over my car, spilling wheat on it like an ice storm, and laughed as he drove away. Because my hatch back was still open, wheat found its way into all my dishes and leftovers.

"He thinks he's so funny," I thought, as I painstakingly plucked dusty wheat kernels from my casserole dishes. "If he wants wheat in his food, that's what he's going to get!"

That same evening when I took out sandwiches, I made sure that this particular combine driver had the "special sandwich" I'd prepared just for him—one that met his daily dose of fiber. I sprinkled whole wheat kernels between the layers of meat and got great satisfaction when I watched him bite into my version of revenge. His eyes widened at first but then he smiled and continued to chew, making a loud crunching noise while the expression on his face said, "I probably deserve this." To my surprise, he finished the whole sandwich—wheat and all. That was the day that the men learned not to mess around with the cook.

Because Matthew and Zach were so young when they took part and helped with harvest, I was concerned that they were spending too many hours out in the field. Their peers were free to play baseball, go to the swimming pool and do all the summer activities that kids do, yet there were my boys spending literally ten to twelve hours a day working with the crew. Matthew and Zach *wanted* to spend their time that way. If they weren't in the fields with their dad, they felt they were missing out.

To ease my guilt and make things a little more special for them, I would fill small coolers with treats that they didn't often get, like cans of pop and candy bars and licorice. I would hand them out to the boys after I served lunch to all the harvesters. The crew gave me a hard time, asking where their coolers were, threatening to take them from the boys, who carried a sense of privilege for getting to have them.

After complaints that Zach was bouncing off the combine cab walls from sugar hyperactivity, the mother in me said it was time to start being more concerned about their health than their sweets desires, so the contents of their coolers changed to more sensible things like juice drinks, beef jerky, and granola bars.

Harvest is always such a big event in our family. We don't only harvest our own crops, but local area farmers' crops as well. We average about two weeks of cutting wheat in the summer and several weeks in the fall to cut soybeans, milo, and corn. It's a big job and it has been great having our boys carry on the farming tradition in our family. In fact, they are the fifth generation of Shorts to work on the Short farm. They decided early in their lives that they wanted to make farming their careers, and we have all worked together to make that happen.

Matthew went to Hutchinson Community College to learn farm management and diesel mechanics, and then on to Kansas State University, where he pursued agronomy, which is basically the study of soil and plant science used in crop production. His education put him in a good position to be the one to run the field sprayer and do the planting.

Zach studied farm management and diesel mechanics at Hutchinson Community College as well. That's where he met Jodi, his sweetheart, who shortly after college graduation became his wife. He, like Matthew, moved back to pursue his dreams of farming in the rural community of Assaria, Kansas, where we live. It was about that time when Chris handed over to Zach the responsibility of managing the custom cutting harvest crew. Having Zach take that on freed up Chris and Matthew to get planting done, and Chris knew Zach could handle the task. That job was a good fit for him.

Whether Zach knew it or not, he was a natural leader, something Chris and I came to realize early as he was growing up. He was observant, mature, responsible, and self-motivated, yet he was fun and playful with a touch of orneriness. His naïve sense of humor made people laugh and he was popular with his peers, yet he never took on an attitude of being better than anyone else— he was sensitive about respecting other's feelings. He was an "old soul," some people would say.

In high school, Zach had a smooth way of getting his peers to fall in line without looking like he was a teacher's pet. His wood shop instructor said that he was grateful to have Zach in his class because Zach would help get the unruly boys to stop their rowdy behavior and pay attention— something his FFA teacher valued as well. She said that she so appreciated his help in assisting students with welding and other technical hands-on skills he was familiar with.

Even as young as grade school, when I was his assistant Boy Scout leader, I saw Zach exhibit leadership skills when he took on the role of patrol leader. Before he was even voted into the position, he started taking charge of his troop during the times he felt that he could make a difference with keeping order.

Zach never missed a detail when something was out of place at harvest time. "Uuh, Mr. Gies, you forgot to fold in your auger," he said over the radio, seeing something in need of correction.

Mr. Gies had been Zach's junior high school English teacher just a few years back and admitted how silly he felt having to be corrected so often by his young former student.

"But he was right!" said Mr. Gies. "He'd catch things I was doing wrong and wasn't afraid to tell me. I appreciated his help."

In Mr. Gies's defense, it was his first time learning to drive the grain cart for our crew—something new to him, but something Zach had several years of practice with.

Every new crew member gets the job of driving the grain cart, a huge wagon that is pulled behind a tractor. The driver must master the skill of driving alongside the moving combines, matching his speed to theirs, as they unload their bins through a swing-out auger (a long, arm-type tube) into the cart while the combine continues to cut. When the grain cart is full, the driver pulls it to the road where the semis are waiting to be loaded. The grain cart driver then unloads his bin into the semis via his swing auger, and then folds it up and races back to the field to find the next combine with a full load.

2

OCTOBER 25TH 2014

*E*veryone was eager to get in a full day's work. Chris was finishing up some planting in a field with Jason's assistance, a farm employee who was a classmate of Zach's. They had grown up together and been friends since preschool.

Matthew was in another field planting wheat and Zach was getting the harvest crew together to cut soybeans.

That day, there were only three guys planning to work the soybean harvest with Zach. There was Lucas, a friend of Matthew's who grew up on a farm and helped drive semis when we needed him. There was John, a longtime family friend who wasn't a usual crew member but had offered to help if we ever needed him, which was perfect because he had a lot of experience running equipment since he's a farmer himself. Lastly, there was Les, a longtime employee at our farm.

Les is someone who I could probably write another book about, but in short, he is a very interesting and eccentric guy with a soft heart (he hides) and genius mind, who can repair just about anything. To me, he looks like he walked straight out of an old western cowboy movie. He's tall with long legs and a lean physique. Even though he's in his sixties, his hair is still light blond and he wears an unkempt, long beard and mustache. He's not appreciated nearly enough by the average person because he comes across a little—well—unique. He is confident in whom he is and really doesn't care what anyone else thinks about him or his opinions. He speaks his mind and sometimes it can be hard to follow his thought process.

One thing Les is infamous for around our shop is telling about his frustrations for things that he says are always disappearing from his house or work place. His favorite word to describe what happened is "Gone!" Not much more explanation than that, just simply "Gone." I always joke that when Les passes away some day, that would be the fitting thing to imprint on his headstone—"Gone!"

On that warm Saturday morning, Zach, Les, and Lucas had spent a good amount of time unplugging a combine header that was packed with soybeans and weeds from cutting the night before. Unplugging a combine header is a task nobody likes to do, especially when everyone is tired and it's dark—the reason why they put it off for the next day.

Once the guys unplugged the header, they continued the regular morning routine of greasing up the equipment and getting things ready to go. Afterwards they went to have lunch at Wendy's, giving the soybeans a little more time to dry so the moisture levels would be better for cutting. John had gone to the farm to get a semi so it would be ready for the driver to use. He brought it back and parked it in the same place they parked the previous night, which was along the road beside the field.

After lunch, everyone headed back to the field ready to go. Les and Zach each climbed into combines, Lucas walked to the semi, and John, who had the job as grain cart driver, hopped in the tractor with the large green grain cart hooked on behind. They'd barely even started cutting when John noticed smoke behind him.

"This is a brand-new tractor and grain cart, what could possibly be wrong?" John thought, before he anxiously called out on the radio: "Zach, I need a fire extinguisher. There's smoke coming from the hitch behind the tractor!" The fact that this was Chris's new equipment probably made John more conscientious of anything being damaged, causing him to react quickly.

Zach was across the field from John when he received the call for help. Trouble-shooting in his head for possible solutions, Zach thought about what could be wrong. The first thing that came to his mind was that it was probably a hydraulic leak that got hot and caught fire. Promptly, he drove his combine over to the service truck that was parked in another area of the field.

The service truck contains all the tools and things needed to repair equipment out in the field, sort of like a repair shop on wheels. Zach drove it up closer to where John and the grain cart were parked, and then swiftly continued on foot toward the smoke.

At the same time, Les was driving up closer in his combine from another area of the field. He too had heard John's call for help on the radio, and being a major mechanic for our farm, wanted to see for himself what was going on.

Instantly he spotted the problem. From Les's view, sitting high up on his combine seat, he had a clear vision of disaster, a situation of life and death! Les saw that the grain cart auger was extended and had caught on an overhead high voltage power line. He realized that the whole cart and tractor were deadly—an electrically charged catastrophe waiting to happen!

Les immediately stopped his combine. He threw open the door of his cab and screamed out, "No, no!! Stop!!! Zach!!!" but he couldn't yell loud enough to be heard over the noisy equipment. Zach was running toward the smoke and Les was unable to stop him.

From his view point of standing under the massive cart, Zach couldn't see anything unusual that would alert him to what was causing the problem. The smoke was growing. Quickly as possible, he needed to get to the other side for a better look. He wanted to jump over the hitch that connected the tractor to the cart, so he grabbed ahold of the cart's ladder to assist his leap when… ZZZZZAAAAAAPPPPPP!!!!! His left hand immediately clamped onto the steel ladder.

Stopped in mid-motion and unable to disengage his hand, Zach's whole body stood stiffly, shaking, locked on to the ladder, while immense jolts of power engulfed him. His eyes jutted wide open and the sound of the electricity pulsated loudly as it surged through and around him. Fire began shooting from his feet on the outside edges of his boots and out of his left shoulder. His body was literally frying from the enormous voltage.

Les, witnessing the horror, was running as fast as he could to get to Zach. The actively moving electricity began to spread and looked to him as though there were sparkly wires all over the tires of the grain cart. Les knew he couldn't touch anything or he too would be in the same situation. His heart raced, knowing he needed to act fast. "Plastic, plastic, something plastic!" The words reverberated through his mind as he frantically searched the bed of the service truck, looking for anything he could use to detach Zach.

This was an almost impossible task, trying to find something helpful in the service truck, as almost everything in there was made of steel, but as fate would have it, he spotted a shovel—a shovel with a plastic scoop and wooden and plastic handle. Quickly, he grabbed it and hurried toward Zach. He paused for an instant, watching and studying, quickly assessing the best plan of action. The fact that Les was a former Marine came in useful. He was trained to keep calm and think through things before acting. It was in his thoughts that he may have already been too late, but he had to do something.

Les realized that the electricity was surging in spurts, some stronger than others, so when it seemed that the surge lessened, he acted. Hooking the hip of the scoop part of the shovel behind Zach's neck, Les gave a quick, hard tug, successfully freeing Zach's hand from the ladder. Zach's back scraped against the hitch as he fell to the ground. He laid there lifeless with hot flames still burning on parts of his body. "He's dead," Les thought as he stood over Zach, stunned by what had just happened.

The fierce heat coming from the flames engulfing the tractor and grain cart snapped Les from his state of shock. He frantically grabbed Zach by the boots, dragging him away through the dirt. Crouching over the body, he patted out the flames on Zach's shoulder and left side. John came running over to assist. He helped Les carry Zach a safe distance away just before the melting power line above them came crashing to the ground.

Both were certain Zach was dead. He wasn't breathing, and they had witnessed something horrific that they were positive nobody could possibly live through. Then they heard a sound: "OOOMPH..." Zach let out a gasp that sounded as if he had been holding his breath for a long time and then finally released. He began twitching, squirmed a bit, and then struggled to get up!

Shocked with disbelief, John recovered and ordered, "Stay down, Zach. You've been badly hurt." Zach collapsed. Les dialed 911. The fire burned hotter.

Of all the fields we farm, we still thank God that this one was close to the city of Salina, a location where first responders and a hospital reside. An ambulance was quickly dispatched, sirens blaring, and help was on its way.

While John and Les stayed with Zach, Lucas acted quickly to move the semi and service truck away from the growing fire. The flames were so hot they had already melted the tarp on the semi parked nearby, and the fallen electrical wire arced and danced on the ground, a continuous threat to everyone in the vicinity.

First responder Shane Pearson arrived on the scene within minutes. Right away, he recognized Zach. It hadn't been that long since he'd been to Zach's house for an emergency call when Brynlee, Zach's young daughter, had a high temperature that led to a seizure. Assessing the situation, Shane was extremely surprised to see that Zach was conscious and struggling to sit up, laboring to breathe. Doing his best to make him calm, Shane coaxed Zach to lie back flat. Then he noticed the holes burned in the outside edges of Zach's boots where the electricity had exited. Intuitively, he perceived the critical nature of Zach's injuries. He radioed the hospital in Salina, telling them to immediately arrange for a helicopter transport to be ready when the ambulance arrived. He knew that because of the severity of the burns, Zach would need to be treated in Wichita, where there was a hospital with a burn unit.

Hastily preparing to check Zach's vitals, Shane asked, "Hey— I'm Shane. Do you remember me?" With eyes startling wide and a dazed expression on his face, Zach nodded almost imperceptibly and began to mumble gibberish between labored breaths.

Wanting to determine if Zach's mind was coherent, Shane proceeded to ask questions. "We're going to get you some help. Can you tell me what your name is?"

Zach looked confused, as if he were trying to understand what was going on, but to Shane's surprise, he gasped, "Zach."

Shane continued the questions: "Do you know your birth date?" Again, Zach gave the correct answer. He told Shane in a breathy whisper, "August third."

Shane was amazed that Zach was alive and cognitive, let alone able to answer questions and remember details. In his twenty-five years of experience as a first responder, he had seen injuries much less severe on patients who did not survive accidents of this magnitude. The vital signs were encouraging, but with Zach's extensive burns and labored breathing, Shane knew time was critical. Zach needed help fast.

More responders soon arrived and worked swiftly to load Zach into the ambulance. Shane, knowing that Zach was Chris's son, felt concern as to whether Chris had been contacted or not, so he took the opportunity to ask one more question: "Are you able to tell me where your dad is, Zach?" Miraculously, Zach showed that his short-term memory was still intact. He managed to get the words out: "Another field, planting wheat."

How was this possible?! How was it that Zach could even be alive after twelve thousand volts of electricity surged through his body for such a length of time? It was nothing short of a miracle that he was alive, conscious and able to speak, not to mention able to remember details like his birth date or what his dad was doing prior to all this happening!

Knowing they could lose him if his lungs were to swell shut, the emergency team began procedures to intubate Zach and quickly drove the short distance to Salina Regional Hospital. At that point, Shane and the rescue crew seriously doubted that things would end well for Zach.

I was at home catching up on neglected house work that Saturday. After being in the tractor for a week, it was so nice to finally have the time to do some laundry and cleaning. I remember being in my bedroom folding clothes on my bed when my cell phone rang. It was Chris. His voice sounded serious.

"Lisa, you need to call Jodi. Zach's been in an accident."

"What happened? Is he okay?" Having been through this before with Zach, I didn't panic but was afraid of what I was about to hear.

"I don't know. He was shocked. You need to call Jodi and go to the hospital. It's bad."

"Shocked?!" I asked, totally confused.

"I don't know what happened," he firmly replied. "You just need to call Jodi and get to the hospital."

My heart sank. I sensed the urgency in Chris's voice and knew there wasn't time to get into the details. We ended our call. "What in the world could have happened? How bad was it?" Visions flew through my mind; my heart was pounding. I immediately called Jodi but tried to sound as calm as possible so I wouldn't cause her to panic.

"Jodi, Chris just called and said that Zach's been in an accident. He doesn't know any details, but he said Zach's been shocked. He said it's bad and he's at the Salina hospital."

Like me, Jodi was caught completely off guard and sounded bewildered and stunned, "Is he okay?—Is he alive?—I don't know what to do! I just put Brynlee down for a nap."

Brynlee is our first grandbaby. She was thirteen months old at the time. Zach and Jodi had only been married three months when they found out they were expecting. They were not prepared for that news and were overwhelmed with the thought of a baby so soon, but Brynlee arrived in September of 2013, and she was as beautiful as could be. We were all in love at first sight!

"I don't know the details of how he is," I answered. "I'll call my mom to come and stay with Brynlee and then be down to get you right away."

Jodi and I raced up the interstate with so many questions on our minds. We had no idea what to expect or even what exactly happened. We were scared to death but tried hard not to let our thoughts get dark.

As we got closer to Salina, we saw a large black plume of smoke in the east, billowing up high in the air. "I think that's where they were working" I said. "I wonder if that fire is from the accident." Seeing that visual only made things worse.

Only about two weeks prior to that day, Jodi and I had been out walking with Brynlee in the stroller to get some exercise in our small town of Assaria. Jodi mentioned to me that she'd had a bad nightmare about Zach. She said she woke up crying because he had been hurt working on the farm. She didn't remember how he was hurt, but she cried and cried because she thought she would lose him. It felt so real to her.

I reassured her, "You don't have to worry. The guys have been farming a long time and they're careful. Nothing has ever happened in all these years."

I didn't say that just to ease her mind. It was true. In all the years that we've farmed, we have never had an event where someone was seriously hurt, but it appeared I would be eating my words.

Flash backs were popping into my head. This was not the first time for me to be racing to the hospital for Zach. As a kid he had so many injuries from accidents (not farm related), that one time when we were in the waiting room at the hospital, an employee began probing me with odd questions. At first, I thought she was a nurse or a clerk needing preliminary information to register Zach into the hospital. She sat down and questioned me about subjects that didn't sound like the normal questions a nurse or clerk would ask. I quickly figured out that she was a social worker, trying to learn what type of parents Chris and I were!

As offensive as that might have been, I had to admit that it probably did look like we could've been abusive parents. Who else visits the hospital so many times for injuries with the same child? Nine times to be exact! Five times were from injuries that resulted in concussions.

The accident that I felt most responsible for happened when Zach was three years old. He was playing with his toys on the kitchen floor while I was preparing supper. I had my hands covered in batter from breading chicken when I noticed a little button cell battery on the floor that must have come out of one of his toys. Looking back, I should've grabbed it right up, but I didn't. Instead I washed my hands off first. We didn't know back then that those little batteries could be fatal if swallowed. He'd just swallowed a penny not too long before that incident and the doctor said the only concern was it getting lodged in his throat and blocking his airway. X-rays showed that the penny went down okay and then he passed it, so I guess I wasn't as concerned about a tiny little battery because I knew it couldn't block his airway, but I still didn't want to risk him swallowing it.

While I was at the sink, I heard Zach make a hacking type noise and then he looked at me sort of guilty-like and said, "I swawowed it." I wasn't sure what "it" was, but I noticed the battery was gone. It didn't appear to be lodged in his throat, but I thought I'd better call the doctor anyway. I had an inner voice tell me a battery is much different than a penny, and I'd better find out what the doctor would say.

I was so surprised when the doctor told me to take Zach to the emergency room right away. I didn't realize things were *that* serious. I was told that the battery acid could eat a hole through his stomach or intestines and had to come out immediately.

Zach was admitted into the hospital where they inserted an IV into the back of his little hand to prepare for a scope surgery. His veins were so tiny that they had to attempt to get the needle in several times, but to my surprise, he didn't seem bothered too much by it. They took him to the operating room in a little red wagon. He didn't cry or seem scared at all. He was enjoying getting to ride in the wagon.

I, on the other hand, was distraught. He looked so tiny in that little blue and white hospital gown as he waved goodbye on his way down the hall, unaware of what he was about to go through. His innocent, big blue eyes framed by his light blonde hair caused my heart to sink as I waved back to him.

Doctors went into his throat with forceps and retrieved the battery. They took pictures which showed that the battery had already eaten into the lining of his stomach. Thank goodness it was caught early enough. The comment the doctor made at his follow up exam told us that he was aware of Zach's high energy when he said, "This little guy didn't need help from a battery. He's already charged."

Charged—my mind came back to the current situation. Here we were, some twenty-one years later, going through it again. He'd been "shocked," we were told. What we hadn't yet learned was that it happened with 12,000 volts of electricity! I have since learned that this amount is six times the level used to put criminals to death on death row. A human being can die from as little as 110 volts of alternating current. I thought that the days of seeing Zach injured were finally behind now that he was an adult. But this was worse than all of them put together.

Once Jodi and I entered the emergency entrance, we were taken back to a private waiting room where there were several young men gathered. I think they were friends of Zach. I didn't know all of them, but apparently, they'd heard the news and headed straight to the hospital. Nobody in the room seemed to know the exact details around the accident, but everyone looked so worried. I was hoping to learn more information from Chris, but he hadn't yet arrived. He was out in a field with only a tractor and no vehicle to drive, so he had to wait for Jason to come and get him.

As we sat waiting for medical personnel to come and talk to us, John, the friend who was driving the tractor that was pulling the grain cart, appeared in the door way. He looked as if he'd seen death. His face was pale and drawn, as if gravity were pulling his mouth, cheeks, and eyes downward. His left arm was hanging stiffly down his side with his hand shaking. He slumped as if he couldn't stand up straight. I asked him what had happened and he tried to speak, but he was overwhelmed with emotion. I could see he had something very wrong with him. "John, are you okay?" I asked. "Do you need to be seen by a doc..." He cut me off and croaked as if he were out of breath, "I'm okay, it's not about me. It's all about Zach—he......." John choked up and could no longer speak. He left the doorway, breaking down in tears.

A hospital worker came just then to tell us that Zach was being prepared for transport to Saint Francis Via Christi Hospital in Wichita. He said that Zach was badly burned and that the Wichita burn unit was where he would get the best intensive care for his needs. He then told us that we would get the chance to see Zach before they took him away.

It wasn't long before Zach was brought down the hall on a gurney and wheeled into a little side room with a curtain drawn. My daughter, Kelsey, arrived just in time to join Jodi and me as we took our first look at him. Zach's body was wrapped in a foil bag with only his face visible. He had a tube down his throat and an oxygen mask on his face. He was out cold. We could smell the pungent odor of burnt hair and flesh, something we'll never forget. His face didn't appear to be burned. He looked as if he were resting comfortably.

"I love you, Zach. You're going to be okay," Jodi whispered through tears streaming down her face.

My mind was in a state of denial and I was trying to be strong and positive when I told him, "We'll see you in Wichita, Zach. I love you." Then they rolled him away.

Chris and Jason made it to the hospital just as a crew was getting ready to transport Zach with the Life Watch helicopter. It's not normal procedure, but believing that it was most likely the last time that Chris would see his son alive, the transport crew allowed him to go up with them to the roof. There, they hustled to get Zach situated so the helicopter could lift off into the sky. Chris stood, watching in disbelief, heartbroken.

By that time, Jodi and I were in the parking lot headed to my car. We could hear the chopper's engine and the blades cutting the wind as it rose into view.

My first instinct was to grab my phone camera. It seemed almost morbid for me to be snapping photos. This was not like taking pictures of Zach at a sporting event. It was a sad and horrific moment, but still I was compelled to do it anyway. I told Jodi, "If Zach gets through this, he is going to want to see these." I took a couple photos and then while I still had my phone out, the thought immediately came to me that he needed prayers.

I'd never been one to post much on Facebook except maybe to share occasional photos of my two grandkids, but I knew social media would be the most effective and quickest way to get the word out there. With shaking hands, I typed out the words: "Please pray for my son Zach. He's being flown to Via Christi for burns from a farm accident. Please pray." Jodi did the same on her phone. We jumped in the car and tearfully headed home.

It was hard to know what and how much to pack into a suitcase. When a person is in a panic, it's hard to think straight at all. The only thing on my mind was that we had to get to Wichita as soon as possible. Jodi had even more to contend with. She had to pack for herself and for Brynlee as well. When a child is only thirteen months old, there are so many things to take into consideration: the bottles, diapers, pacifiers, stroller, blankets, baby food. And who knew how many days we needed to pack for? Nevertheless, she was ready by the time Chris and I drove to the farm to pick her and her daughter up. The hour drive to Wichita is still a blur in my mind.

The Facebook messages Jodi and I sent out had served us well. By the time we arrived in Wichita, our phones were lit up with comments. People in our community of Assaria and Salina had heard the breaking news on the radio of a young man being electrically burned in a farm accident. What they didn't know was who it was until they put it together with our solicitations for prayers for Zach.

Because the huge burning tires on the tractor and grain cart had emitted such a deep black plume of smoke that billowed way up high in the sky, people from miles away could see the accident site. Once they knew what was going on and who was involved, they immediately became engaged with us. The comments went on and on by the pages:

"All of our family is praying for all of you."

"Oh no! I heard about the accident but didn't know it was Zach!"

"Praying for Zach. He's a fighter."

"Praying hard. Keep us posted."

The news traveled fast and before long, we had an army of prayer warriors. They were all so good to us. Our friend and farm neighbor, Justin, was out harvesting in his combine when he received the news on his phone that Zach had been injured. He immediately thought of the biblical scripture, "Where two or more are gathered in my name, there am I amongst them." He radioed to the others working in the field with him. They all stopped, climbed down from their combines, and prayed together. That was the beginning of a critical mass of support for Zach and our family.

The waiting room in Wichita's intensive care unit was large. There were lots of wooden chairs lining the walls, with tables placed here and there. A small kitchen area complete with refrigerator, sink, microwave, and cabinets to store belongings was located on one end of the room. A flat screen TV hanging from the ceiling caught our attention as our family and several friends sat waiting to hear about Zach's condition. The channel 12 news station was reporting on the accident. They were showing pictures of the black smoke and the tractor and grain cart on fire, which were the first we'd seen. The reporter mentioned that they didn't know Zach's condition; something we also were so frantically wanting to know. It all felt surreal as we watched, waited, and worried, helpless as if in a nightmare. The medical personnel had Zach in the surgery ward, cleaning his wounds and trying to assess his injuries.

After some time, we were introduced to Dr. Robert Bingaman, Zach's doctor. He was a tall, attractive man with thinning salt and pepper hair and a mustache. He reminded me a bit of Tom Selleck. When he began to speak, he had our full attention. He informed us that Zach was alive and had survived because he was healthy and young. Those were definite factors in his favor. Then some bad news followed. Zach had third and fourth degree burns on over 54% of his body and Dr. Bingaman was certain that Zach would lose his left foot because it was so badly damaged.

Dr. Bingaman stood in his mint green scrubs with his hands in his white lab coat pockets as he went on to tell us that the electricity entered Zach's left hand where he grabbed the ladder, then exited out of several places: his left shoulder, his back over his left kidney, his right thigh, and both feet. Later we learned that it had also exited from his head.

Dr. Bingaman went on to explain that with electrical burns, the exit wounds are far more damaging than where the current enters the body. Tissue is blown apart where the electricity exits. Electrical burns are also far more complex than regular burns because the damage is done from the inside out, and it is difficult to tell the exact path the electricity took or the damage done on the inside of the body.

"Electricity takes the path of least resistance," Dr. Bingaman told us. It appeared to have traveled primarily through Zach's left hand, down his arm and onward down his side, into his left leg, and out of his left foot, but it had to have crossed somewhere through his body since he also had exit wounds out of his right leg and foot. That was a huge concern because it was hard to know if damage was done to his major organs when it crossed. As far as Dr. Bingaman could see up to that point, it appeared that Zach's lungs and heart were functioning normally, but his kidneys were the big concern. There is something called myoglobin that the body produces when damage has been inflicted. It's a substance that's formed by all the dead tissue—the burned muscle, flesh, and other internal parts. It travels in the blood and then is filtered through the kidneys. If bad enough, it can cause the kidneys to shut down. Zach's myoglobin levels were off the chart, which registers as high as 40,000. Dialysis is always necessary in those situations, we were told, with the high possibility of a kidney transplant.

"The next six hours will tell us more about his kidneys," said Dr. Bingaman, "and if he makes it through the night, we will proceed forward."

"What?... *if* he makes it through the night!" The reality of it all had not yet soaked in. We were stunned and in disbelief that things could be so bad. Nobody had told us any kind of percentage rate for his survival—we hadn't asked. None of us were to a point that we could even think about losing Zach. We just couldn't look at things that way. We weren't in denial—we just weren't ready to accept anything different than the fact that Zach was going to be okay. So he might lose his foot—that we could live with—but we weren't going to lose Zach!

By evening, many family and friends began to show up and congregate in the waiting room. Jodi's parents, George and Staci, and her brother and sister arrived at the hospital from where they live—two and a half hours away. Chris and I, Kelsey, her husband Broc, Matthew, some of Zach's friends, Chris's brothers and their wives and kids, all sat together feeling helpless. There was nothing we could do but pray and hope for good news.

The night went on and fatigue was getting the best of us. Visitors left and Kelsey and Broc went to find a nearby hotel. The rest of us stayed at the hospital in case something came up. Jodi and her family took Brynlee and found a small, private conference room where they could sleep on the carpeted floor.

Chris sat upright in a chair and I stretched across a wooden love seat in the waiting room and tried to catch a little rest. I remember seeing Matthew lying on the hard linoleum floor—no pillow or blanket, resting the best he could. My heart ached knowing he was worried for his brother. "What is going through his mind?" I wondered. Matt and Zach have spent most of their lives working and playing side by side. It's often not until something like this happens that the value of a relationship is realized.

The two aren't the type to generally show their feelings, so when Matt shared what he'd written when giving the Best Man speech for Zach's wedding toast only two years before, it melted my heart. He described the great times they'd had growing up together and said that even though they hardly acted like it—or either of them would generally admit it—at the end of the day, they were the best of friends and could always count on each other.

I live for moments like that one. That speech made me realize that Chris and I have been successful in raising our kids. At least that's my definition of success. Knowing our kids are loving people who care about others is more important to me than what they choose to do for a living or how much money they make.

Looking at Matthew lying on that hard floor, I thought to myself that his discomfort was nothing compared to the pain he had to be feeling from the fear of losing a best friend and brother.

I must have managed to fall asleep because I was awakened by the sounds of people talking in the dimly lit room before the break of dawn. I felt like I was in a fog. I was so sleepy and trying hard to wake up—so stiff from lying all curled up on that hard, wooden seat. We'd made it to the morning and had not heard any news. That was something to hold on to.

The sun came up and lit the room. Jodi and her family, including Brynlee, joined us in the waiting room. A nurse came to tell us we could see Zach. Chris, Jodi, Matthew and I eagerly approached the entryway to the intensive care unit.

For security reasons, we had to use the phone at the entrance to get permission to enter. The double doors made a loud "click-click" noise, then unlatched and opened automatically to give us access to the burn unit. I'm not sure if it was the medications or cleaning compounds used to sanitize the area, but there was a pungent odor within the burn unit that made us aware we were entering a distinct area of the hospital.

As we walked past the nurse's station, we glanced into a couple of rooms that were occupied with two burn victims propped upright in their beds. They looked like mummies, all wrapped in gauze. Not a bit of flesh was revealed. They were a father and son who were severely burned when the hot water heater they were trying to light in their basement exploded. Their entire house was lifted off the foundation! They managed to survive, by the grace of God, and ended up in rooms next to each other.

It was disturbing to see the two injured men. We walked by, trying not to stare, on our way to Zach's room, which was the next room down the hall. As disturbing as it was, it was not nearly as devastating as seeing Zach. The sight of Zach in that hospital bed caused emotions that I can't even put into words. There were so many thoughts and feelings tumbling through my mind all at once that no single word can accurately describe what I felt at that moment. It was a heart-breaking sight for us all.

Tubes and wires attached to monitors displaying blinking lights surrounded him. His legs and feet were firmly wrapped in ace bandages with little red drain tubes sticking out next to the ends of two exposed toes. His left arm and body were wrapped in oily, bloodstained gauze. There was a white creamy lotion covering his face. A tube snaked into his nose with a wet strip of cotton to hold it in place, along with a tube in his mouth disappearing down his throat. The room was filled with the wheeze of a machine pumping air into his lungs, along with the beeps and blips of other monitors. "Oh, my dear God….Oh Zach." This didn't look like our Zach. His face and lips were swollen. The nurse in the room told us that he was put into a drug induced coma for his protection. His body was working so hard in response to his injuries. He was very critically sick, and now that we had seen him with our own eyes, the reality of it all hit us like a blow to the stomach.

The nurse explained that during surgery, doctors had to do a sclerotome on his left arm and leg, a procedure that involves making an incision from one end of the appendage to the other to relieve swelling that cuts off the blood circulation. The gross vision came into my mind of the way a hotdog looks when cut down its length after it has been cooked in the microwave. The meat literally separates, releasing the pressure of the swelling. I could hardly imagine Zach going through something like that. It was awful to think about all the torture his body was enduring.

We stood there filled with grief, trying to comprehend what our eyes were witnessing. We allowed time to let the sight soak in and become real to us before speaking. What might Zach be feeling? Did he know of our presence? Eventually, not knowing if Zach could hear us, we spoke to him as if he could. We wanted to believe that he could hear us.

On the positive side of things, we were told that Zach's myoglobin levels came way down through the night, from off the charts above 40,000 to 17,000. That was great news! Still dangerously high, the doctor cautioned, but he was impressed at how much it improved. Not out of the woods, he said, but indicative that there was more of a chance that conditions could turn around for the better. No further surgery would take place until Zach was more stable.

We visited Zach's room two at a time and watched the nurses perform their routines of checking vital signs, changing out bags of fluids, and resetting monitors. They were so tender while applying fresh cream to his face, and they compassionately answered our many questions. Another question popped into my mind while they worked: was anyone aware that Zach wore contacts? The two nurses glanced at each other, surprised expressions on their faces.

One hurried over and lifted his eyelid. Sure enough, the contacts were still on, and she began the process to remove them. "I am glad that you mentioned it," she murmured. It was just one of those mothering instincts that made me think of that. One never stops thinking like a mother once you have kids. Looking back, I still wonder if the contacts protected his eyes from the flames. On the other hand, it's a wonder that they hadn't melted to his eyes!

Another question we had for the nurses was about the monitors and all the numbers tracking Zach's vitals. Once they explained how to read them, those screens became the objects of our full attention. We were obsessed with watching his blood pressure and heart rate. We'd also keep checking the catheter tube for signs that his urine was clearing. The blood and myoglobin ran dark in color through the tube. It was critical for that to start clearing up.

Baskets of food started to arrive at the hospital along with more and more caring friends and relatives. Concerned chatter filled the spacious waiting room, and conversations carried on as if it were a family reunion.

Little Brynlee had been completely removed from her routine. She had no bed to lie down for naps, and with all the noise and activity, it was hard to get her to sleep. At one point, late in the day, we realized that the poor toddler had not even been fed her lunch. Being so wrapped up in all that was going on with Zach, we had not realized how the moments slipped away. Time and schedules didn't seem to exist. Brynlee was passed from one person to the other. The only way to get her to sleep was to push her around the hospital in her stroller. That was something I was very willing to do. It gave me alone time to regroup and meditate, a way to escape the crowds of people and noise. It was helpful to have the support of everyone there and I knew they wanted to show how much they cared, but it also became overwhelming at times, and I didn't always feel like being social.

The hospital, Via Christi, surrounded a beautiful Catholic church, enabling me to look out the windows and see its peaceful presence as I pushed Brynlee in the stroller. The church was built of blonde stone and featured ornate windows encompassed by a well-groomed lawn with religious statues dotting it here and there. It gave me comfort to see that faithful structure. I prayed as I pushed Brynlee in the stroller and felt more connected to God. Brynlee would eventually fall asleep, and I just kept walking and walking the halls to give her and myself peace and quiet.

Channel 12 News, the local Wichita station, managed to get in touch with Jodi by phone. They wanted to do an interview with her about Zach and his accident. Jodi had always thought of herself as a shy person, and

the idea of an interview scared her. She pondered the request several hours, then decided she could do it.

I never thought of Jodi as shy, but I was just really getting to know her. Zach dated Jodi in college for two years before they were engaged, but he'd never even mentioned much about her throughout that time, let alone brought her home for Chris and me to meet. I most definitely learned he was serious about her the summer before his third year of college. He casually mentioned that he wouldn't get to see Jodi over the summer once school was out. Nonchalantly, I told him that maybe it would give each of them a chance to date around a while. Boy, was that the wrong thing to say! He came back at me as if I had just said something terribly insulting. "Why would you say that, Mom? Jodi is my girlfriend! Why would we want to date around?" He shook his head and walked off all miffed at me. That's when I first learned how he felt about Jodi. He hadn't dated many girls, and I thought he was just getting his feet wet. I had no idea that he was already head over heels for her.

The first time Chris and I met her was at a college track meet. Zach wanted us to watch Jodi run and meet her parents, Staci and George, who were at the meet as well. That was another indication of how serious he was—his wanting us to meet her parents. Chris and I were impressed with her grace and speed as she took off around the track. She was so fast! It was fun to watch her. We thought she was such a cute girl too with her long dark hair and sweet smile. She was a little shy about meeting us, but most girls that age would be a little nervous to meet their boyfriend's parents for the first time.

Looking back, I see how quickly Jodi had to grow up. She experienced several major life changes in rapid order. Within two years of graduating from college, she moved to a new city, joined a new family, and became a

farm wife, a very different lifestyle than how she'd grown up. Jodi became a mother only three days before her first wedding anniversary, and then Zach had his accident, leaving her to face a world of uncertainty

and nearly making her a widow at the young age of 23. That was an awful lot for a young woman to take on in such a short time.

The woman from Channel 12 News came and set up for the interview at the hospital that evening. Jodi calmed her nerves, stayed composed, and did a very credible job of answering the questions the reporter had for her. It sure didn't hurt to get the word out even more that Zach was struggling for his life. We were thankful to have all the prayers we could get, and the interview broadcast from the news station helped to make that happen.

October 25th 2014

The second day at the hospital was coming to an end. Kelsey and Broc went back home to Assaria. Their four-month-old son, Liam, our first grandson, had been left with Kelsey's in-laws. It was the young parents first time to be away from Liam overnight, and since things were looking more positive for Zach, they wanted to go be with their baby. They knew we would keep them informed of any changes.

People stayed late into the evening with us. We were exhausted and running on adrenaline. Zach was resting and holding his own. We were still in the "wait and see" mode, but we had made it past the dreaded six-hour deadline that first threatened us. Not much was being done other than monitoring and keeping him stable with fluids and medications. It was an eye-opening revelation when we were told that if Zach survived, he could expect to be hospitalized for months. Not days, but months! That was hard to swallow, but we were ready to do whatever was necessary to get him well.

3

THE THIRD DAY

We practically lived in the waiting room at Via Christi. There was a bathroom in the hall where we could shower, and with all the kitchen conveniences in the waiting room, we could eat there—especially since we had food that people brought in for us. Chris's brother Randy came to the hospital many evenings with meals he had prepared in a crockpot.

Because it was a public waiting room, several visitors came and went, but there was one woman who had frequented that room each day we'd been there. We had often seen her sitting and working on hand stitching. As we began to talk, I learned that she was the wife and mother of the two men wrapped like mummies in the rooms next to Zach's. Her name was Sally and she was a nurse practitioner, which was beneficial to us because she could explain the medical terminology that we wanted to learn more about. She had already been at the hospital for two weeks with her injured husband and son, Scott and Alex, so she was familiar with the day to day procedures and helped us understand what to expect and what was considered "normal."

It turned out that Sally's son Alex was a farm kid like Zach and nearly the same age too. Zach was twenty-four at the time.

The Third Day

Those two young men lay in beds right next to each other, fighting for their lives. "Someday," I told Sally, "I hope this all becomes a bad memory and that the two of them will get the opportunity to meet and talk." We hugged and cried together several times. It was somehow comforting to have Sally there going through the same thing. We were both grieving mothers—only she had a husband fighting for his life as well!

Sally warned us that the third day with "her boys," as she called them, was the hardest. It was a day that their medical conditions came to a crisis and she'd nearly lost them both. It was a sad and stressful day for them all.

I felt confident that Zach was remaining stable. This was going to be his third day, and we had no reason to feel that things were going to change, except to expect that he was going to get stronger. The doctors were pleased with his progress. They said he was still alive only because he was young and had been in good health, and that was in his favor. I didn't believe that Sally's fate of a bad third day had any parallels with the way things would be for Zach.

Unfortunately, my hopes and beliefs didn't hold true. The third day for Zach *did* take a bad turn. Conditions changed very quickly.

Chris and I had Brynlee with us in the hospital cafeteria at noon on Monday. The three of us had just sat down with our trays to eat lunch. Jodi was in the waiting room with her parents and Matthew. A frantic nurse burst into the room. "Jodi, come with me now!" Worried and alarmed, Jodi raced after her; Matthew joined them. They hurried to Zach's room—it was filled with nurses and other medical personnel working frantically. One was on top of Zach giving him chest compressions. Zach was in cardio pulmonary arrest—code blue!

In the cafeteria, my cell phone rang; it was a call from a nurse: "You need to come up to Zach's room as soon as possible." I didn't have any idea what was going on. Nobody from the hospital had ever called my phone before, so I guessed this must be serious. Chris said he'd watch Bryn so I could go up to Zach. I took the elevator, then ran down the hall toward the trauma center/burn unit. Once there, I saw the urgency of the situation. Everyone was scurrying around. A nurse was bearing her weight down on top of Zach, giving him resuscitative treatment. There was a crash cart nearby with someone holding paddles in their hands. All the staff was working swiftly together, calling out commands to each other and reporting Zach's vitals. Jodi and Matthew were standing at the head of Zach's bed, looks of terror and confusion on their faces. I hesitated in the door way, but a nurse told me that I could enter the room to be closer to Zach. The room was already filled with staff and equipment and I feared I would get in the way and slow their efforts, but I slipped through to where I could stand next to Jodi and Matt.

Zach's heart had quit beating. The room was filled with an aura of urgent yet controlled team work. They were trying to get Zach's pulse back. The nurse administering chest manipulations became fatigued, so another took her place. With one hand on top of the other, the second nurse pushed down on his chest. Zach's body bounced off the mattress as she applied pressure with each compression, yet no response from Zach was apparent.

"Come on, Zach! Come back to us!" I demanded urgently. Jodi chimed in, "Come on, Zach! Fight! Keep fighting! Come on, Zach!" We chanted this mantra over and over as we watched for a change in the terrifying situation. Matthew stood frozen, speechless in disbelief. Time slowed to a crawl. Nine long minutes later, a nurse called out, "We have a pulse!"

"Thank you, God!" Those words were music to our ears. We gasped deep breaths of relief. Somehow, I just knew that Zach's heart would get going again. It was a scary moment in time, but it didn't feel possible that it was the end. Maybe I was in a state of denial or in shock—I don't know.

Sophia, one of the nurses who did the CPR and whom we were blessed to have on duty that day, told us that she had been watching Zach closely that morning. She noticed that his blood pressure was steadily dropping, and said that if she'd been gone for a short time—even just to go to the restroom—when he coded, he would have died had she not started CPR immediately. Sophia was conscientious and prepared, and for that we are forever grateful—she was our angel.

Because Zach made it through the first two nights, we were encouraged that he was past the worst. He was a fighter and we were sure he was going to make it, but after that last episode, uncertainty and fear entered our heads. Sally's traumatic third day became our story as well.

Jodi was traumatized after what she had witnessed; she couldn't get the vision of Zach without a heartbeat out of her mind. She decided that the best thing she could do was inform all her connections on Facebook of Zach's close call and ask for their help. She pulled out her phone and desperately typed, "Zach needs prayers now!"

This was a move that created instant reactions. In almost no time, responses poured in on Jodi's and my Facebook accounts. The message that Zach was in need of immediate prayers flew through the air. It amazed me that so many people cared—individuals whom we didn't even know sent word they were praying and asked how else they could help.

I was especially moved when I heard how individuals dropped what they were doing to pray. My neighbor Lori from across the street was in the middle of a meeting at her place of employment when Jodi's plea came across her phone: "Stop what you're doing and pray for Zach." Lori later said that the meeting screeched to a halt and all fifteen members present bowed their heads.

The prayers made all the difference for our family. They gave us strength and support. One positive thought flashed through my mind and lingered: if it was Zach's time to go, wouldn't he have died in the field when 12,000 volts surged through his body for as long as it did? It's a miracle that he survived! If Zach's time in this world was truly up, it seemed that would have been the time—yet he was still with us. There must be some reason he survived, I reasoned, which made me wonder about God's plan for him. Whatever it was, I was holding on to the hope that Zach was meant to keep living. We all were.

Zach appeared to be recovering as the afternoon went on. It was a Monday, so visitors started showing up when they got off from work and lingered in the large waiting room, taking turns to see him. Kelsey skipped work and headed straight back as soon as she got the word that Zach had coded.

Even though Zach was in a coma, we all treated him as if he weren't. We would let him know when we were there, and we'd talk to him and to each other so he would hear our conversations. A group of his friends went together to his room. It was their first time to see Zach since he was injured. When they came back out, I could tell they were trying to hold it together for our family's sake, but it was obvious that they were devastated to see him looking as he did. All the gauze wrappings, tubes, wires, and monitors were hard for anyone to overlook.

A doctor approached Jodi while Chris and I were standing in the hall just outside of Zach's room. He asked what plan of action she would like them to take if Zach were to crash again. "Do you want us to do CPR and work to revive him again?" It was a legitimate question, but seemed strange to us that they would even have to ask. Of course we would want them to revive him!

The Third Day

We hadn't yet even thought about the possibility of Zach crashing *again*. We were still recouping from the last episode, grateful that he made it through. Predictably, Jodi's response was that she wanted them to do CPR again if necessary.

Thank God that awful event didn't repeat itself, but as the day lead on into the evening, we were presented with something even more disheartening.

4

LETTING GO

A doctor, not Dr. Bingaman but an intern or some other doctor we hadn't met, directed Jodi, Chris, and me to a monitor in the hallway outside Zach's room. On the screen was a picture of Zach's lungs. The doctor pointed out that they were more than three quarters filled with fluid. He explained to us that the ventilator was no longer adequate to supply air to Zach's lungs. The machine was set at one hundred percent oxygen and yet it wasn't enough. The only way that air was going to get into his lungs was by force—by use of a pressure bag. The doctor went on to caution that there was a risk that Zach's lungs could burst if air was forced into them, but it was the only way Zach could get enough oxygen to breathe.

This was devastating news! We weren't aware, up until then, that his lungs were filling with fluid. It had happened quickly. Immediately, the thought of my dad came to mind. He had been losing his battle with Leukemia when his lungs began to fill with fluid. I remember that his doctors removed the fluid through a procedure called Lasiks. I asked Zach's doctor if that were something they could do for Zach. The doctor explained that Zach needed to keep receiving the fluids to keep his veins from collapsing. Fluids are essential to burn victims for that reason, we were told, so Lasiks was not an option. What were we to do? The news was sickening. It felt as if my heart had sunk into my stomach.

"We're doing everything we can but we're at the point where a decision has to be made," said the doctor. "We can use the pressure bag or we can opt to just keep him comfortable. We'll leave that decision up to you."

Jodi, Zach's wife, was the one who had to give permission for them to proceed with using the pressure bag. I distinctly remember my feelings at that moment. Doctors weren't asking me or Chris how to proceed. Even though Zach is our son whom we raised and cared for all his life, at that crucial moment, neither I nor his dad had any legal say as to how to proceed. That life and death decision was left in his wife's hands. It made me aware for the first time that our "parent card" had expired, and that was a little hard to swallow. Zach was, after all, an adult who was married, but he was only twenty-four years old, and it just didn't seem that long ago he was still in our care.

"I want you to do everything you can to keep Zach alive," Jodi said with conviction. Chris and I agreed with her decision, but I didn't feel one-hundred percent certain that we were about to do the right thing. How does one know it's okay to take the chance of blowing out someone's lungs? But to do nothing meant we would lose Zach for sure. Maybe, as it turned out, it was a reprieve to not be the ones who had to make that call.

Once the equipment was in place, a nurse began to manually squeeze a rubber bag which resembled a thick white balloon and was connected to the ventilator tube going into Zach's mouth. Using both of her hands, she had to keep up with each steady breath, slowly forcing air in, and then releasing the bag to let air flow out. Every time she'd squeeze that bag, Zach's chest would rise, and then the bag would make a long, slow groaning noise when it was released and drew air back into itself, causing Zach's chest to fall back down. This went on and on until the nurse's hands were fatigued and she was relieved by another nurse who picked up the rhythm.

Watching the process of the pressure bag was grueling. I will never forget the mournful groaning sound it made each time the air drew back inside itself. How long could it go on? Would it even help clear his lungs? The tension was palpable.

A catholic priest approached me outside of Zach's room. "Are you Zach's mother?" he asked. I acknowledged that I was. "I hope it was okay that I took the liberty earlier today to give Zach his last rights. I also anointed him with oil. I noticed on his chart that he was baptized Catholic and I didn't see anyone around ministering to him, so I wanted to do that for him. I hope you are okay with that."

Looking back, it's strange that I didn't take that as a sign that Zach was failing. Instead, my thought was that I was grateful that someone was looking out for him spiritually.

"Thank you. I do appreciate that," I told him.

We visited for a while about Zach and how he was injured. It wasn't long before a Methodist pastor showed up as well. The priest was standing on my left and the pastor was on my right. The pastor introduced himself to me. I remember telling the two men that it seemed very appropriate to have them both there representing each faith. Zach had been baptized Catholic and was confirmed Methodist. I was comforted by having them there to pray for us and with us, and their company was a positive distraction for me.

Zach's room and the hallway began to fill with family and friends as well as doctors and nurses. The atmosphere was progressively changing. It felt like we were on a ship headed toward a storm. A question entered my mind: "Why did that priest and pastor come here? Did someone tell them that Zach was nearing the end? We knew his condition was critical, but nobody confirmed to us that Zach was dying!"

Unfortunately, as the evening wore on, it became more and more apparent that his condition was changing for the worse. It wasn't long before another startling update reported that Zach's kidneys were beginning to shut down. From that point on, everything went downhill quickly, and that's when we finally faced reality. Fear and defeat crept in and showed on the faces of everyone present. They began embracing, praying silently and crying.

Zach's appearance changed quickly. His body was swollen to a point beyond recognition. He looked as if he were a buffed-up weight lifter who was maxed out on steroids. His lips were huge and swollen, and the girth of his arms was at least twice their normal size. His skin was so taut that I was afraid that he was going to burst open at any moment. When I touched his arm, it felt like a mannequin—cold and hard.

It was the most helpless feeling, standing there watching at Zach's side. I could hardly tolerate the sound of that pressure bag, and I didn't want Zach to have to listen to it either. I had a burning desire to wrap my arms around him and hold him, as if he were my baby again. I wanted to soothe him. I think only a mother, especially a mother who knows she's losing her child, could understand this strong yearning. I went to a faraway place in my mind and regressed back in time. My mothering instincts overcame me as I softly sang in his ear so that others wouldn't hear, so that he could listen to the sound of my voice over that bag! I didn't sing anything in particular, just wordless melodies that rolled off my tongue. I leaned gently against the bed, causing it to rock back and forth as I sang. In my mind, I was comforting my son, rocking and holding him close to make him feel loved. It felt just for that short while like we were in a place all alone without all the chaos and people, like everything was okay. I was comforted knowing he was with me. It was a sacred moment.

Jodi brought me back to reality when she moved up to be next to Zach. She asked why his bed was rocking. I'm sure she must have wondered what the heck I was doing. I knew that I was responsible but didn't say anything. The moment was too personal and I didn't feel the need to explain, but I did become aware that I had been selfish about taking time and space from her. Every second was precious, and she wanted to spend it next to her husband, alone.

I'm not sure how much time passed—it felt like forever. The pressure bag continued to groan, and Zach's chest expanded bigger and bigger as the nurse forced in air. Watching his chest lift up and down off the mattress made me think that his body was being forced to do more than was morally humane. I couldn't bear to watch anymore, so I turned away and went to find Chris, who was standing in the hall. He looked so heartbroken. We were both at our wits end and felt so absolutely helpless.

I put my arms around Chris's neck and sobbed uncontrollably against his chest as he held me. I cried with him until I couldn't cry anymore. Empty, defeated, and shocked, we simply clung to each other. There was nothing we could do—it was all out of our hands, and Zach was slipping away. We didn't have to say it to each other; both of us knew it was nearly time to let him go. It was all so surreal. I wanted to wake up and find it had all been a horrible nightmare. Never did we dream we would have to go through losing one of our kids, especially not like that. Parents always worry about their kids, but they never want to believe that they will lose their child to death. That only happens to other people.

Once we pulled ourselves together, Chris and I walked toward Zach's room. Jodi was standing in the doorway with her mom who was trying to comfort her. Someone suggested she sit down because she was turning pale. I peered into Zach's room and when I saw the

LETTING GO

vision of him there on the bed with medical staff all around him, forcing his body to go beyond its capability, I felt he was being tortured. My heart began to pound out of my chest and I said to Chris, "I can't do this anymore! I can't stand to see him pushed like that." I barely got the words out of my mouth when Chris broke down as well, feeling the same thing. Overcome with emotion, he went straight over to Jodi and pleaded with her: "I can't take this anymore! I can't watch Zach go through this anymore."

Jodi gazed in at Zach from the doorway, her face frantic as tears ran down. The pressure of what to do was immense. Chris's plea gave her the permission she needed to call it all off, but she had to make sure it was what she knew she wanted. She paused for a moment, then she too broke down: "Let's just do what will make him comfortable." We had all come to the end of our rope. We couldn't keep it up any longer. It felt as though we had squeezed every bit of life possible from his body and it wasn't right to carry on expecting more. The decision to stop fighting felt right. We loved Zach way too much to watch him go through any more. Jodi let the medical staff know what she had decided. As hard as it was, it was time to turn Zach over to God and put him into His hands.

Dr. Bingaman entered Zach's room, compassion on his face. He promptly took charge of the situation, ordering the pressure bag and fluids discontinued. The process of using Lasiks began, the procedure I was earlier told he wasn't a candidate for. Now that we had decided to let him go, fluids weren't necessary to keep his veins from collapsing. Once Lasiks started, the fluids literally oozed from his body. They ran off his bed, dripping into pools on the floor. Nurses moved to reset the monitors and take care of Zach's basic needs. The plan was to make sure he remained as comfortable as possible and let nature take its course.

Dr. Bingaman tried to comfort us by letting us know that he felt we were making the right decision to let Zach go. As he stood next to Chris, he described all the things he believed would've been Zach's fate if he continued to live. "Zach will lose his left leg and almost positively his right one as well. His left arm is very questionable as to whether it can be saved. If amputated, it would not be at the shoulder but deep into the chest." He went on with more dark details. "Zach's back will be an issue because of the muscle he lost over his kidney where the electricity exited. He will more than likely also need a kidney transplant because of the damage sustained by dealing with the myoglobin. There are quite possibly other problems we don't even know about. Would that be the quality of life Zach would want?"

We absolutely knew that would not be the way Zach would want to live. Zach was the most energetic, high performance, go-getting individual we'd ever seen. Chris called him the Tasmanian Devil when he was a child because he moved like a little tornado. I always said he was like a bull in a china shop. When he was in the third grade, his teacher put him in the back of the classroom so he could stand up and move around without disturbing the other kids. We still laugh when we remember how the teacher told us he tipped over backward, desk and all, because he was wiggling around too much one day.

Zach was an athlete all his life and excelled in the sports he participated in, especially wrestling. He loved to ski, both on snow and water, and he loved to get out on his motorcycle or four-wheeler and ride like a maniac, catching air way up high as he flew over the hills that he and Matt had pushed up with a tractor in the cattle pens.

Zach was never still unless he was sleeping. Even then, he was restless. When he was little, he'd jump in bed with us because he was frightened of lightning and thunder during storms. It was like sleeping with a wild animal the way he'd throw his arms and legs across us and toss and turn sideways in the bed.

Until Dr. Bingaman shared all the details of Zach's fate, we hadn't known that he was facing so many issues. We absolutely knew then in our hearts that it was the right thing to let him go for his own sake. Truth be known, it really wasn't our decision anyway. God was the one in control. This exhilarating soul that was gifted to us and who brought so much joy and love into our lives was not ours to hold onto—he belonged to God. Our faith was strong enough that we believed Zach would be much better off in Heaven. It felt selfish for us to expect him to stay, knowing he'd have to suffer and give up the life he had always known.

Jodi went to get Brynlee. Next to saying goodbye to Zach, it would be the hardest thing she'd ever had to do in her life, to tell Brynlee that Daddy was going to go to Heaven and become an angel.

Chris and I both took a moment to talk to Zach. With tears pouring down our faces and our voices cracking, we let him know that we were so very proud of him and that he was the best son we could ever have asked for. We let him know how much we loved him and how much joy he brought to our lives. We told him that we would take care of Jodi and Brynlee for him, that he had nothing to worry about. We went on to say everything that was on our hearts but it didn't feel like enough. We simply could not express with words what our hearts were feeling. We were broken. We just stood next to him and cried.

It was getting late in the evening. Each person who came to the hospital took a moment to say beautiful things to Zach and tell him goodbye. Some of our friends went home to give us private family time. Others stayed a while longer to support us however they could. The nurses were so accommodating. They took care of Brynlee so we could concentrate our time on Zach.

Jodi, Chris, Matthew, Kelsey, and I all stood in Zach's room with Dr. Bingaman while many other family members stood in the hall outside his open door, waiting for the saddest moment of our lives to take place. When I looked over at Jodi's mom, Staci, standing in the doorway, it occurred to me that our family dynamics would change completely. I went over to her and expressed my sorrow: "This means that Jodi and Brynlee will move back to Topeka with you, and we won't see them as much. Our families won't be together anymore. We've really come to love your family."

Staci and Jodi's dad, George, had become our friends in the short three years since we had first met them. We'd hit it off really well and enjoyed their company immensely. They drove the two-hour distance frequently to Assaria to visit Zach and Jodi, and we'd all gather together and visit. Staci assured me that we would always be family. We hugged and cried together.

As the evening went on, we kept our eyes on the monitor screens, watching to see if Zach's vital signs changed. I asked a male nurse what we could expect to take place. Would it be like my dad—that awful 'death rattle' as he neared the end of his life? I wanted to be prepared. The nurse explained that everyone is different. "Zach's vitals will slowly drop, but he won't feel any pain. He should go peacefully," he said. Hearing that helped some. It's odd, but by that point, I was in a place of acceptance and peace, as if God had calmed me. Chris seemed better too.

I saw Matt, completely absorbed in his thoughts, and went over to him. "This is so hard to believe. It doesn't feel real," I said to him. I looked up at the clock on the wall: 11:35 pm. "I was there when he came into this world on Saturday, August third, 1990, at 10:50 am, and now I'll be here when he leaves on this date, Monday, October 27, 2014." I don't know why I needed to say that just then. Everything just seemed unreal—like a bad dream—or maybe I was trying to get a grip on actually being there in the moment.

After standing around Zach's bed for probably an hour but not seeing many changes, a few of us went across the hall to a private waiting room so we could sit down for a while. We were talking about memories of Zach and how much we'd miss him, as though he'd already left us and we were grieving already. Jodi pulled out her phone to look at pictures of Zach. She played a little recording she had of his voice. It was Zach talking to Brynlee: "I love you, Bryn. I loooooovvvve you" he said in a sing-song way. We laughed and cried at the same time. Jodi played it over again and then again. We couldn't get enough of it. It was the only recent thing we had to remember his voice by. It was so sweet and comforting, yet painful as well.

Back in Zach's room, Chris and Dr. Bingaman were carrying on a conversation about farming and what kind of guy Zach was and what he did on the farm. Stopping in mid-sentence, Dr. Bingaman paused their conversation. With a puzzled look on his face, he switched his attention to focus on the monitors and then ordered the nurse to start a unit of blood for Zach.

When I heard what was going on, I was confused. "Why are they messing with that? Zach is dying—what good would more blood do now?" It didn't occur to me that his condition could turn around. I'd learned my lesson with how things go at the end of life when my dad passed away. After he was removed from life support, his vital signs improved so much that we thought he was going to get better. We got excited, only to see him plummet into death. A doctor told me that sometimes happens with patients and wasn't unusual. Because of that memory, I protected myself from false hope and didn't let myself get excited when we were told that Zach's vitals were slightly improving.

The new unit of blood was hooked up and administered to Zach. "Maybe he's trying to prove me wrong," mused Dr. Bingaman as he observed Zach's vitals improving a little more.

For some reason, that statement didn't jumpstart our hearts. We were resolved to the prediction that we were going to lose Zach.

Then Zach's vital signs improved even more. His blood pressure started to rise, his oxygen saturation levels started to climb, and he began to stabilize. Seconds became minutes and minutes became hours, and Zach was still hanging on! It seemed crazy, but I wondered if anyone else was thinking the same when I quipped, "It feels like we aren't waiting for Zach to pass anymore." No one really knew what to say, not even Dr. Bingaman. Bewilderment sat on our faces. We were afraid to get our hopes up too high, so we just waited it out, moment by moment.

It was in the wee hours of the night when Dr. Bingaman reported that Zach was remaining stable and appearing to hold his own, at least for the time being. He told us that they would continue to monitor Zach throughout the night and see how things looked in the morning, then left the room, leaving Zach in a nurse's care.

Between feeling confused as to what we were experiencing, being drained emotionally, and not having any quality sleep since the night before the accident, we were in a fog, a sort of twilight zone. Chris and I decided that we didn't want to sleep in the waiting room again for the few hours left of the night. We felt like it would be okay to go to a nearby hotel, knowing that Jodi and Matthew would stay with Zach and call us if anything changed.

Morning came and there were no calls. Chris and I got around early and headed straight back to Via Christi. Matthew and Jodi were in the waiting room and greeted us with an update that Zach was still holding his own and appeared stable. Chris and I were relieved but not surprised. We would not have left if we had felt he was not going to hold on. We sat down and rehashed what happened the night before. It just didn't make sense. We couldn't understand what was going on with Zach. He had been dying in that room—his body was shutting down. Every effort made to help him, came to a halt when nothing more could be done. Then he improved. What had happened?

5

AMAZING GRACE!

By late morning, Dr. Bingaman entered the waiting room wearing his white lab coat. He pulled a chair out to the middle of the room and asked us to sit down with him. We were eager to hear what he had to say. We were perplexed and wanted some clarity. He leaned forward with his elbows on his knees and spoke calmly with a serious look on his face, "We were all in that room together last night," he said, "and you saw what Zach went through....I want you to know that it wasn't me that turned things around to bring Zach back...that was a God thing. I didn't have anything to do with that."

We were so overtaken that we couldn't even respond. Emotions ran high and tears welled up in our eyes. Dr. Bingaman went on to say, "Zach has shown us that he wants to live and I'm going to do everything I can to help him. We are going to go forward with things and see what develops."

That was a powerful moment. To have a man who believes in and works with science and the physical body tell us that it wasn't science that was responsible for saving Zach, but instead, God…well, that's just something you don't see or hear every day. We believed that God had everything to do with what we saw, but our doctor had confirmed it in his own words! We—us and the doctor—had witnessed a true miracle!

Dr. Bingaman stood up and asked if we would all join hands for a moment in prayer. We stood and bowed our heads as he humbly gave God all the credit and asked for His blessings on Zach in the days ahead.

I had never heard of or seen a doctor pray with families as Dr. Bingaman did. It was a Catholic hospital, so I'm sure that had something to do with it, but the fact that our doctor wanted to pray with us—wow—that was moving! It confirmed that he meant what he said when he told us that it was God's doing and not his own.

After we took time to absorb the news we'd heard, Jodi and I grabbed our phones. We wanted to inform everyone what had happened. We knew that things could still turn on a dime, but we wanted to shout the good news from the rooftops! We knew people would be so surprised to hear what we had to say because the last they knew, we were telling Zach goodbye. Even the ones who left the hospital the night before didn't know of the miracle.

I posted my message on Facebook:

> I don't understand what's happening. After watching doctors work so hard to force air into Zach's fluid filled lungs, we could no longer take it. We decided to opt for letting nature take place and just keep Zach comfortable. They stopped forcing the fluids and pressure bagging air, we prayed around Zach and said our goodbyes and instead of his vital signs slowly giving way to a peaceful stop, they got better! Still this morning he is trudging on! I don't understand God's plan here. Perhaps it is because of all the prayers he

stays the fight. We were so convinced his body had been through enough, yet his strong heart continues to beat and he looks so much more peaceful! I'm guarding my heart by staying realistic, knowing we may only get to keep him a short while, but it's absolutely amazing to watch this trooper of ours prove science wrong. We are overwhelmed with all the love and support you all have given. I believe your prayers have added quality time and graceful peace to Zach's life. We know you all hurt the same as we do, and you've let us know that by your outpouring hearts. Just to say thank you doesn't seem like enough to show our gratitude. God bless you all!

It didn't take long before the positive comments came back to us:

"I am overwhelmed to hear your encouraging news! We will keep the prayers flowing."

"Praying for Zach and your family as you go through this time. Praying that God will heal his injured body and allow him to live."

"Lisa Short, I don't pray for much, but I am for Zach and your family."

"This tragic accident has rocked our little community and far beyond to the core. Our hearts are heavy as we keep Zach and all of you in our thoughts every second of the day. Know that as hard as it is to post these updates, we all truly appreciate it beyond words."

"There are literally thousands of people in the Salina area and around the nation, praying for Zach and all of you as you go through this challenge. We are all behind you, with our support and love, and prayers for healing and strength."

These were just a few of the many messages from our community, family, and friends. They were incredible about letting us know how much they cared.

Our friend Justin, who stopped his harvest crew to pray the first day the news came that Zach was injured, said an idea came to him. He felt he wanted to do more to help Zach, so he posted his idea on Facebook. He wrote:

> I know many are praying constantly for Zach Short and his family. I believe there is tremendous power in a community praying together. Our farm is going to pause each day at 10am and 4pm to pray for Zach and Jodi Short, Chris and Lisa Short, Kelsey (Short) Tanner, and Matt Short. I invite everyone to set an alarm on your phone, and pause your day at 10 and 4 to pray. I invite all other farmers to stop their tractors and combines with us at those times to pray.

Soon everyone that followed our story, farmer or not, was responding with comments that they were stopping whatever they were doing and praying for Zach at 10:00am and 4:00pm. It was a beautiful idea. We felt so fortunate and loved. We had people tell us that they'd be out driving near where the farmers were harvesting and see their equipment come to a halt at those specific times of the day. They knew what was going on, and it moved them to tears.

Looking peaceful, and lying there on his back, still in the comatose state, Zach continued to hold his own the whole day through. Even though he was still very critical, we had new confidence that maybe things were going to be okay. Maybe God was still not finished with Zach here on Earth. Three times now, he had lived through the impossible and defied the odds.

After people received word that Zach made it through the night, more visitors than ever showed up at the hospital. They came with gifts of food and comfort items for Brynlee like blankets and stuffed animals. They asked what they could do to help, always offering their prayers but wanting to know how they could do more. The Facebook comments were coming nonstop. Jodi and I wanted to respond to each one personally, but it was impossible to keep up with them all.

Love and support came out of everywhere. Back home in Assaria, we had left everything we were doing on the farm. Harvest and planting are a crucial time of year that we schedule everything else around—it's our income. All our time and expense had been put into growing our fall crops and there was only so much time to get them out of the field. Same goes for planting; there's only a certain window of time before the seed needs to be in the ground. The busy farm season wasn't too far off from being completed when the accident happened but still wasn't finished. The wonderful thing was that our work was never abandoned. Several friends and neighboring farmers joined our crew to pick up where we left off on the day of the accident. Some loaned their equipment, and others gave their time to finish harvest and planting for us. That was a big need of ours at the time, and our farm community generously came through.

It was so different to be on the receiving end of the spectrum. For us, it was usually the other way around. Chris has always been known as the guy with a generous heart who protects the backs of his friends and farm neighbors. I don't know how many times he has been there to cover for others in their time of need. Several times, he had volunteered his crew and equipment to help friends who were ill or had passed away and left behind their wives with crops remaining in the fields.

He has always been extremely generous with loaning his equipment out to farmers who had break downs with their own equipment and nowhere else to turn in a busy time, or he'd drop his own work to do their repairs and get them going again. He has given large amounts of his time taking care of area widows and elderly neighbors' needs. He'd do home repairs, snow removal, vehicle repairs, and other various jobs. He's even used his equipment to bury beloved horses which had died.

Chris and I have always felt that doing what we can to help others is the right thing. We've learned that eventually, good deeds come back to us in some form or another. In the case of Zach's accident, things did come back—they came back to us ten-fold! When I took the time to think about it, I could see all that was taking place and felt there was something bigger beginning to unfold inside of all the tragedy. I posted my thoughts on Facebook:

To all friends and loved ones. I feel compelled to acknowledge something today. We are in the midst of a miracle! Obviously just the fact that Zach is alive is one, but there is more going on here than meets the eye. I'm beginning to see a higher purpose in all that is happening. Love is pouring out through people, coming together to hold Zach and his family up. People of little faith are beginning to pray. Those who have let their belief in God get lazy, are becoming prayer warriors. And those who have never taken time to get to know God, are waking up to who he is and how he works in our lives. I know that it appears Zach could rally to make it, but if he doesn't, I believe he's fulfilled an amazing task that God is using him for. If Zach lives, we will be most grateful for that gift, and pray that he can endure what's ahead. If God takes him home, we will be grateful for the time God gave us, and for all the love he's facilitated through Zach. I don't know what to tell you when you ask us what special prayers you can send up. Just thank God for all he does in all our lives. He's an awesome God!

What a great day it had been. We knew it was possible that conditions could change in a heartbeat, but it was one more day that we got to spend with Zach. It was another day that we felt the love and support of so many wonderful, generous people. My heart swelled with gratitude for the many prayers. I felt that prayer had everything to do with why Zach was still alive and why I'd had the strength for all that was happening. I wanted to see the graphic photos of what was under Zach's bandages. Believe me, that took strength! I needed to know what he'd suffered and what we were looking at in the way of future repairs. As horrific as the photos were, they didn't repulse me. Instead, they helped to make it more real for me to understand why the doctors had to do what they said would be needed.

Doctors needed more time to keep Zach stable and to see if his internal organs would continue to function normally. The next plan of action was to do surgery to clean out the deep exit wound on Zach's back and to explore his arm to see if it was merely skin damage or deep muscle damage. I knew by what I saw in those photos that Zach was going to need more miraculous healing. He was facing the loss of his right foot, and his left leg and arm did not look promising. It was obvious that half of his left thumb would not survive; the end was barely hanging on. Because God had spared him, and Zachary's will to live was so strong, I had to believe he'd make it through the trials to come. And because of the miracles we had seen up until then, I wanted to believe God would heal those limbs as well.

Kelsey, Matt, and I went in to see Zach and tell him goodnight after a long day. He was heavily sedated; the induced coma was used to dull the pain of all the burns and injuries, and the ventilator was still pumping air into his lungs. It was hard to have a one-sided conversation with him. We so wanted to see him open his eyes. We wanted to know if he was aware that we were there with him, but there was no way we could tell. We hadn't been able to communicate with him since the day of the accident, three days prior, and we were missing his voice and his fun personality. We wondered how much longer he would be in the state we were looking at.

We said our goodnights and began to walk away when the most amazing thing happened! Zach slowly and steadily raised his right hand up off the bed! It was as if he were trying to extend it to us! We could tell it was a big effort for him, because his hand shook and looked as if it was too heavy for him to lift, but he lifted it!

Our mouths dropped open and tears of joy flooded our eyes—we were so excited! "We see, Zach!" I cried. "We see your hand! You can hear us!" Matthew grinned from ear to ear, and Kelsey chimed in with me, practically giggling, "We love you, Zach! Thank you!" We left the room, and went straight to Jodi and the others in the waiting room to share the exciting news.

It was three days after that dreadful Monday night, and Zach's vital signs maintained as normal. It was becoming more evident that his internal organs were working as they should. Even his kidneys were functioning despite the high levels of myoglobin that threatened to shut them down. Dialysis had not been needed up to that point, although the doctors said it was the usual protocol. Neither we nor Dr. Bingaman knew for sure if the worst was over, but we all continued to be amazed. It was still early to be dismissing problems that weren't yet visible, so we were hanging on day by day and being thankful for any good news we could get. Zach was still considered to be in critical condition, but because his vital signs were stable enough, Dr. Bingaman said it was time to go in for a second surgery.

6

COPING WITH THE NEWS

It felt like a long time, but we waited as patiently as we could, eager to hear the diagnosis once surgery was finished. Dr. Bingaman finally appeared in the waiting room to deliver his findings. He told us that all went well; he cleaned out the deeper wounds, and learned that the bad one in Zach's back did not go so deep that it got into the kidney. He went on to say that he was correct in his prediction that Zach would lose his left foot. We were prepared to hear that, but it was devastating for us to learn that the amputation would need to be done clear up to above his knee! The news grew worse when Doctor said that Zach would also lose his right foot, and at that point, he was not sure how far up the leg he'd have to amputate. Next came the report on Zach's left arm. Dr. Bingaman told us that he believed the arm might possibly be salvageable, but it had deep muscle damage. He wanted to give it a little more time to heal, but because of all the damage, Zach would not be able to lift it. Wrapping up the conversation, Dr. Bingaman said that he'd stay in touch as things developed, but for the moment, that was everything he knew.

Coping with the News

I suppose things could have been much worse, but there was not a lot of good news in that report. We hung our heads in disbelief. It felt like someone let the air out of our tires, leaving us completely deflated. I guess we were hoping that things weren't as bad as they seemed. We were hoping that our Zach was going to be well again and not have life-lasting complications. We sat and grieved. We still had Zach, but it sounded like he was going to be dissected piece by piece. It really worried us that it didn't sound certain his arm would survive. That would be even more devastating! The thought of Zach losing his arm, on top of everything else, made us think that he might not want to live. It was hard enough to imagine him without his legs. We were so concerned over how Zach would take the news once he woke up. Would he still be able to farm or live a life he would be happy with?

It sickened us to think about all that was wrong, but it didn't serve us well to dwell on the things we had no control over, so we decided to focus on the things we were grateful for. We did still have Zach—after all, we thought we had lost him forever on Monday. We thought we'd never hear his voice again and that Brynlee wouldn't get to know him. How many people have lost a loved one and wished they could have just one more day with that person? Well, it was looking more promising that we might get that second chance. That in and of itself was a miraculous gift. We also had the good news that his organs were all functioning normally, and that was HUGELY a blessing to be thankful for! This would slow Zach down, but it would not stop him—he would manage somehow. It would be tough, but he would figure it out. We couldn't know God's plan in all of this, but we trusted that He was looking out for Zach and chose him because He knew that Zach was capable. He was a trooper!

I loved the fact that the hospital had a church that we could visit right there on the campus. All we had to do was go down the elevator to the bottom floor and there it was, with its doors wide open, to welcome anyone who needed to find sanctity in a place that made them feel close to God. The candles were always lit and flickering in the dark entryway, and there was a familiar statue of Mary holding Jesus on her lap, her face so mournful as she compassionately looks over her son who'd been crucified. That statue, called the Pieta, spoke loudly to me every time I entered the church. I had seen it many times before, but each time my focus had always been on Jesus and his pain. But now when I looked at it, I felt the same sorrows for Mary. She felt just as wounded and crucified on the inside as Jesus was on the outside. I felt that same anguish when I looked at my own son. Of course, God too, surely felt the pain of knowing how much His son, along with all those who loved him, suffered. And he did it all for us! God works in such mysterious and wondrous ways. I've always known that but now, we were greatly experiencing it.

I had that same statue on my mind when I was reading Facebook and noticed that I was receiving messages from so many mothers who had lost their children. They were lovingly reaching out to comfort us. I always had feelings of great sorrow for them before, but with what we had just gone through, my heart bled even more for them. On that dreaded Monday, we did experience the hurt of losing a child and saying goodbye. Thank the good Lord it was brief, but we felt it. Saying we're fortunate Zach's been given another chance to live was a gross understatement. Words couldn't express how grateful we were. I know it's not my job to figure it all out or question God, but I sure didn't understand why things happened as they did. I don't believe that God took those other mother's children home to Heaven because of anything they did or didn't do differently than us. I do believe everything happens for a purpose, and perhaps in Zach's case, we had already experienced that purpose. The community uniting in love to pour

COPING WITH THE NEWS

out their hearts and the strengthening of people's faiths became very evident. My heart goes out to all those parents who have been separated from their children. They know they'll be together again someday, but that wait must feel like an eternity to them.

People continued to let us know that they were praying for Zach and for all of us. I believe that was the only reason any of us had any strength at all. We had been operating on so little sleep. We'd stay late at the hospital each night and with the stress, we didn't really rest well when we went to bed. Chris and I had been staying at a nearby hotel the previous three nights but Jodi, her parents, Brynlee, and Matt had been sleeping on blow up mattresses on the hospital floor. Kelsey drove back and forth from her home.

It was a true Godsend when Sharon and Jim entered our situation. Sharon and Jim are a sister and brother-in-law to Chris's brother's wife. They own a guest loft next to one they live in that's located just a couple blocks down the street from the hospital. Sharon and Jim knew that we were going to be there in Wichita for a long time, and because we live an hour away, they offered us the loft to stay in for however long we needed it! What a much-needed blessing that was! We had never been offered something that generous before. We had never been in a situation where we needed help like that before. Jim and Sharon not only provided a place to stay, but also stocked it with food and drinks and had the Wi-Fi connected as well as satellite TV. Their kindness reminded me of the Bible story of the good Samaritan, who not only came to the aid of a dying man on the ground, but also provided for all his needs until he was well. It felt like too much to accept from Jim and Sharon, but we were desperate and graciously took them up on their offer. It made our stay during those hard times so much more bearable and we will be eternally thankful for their kindness.

After five days in Wichita, Chris and I needed to make a trip back home and felt it would be okay to leave for a short time. We needed a fresh supply of clothes and other things we wanted to have with us in Wichita. Chris needed to check on how things were going on the farm. Even though the season was finishing up for the year, we have a machine shop and a combine refurbishing business, so there's always a lot going on. I manage the bookkeeping, payroll, and business in the office at the farm and was sure that in the time we had been away, things were piling up along with the regular household bills. Even though our world came to a halt, life as usual was still going on around us.

It was wonderful that Jodi's parents took vacation time to stay with her and help care for Brynlee at the hospital. Jodi needed them more than ever. Since they were there, Chris and I could leave without worrying about her. She and Brynlee could stay with Zach, and we could get the list of things Jodi needed from home.

It was nice to see home again when Chris dropped me off and left to go to the farm. It was my first time to be alone since the accident, and I felt that being home was going to lift my spirits by surrounding me with everything that felt normal.

But that's not what happened at all. Being there in the quietness of our home opened my eyes to a reality that came on totally unexpectedly. Photographs or anything I saw that reminded me of Zach caused me such deep emotional pain that it was as if he had died, and I was mourning his death. While I gathered up things in my room, an incredible sense of sadness came over me, and I started thinking of what life would be like without him. Knowing that no one else was there or could hear me, I started crying as I began a conversation out loud with God. All the harsh events of the past week flashed through my mind like a raging storm, and my sadness was soon replaced with anger. I was thinking about how Zach did not deserve all he was going through. He was such a good person, and now he was suffering. His life would be changed forever. I began to yell at God, asking Him why this had to happen to Zach. I threw the pillows off my bed and then picked one up and punched it over and over as hard as I could while screaming at the top of my lungs. Finally, my anger gave way to sobbing. Falling to my knees on the floor, I cried long and hard until finally a sense of calm took over and I no longer felt anything inside—not anger, not sadness, just emptiness. It was as if I had purged everything that built up inside since the beginning of the whole tragic event.

When Chris came back to get me, he shared that he too had a terrible experience when he went back to the farm. He said that everywhere he looked, he could see Zach. He could see the fields Zach had worked, the projects he had helped build around the farm, and the dog Milo, the stray Zach rescued when it was abandoned. Then he'd seen the thing that hurt the most. It was Zach's new Ford pickup that was parked in his drive way in front of his house. Zach had purchased it only a few months before his accident. It was his first new vehicle to own, and he was so proud of it. Chris had the same overwhelming emotional experience that I had. Even though Zach was still with us, the fear of losing him still hung over our heads like a dreary, black cloud. There were still so many questions about his future—if he even had one. We knew he was in critical condition and that there were no promises. Each day with him was a gift and we knew it.

7

MOVING ON

For the first time, we could all stay together in comfort and still be near the hospital. In the loft, there was a couch that pulled out into a bed in the living room next to the kitchen. Jodi set up her things there, as it would be handier for her to have the kitchen nearby for Brynlee. Kelsey could share the bed with Jodi when she visited, Matthew could sleep on the other couch, and there was a loft bedroom at the top of the long stairway that Chris and I moved into. We had a small washing machine and dryer to use in a closet next to the kitchen. Everything was clean and modernly decorated—it was perfect. I don't know what we would've done without it. Hotels were expensive, and we had no idea how long we were going to be staying in Wichita.

Halloween came, and Jodi was anticipating dressing Brynlee up in her cute little owl costume she had eagerly purchased in advance. It was going to be Brynlee's first time to participate—she was only one-month old the previous year. Since Zach was holding his own and resting well, we decided not to let the fact that we were in a hospital stop us from taking part in the fun holiday. We couldn't go trick or treating around the hospital neighborhood; that would be too dangerous. The area the hospital was located in wasn't a safe part of town, so we thought of a different idea. Instead of asking for candy at unfamiliar houses, we'd pass it out to the patients in the children's ward.

Brynlee was adorable in her little tan hoot-owl costume with big green eyes located on the hood on top of her head. As we went from room to room, Jodi, Staci, Ashley (Jodi's sister), and I followed behind Brynlee and her cousin, Braedyn who was dressed as a ninja turtle. Watching the pink wings on Brynlee's back flutter up and down as she toddled along toting her candy bucket was entertaining. Her short little legs carried her quickly down the halls even though she was fairly new at walking. At times she'd stumble, then go rolling across the floor because of all the padding around her tummy and back. We knew we'd made a good choice when we visited the children's rooms that Halloween. We saw the atmosphere change for the kids lying in their beds when Brynlee and her cousin handed out candy and put big smiles on their faces. The nurses and staff were amused as well. It was so nice to break away from our stress and have a little normality, even if only for an evening. We were starting to relax a little bit.

Part of Jodi's routine for putting Brynlee to bed was to use a digital music machine. It played the song *Rock-a-Bye Baby* in a loop over and over and over. Even though Jodi turned the volume down, it was still audible from Chris's and my bedroom in the loft. We had no problem falling asleep because we were usually mentally exhausted each night, but it never failed that I would wake up about 4:30 or 5:00 each morning to hear that song playing. "Rock-a-bye baby in the tree top...." I'd sing along with it in my head, over and over. While I listened to that melody repeating again and again like a mantra, my mind pictured what Zach was going through—what we were all going through. As I lay there, trapped in a dreamworld twilight zone, my mind played host to a world of emotions. They were thoughts that compelled me to get up and put into words the feelings I wanted to share with others on Facebook. I began to do that every morning before dawn—so strange for me, considering that I'm not a morning person. Chris grumbled sleepily that I needed to stay in bed, but I couldn't sleep. I wanted to share the thoughts while they were fresh in my mind. It was like my heart was talking to me and saying, "This is important. Take care of it now!" I started going into the bathroom and shutting the door. I'd sit on the toilet seat in the dark with my phone, posting to Facebook what came to my mind each morning, then I'd go back and lie down, careful not to wake Chris.

One morning when I woke up, a rush of gratitude rustled my heart. The night before I had read the postings about different ways people were showing support for Zach and our family, and I felt compelled to express my appreciation. I went into the bathroom and typed to Facebook:

> *I keep waking up before the sun comes up because things are heavy on my heart. This time I woke up with the overwhelming feeling of gratitude. Of course, you all know and have felt along with us, the over abundant joy that God has given us our Zachary. I can't even form the right words that can express the gratitude we feel for that.*

I'm slow to let you know, but it's something that's been there all along, and that's our feeling of gratitude for all of you. I can barely type out the words because I can't see through my tears and my fingers are shaking. I don't know how to form a message to you that would possibly say it strong enough, how our family feels for all you have done for us and for Zach. I know that God is taking care of us, through all of you. Over, and over again, we'll read or hear about something that you have done to show how much you care. The best way I can describe how it feels each time news is delivered about what you've done or said or prayed, is that it feels like my heart has been given a warm embrace; it swells with love; chills come over me; then tears come to my eyes; my fatigue melts away and adrenaline pumps strength back into me. I know I speak the same for the rest of my family. The things you have done to support us are leaving us awe struck. Back home our friends and neighbors are working long hours to harvest our fall crops and plant our wheat so that Chris and Matt can be here at the hospital. There have been fund raisers and monetary donations collected for Zach's family at a chili feed, a football game, at local banks, and online. My friend gave her entire day's earnings from each client at her salon. Friends and family sent meals to feed us at the hospital and have brought buckets and plates of snacks. A song has been dedicated in Zach's name. The school where Zach attended stopped for a minute of silence to remember him, and children have colored get-well pictures. We have been given the use of a beautiful loft to stay in near the hospital which has been stocked with food. These friends say we can stay there for however long we have the need. When we went home to take care of some business last Wednesday, we saw our lawn was mowed. We've seen signs posted that read "Pray for Zach Short." The visits, cards, calls, texts, and posts continue to come and remind us of your love and support. And I've left it for last but not because it's least...quite opposite...the prayers! You have formed prayer chains in your churches, schools and organizations. Our farm neighbors started the idea of stopping their combine crew at 10:00am and 4:00pm to pray, which led many others all over to do the same. I know there are things I've left out or am probably not even aware of yet, but please just know that each and every act, that every one of you has done, makes a difference in coping with this tragedy. You've all been there for us and we feel how much your hearts ache along with ours. Thank you, thank you, THANK YOU! We can't say it strong enough. God bless you and thank you!

Not only were people at home doing wonderful things to support us, they were making visits to the hospital to offer their companionship or help. One lady even brought holy water from a trip to Israel and sprinkled it on Zach.

Some of the first responders to Zach's accident visited to follow up on him. One, brought her friend whom she said was gifted with spiritual abilities to pray over sick patients and help them heal. She asked permission for her friend to pray over Zach, so Jodi and I said that of course she was welcome to do that. We hadn't ever experienced anything quite like what we saw her do.

After introducing herself to Zach whom was still deep in a comatose state, Jodi and I watched as this woman circled around his bed, waving her arms over him while chanting words that we didn't understand. Maybe she was praying in tongues—we didn't know. Then I saw a tear fall from the outside corner of Zach's eye and run down his hairline. I wasn't quite sure what to make of that. "Maybe the nurses had just recently put in some eyedrops," I thought to myself, "or maybe it has something to do with the chanting!"

Next, the woman held up something long and pointed, explaining that it was the horn of a ram and called a shofar. She asked if it would be alright to "Seal the prayers," as she put it, "by blowing the horn which also would signify victory over death."

Jodi and I looked at each other with amused, questioning eyes. We weren't quite sure what all this entailed. Visions of nurses running down the hall to Zach's room to see what the commotion was danced through my imagination, but letting her know that it would be okay, Jodi and I shuffled over to the doorway, nervously looking over our shoulders for personnel that might show up. After reassuring us that she would try not to be too conspicuous, the woman put the horn to her mouth and blew out a short, anticlimactic "honk." She usually made a louder and longer call, she explained, but she wanted to be respectful of the hospital peace.

After visiting a bit with this woman who seemed to possess such a positive aura, we thanked her for taking the time to pray for Zach. Before saying goodbye, she carefully wrapped her shofar in a soft cloth and then paused for a moment before she left the room. Looking in Jodi's direction, she smiled as she revealed to us that she saw a vision of a baby boy in Jodi's future. Not certain how seriously to take that comment, it did give us a ray of hope. Jodi and I were moved by her compassion and open to anything that might help Zach heal. Who knows? Maybe it did!

Most of the support we received continuously came from those following Jodi's and my posts online with our updates on Zach. Some said they would start their day by first checking Facebook to see how Zach was doing. Jodi had so many "friend" requests, including people whom she didn't know, that her newsfeed began to clog. A friend took care of that for Jodi by creating a separate Facebook account, called "Prayers for Zach Short."

The support and prayers of our community was a boost of strength we needed for what we had ahead of us. The day came that we knew could no longer be put off. Dr. Bingaman approached us in the waiting room to explain his plan for surgery. His voice cracked when he reiterated the previous Monday's events, reminding us that he had gone into the room to watch Zach through the dying process, but instead, witnessed something he had never seen—a complete turnaround. Again, he stated that he had no explanation for it other than it was a miracle—it was God.

We had all come to love Dr. Bingaman more with each day and appreciated his knowledge and compassion. He knew each of us by name. He hugged us, cried with us, and led us in prayer. We felt confident in his decisions. That's why, when he told us it was going to be necessary to remove parts of Zach's legs to save his life, we trusted him. Of course, It was extremely hard to accept that information, but Dr. Bingaman helped us understand it was the right thing to do by explaining that the damage from the burns on Zach's legs was too severe and that the infection was a threat to his life. He said that the right foot was unsalvageable from the ankle down. The left leg was much worse with the most damaging burns being from the knee to the end of his toes. We asked him if it was absolutely necessary to amputate the knee. Dr. Bingaman replied that it was his experience that people who tried to save an unhealthy knee which had been grafted had a difficult time attaching a prosthetic and would end up having to go back into surgery to amputate above the knee.

We wanted to move on with whatever it took to make Zach well. So, that day at 1:30pm, the medical team began the process to remove Zach's left leg above the knee and his right leg above the ankle. Dr. Bingaman said he would use all the salvageable skin from those legs to graft onto burns on Zach's left side and upper legs. He also intended to clean up the deep laceration on the left hand that had grabbed the metal ladder on the grain cart.

We sat in the waiting room all afternoon waiting for news from the surgery that would forever alter Zach's life. The thought of Zach without his legs saddened us deeply, but there was no other choice if we were going to save him. We had to accept what we were given and move on, hoping for the best. Little Brynlee kept us occupied and distracted during the wait. She would never remember her daddy any other way than without his legs.

As I waited with the rest of the family, my thoughts went back to all the other times Zach was injured and ended up in the hospital. I'm not sure why that kid was so accident prone. One might think we were inattentive parents, but we have two other kids who never made even half the trips to the doctor that we made with Zach. It wasn't like Zach was uncoordinated and clumsy; he was quite the opposite. He was fast and fearless and highly focused on his goal, which possibly distracted him from the consequences of his actions. That may have been the reason for some of his accidents, but otherwise it was just plain bad timing or bad luck. For instance, when he was six years old, he was told to take the trash out to the burn barrel. Seeing that it was already full, he got inside the blackened metal barrel, held onto the edge, and jumped up and down to pack the trash, attempting to make room for more. He was so focused on watching his feet squishing the trash that he hit his forehead on the edge of the barrel, and the resulting gash between his eyes ended up needing four stitches.

There was also the time I received a call from the school nurse when Zach was in the 1st grade. She told me that he was in an accident on the playground. He was playing football at recess and collided heads with another classmate. The other little boy's face was cut from the smashed glasses he was wearing, but Zach appeared to be okay. After school, he complained of a headache, became nauseated, and threw up. We made a trip to the emergency room where he was diagnosed with a concussion.

Then there was the time when Zach was seven and fell off his mini four-wheeler somewhere out in the barnyard while I was inside the house. He and Matthew loved that little four-wheeler. They buzzed all over the farm and had great fun driving it. One day my parents came for a visit and noticed that Zach wasn't running up to greet them, but instead was lying out in the grass. Mom asked, "What's Zach doing out in the yard? He wouldn't come over to say hello." "That's strange," I thought to myself. He always came flying up to his grandparents with hugs and kisses when they arrived. I went outside and sure enough, he was out in the grass lying there as if he were studying the clouds. I walked out to him. "Zach, Grandma and Grandpa are here. What are you doing?" "Nothing" he replied. I grabbed him under the armpits to stand him up. He wouldn't put his feet down to bear his weight. "Zach, stand up. Don't you want to go see Grandma and Grandpa? They're here. C'mon, let's go inside." I thought he was stalling or messing around with me. "C'mon, Grandma and Grandpa want to see you, let's go...." It finally hit me. "He's not playing—something is wrong with this kid." I looked into his light blue eyes and noticed that they didn't seem to be focusing correctly. "Zach, did you fall off your four-wheeler?" He looked away from me and said, "Nothing."

I turned his head to face me. "Zach, did you hurt yourself on the four-wheeler?" He answered as if he was frustrated by my questions. "Nothing!" he said back. That was a strange answer, I thought. He finally began to walk, but it was as if he were drunk. I scooped him up, put him in the car, and Mom and I raced to the hospital. His symptoms got worse while we were there. He began to vomit over and over. When the doctor asked Zach who I was, he said that he didn't know. The doctor then asked him who his grandma was and he replied, "My teacher." There were no visible bumps or bruises on his head, thanks to his helmet. A cat scan was done, as well as an EEG in case it was a seizure, since we really didn't know what happened to him. Tests came back normal, but Zach was kept overnight for observation.

Another concussion was diagnosed when Zach was eight. He was playing basketball and ran smack into the goal pole when he was reaching for the ball in the air. By evening, his words began to slur and he started the vomiting that signaled his brain was injured. Again, we ran to the ER where he stayed overnight for observation.

Concussion number four made Chris and I shake our heads in disbelief. Zach was merely filling the dog bowl with water. The large flat rock it sat on below the spigot became slick when the water ran over. Zach slipped and fell, hitting the back of his head. He spoke gibberish all the way to the hospital. He was talking, but it was as if he was speaking another language. We began to think this boy should wear a helmet full time! Thank goodness I'm a licensed cosmetologist, because I have saved myself a bundle of money coloring the gray hairs that boy caused me!

When it came to junior high football season, Zach's doctor would not sign the physical form giving permission for him to play the game. She said he had already suffered too many concussions, and she wouldn't okay it. That bummed Zach out. He loved sports so much, and had played football with the YMCA and Recreation

Department all his grade school years. He was good and probably would've excelled in it, but honestly, I was relieved to think that I wouldn't have to worry about him getting concussed or hurt in that sport.

Unfortunately, keeping him out of football didn't fix everything. Chris and I were on our way to Zach's high school wrestling meet when we received a call that he was taken to the hospital in Newton, Kansas. He had been picked up by his opponent and slammed down on the mat, hitting his head hard enough that it caused yet another concussion.

Concussions weren't the only injuries that Zach sustained. At only nine months old, he ended up in traction for a full week in the hospital. Both his little legs were suspended in the air while his body was pinned down to the bed with a diaper across his hips so he couldn't move. He fell out of a swing at his grandparents' house when his older sister, Kelsey, lifted the bar that held them in, causing them both to fall on the ground, her on top of him. Zach's femur, the thigh bone up near his hip, was fractured. That incident was probably harder on me and his grandma than it was on him. He'd cry and reach his little arms out for me to pick him up from the bed in the hospital, but I couldn't do anything but lay my head close to him and utter soothing words or sing. I slept next to him on a cot each night, wanting to be near. After a couple days, he quit crying to be held. I guess he finally realized it did him no good. We were never so happy as that day they took him down from traction and put a full body cast on him, allowing him to go home. At that age, he hadn't walked yet, so he crawled around in the blue cast that wrapped around his tummy with his leg protruding stiffly behind him. He looked like a turtle with a bum leg.

When Zach was 20 months old, I remember getting out of the shower and toweling off when I heard a thump, then a cry. I ran into the bedroom that he and Matthew shared, where Zach had fallen from his crib. He had never attempted to climb out before—that was the first time. When I picked him up, he held out his tiny wrist and said "Hurts." I took him into the bathroom where there was better lighting and could tell right away that his wrist was broken. It looked flattened and crooked. He wore a little green cast for a few weeks on his forearm. We still have that tiny cast, as well as the blue body cast and the battery he swallowed. I'm not sure why I kept them—maybe to show Zach what all we'd been through together and to remind me of how resilient he was. That reminder came in handy as we waited through the devastating surgery that removed his legs.

After three hours, the doctors reported that the surgery was completed, and that Zach was doing as well as could be expected. The next twelve hours were the most critical for watching his response, they warned us, mostly blood pressure and kidney function, but they felt he would do fine. Praise God!

It was done. The anticipation of that awful surgery to remove the unrepairable parts of Zach's legs was a large part of our anxiety. Knowing it was over and that he was resting gave us some relief. It was helpful that Zach remained in the induced coma. It gave us time to handle the emotional aspects that we were dealing with before we had to face Zach's ability to deal with the loss of his legs.

I thought that I was prepared to see him the next day. I told myself I could withstand anything, after going through that near-death experience, but that was not the case. When Chris and I walked into Zach's room and laid eyes on him for the first time after his surgery, we weren't at all prepared for the reality of what was before us.

Zach's body was covered with a crisp white sheet, but it didn't hide the fact that where his legs should have been, there was nothing. The contours of his body and upper legs were visible, but the sheet went flat on the bottom half of the bed. He didn't have to be uncovered for us to know what was not under that sheet. His legs had been so long before! it was as if he'd been sawed in half. Chris and I felt gut-wrenching sadness to see him that way. A part of Zach was gone forever—we would never again see or experience him as he was. We thought we were prepared, but it was much harder to accept than we'd expected.

I was so broken hearted and disappointed by what I was looking at. At the same time, I felt ashamed of myself for having those feelings. God had spared Zach's life and all his bodily functions, so to be disappointed that we couldn't also save his legs caused me to feel like I was being greedy for wanting more. I wanted it all! I wanted him to be the way he was before!

Chris and I choked on our tears as we stood there in a state of shock, trying to process what our eyes beheld. We were speechless. The nurse in the room could see our pain and did her best to comfort us. She told us that it was okay to cry, to let it all out because it was a loss, a grieving process that was a lot like losing someone to death. We needed time to absorb the reality, and then we'd need to be strong enough to help Zach get through it once he awoke and learned his fate.

Jodi warned us it would be hard to see him. I admired how she had managed to hold things together despite what she saw and was going through. What a tremendous emotional impact it was for her to have to sign the forms authorizing the amputation of her husband's legs. How could he be a farmer without his legs? She longed to be able to talk to Zach about such a weighty decision, but there was no time with the threat of spreading infection, so she took a deep breath and signed on the line. Jodi's love for Zach was holding strong and true. She vowed that the two of them would get through it all together, that she loved him for who he was and not for his legs.

After that big surgery, doctors started focusing on other areas that needed attention. They put a wound VAC on his right thigh where the electricity exited and blew apart the flesh on his leg, leaving a wound that nurses told us was "soupy." A wound VAC (vacuum-assisted closure) was something we had never seen. Basically, it was a tube connected to a large bandage that covered the wound. Through a vacuum process, it's used to pull wounds together that are too large or deep for stitches or staples. The tube attached to Zach's leg looked like something out of a science fiction movie.

Zach had another exit wound above his forehead in his hair on the right side of his head. The doctors cleaned out the dead flesh, a procedure also referred to as debriding, which left him with a gaping hole about the size of a silver dollar. They stitched it together, but as time went on it slowly pulled apart, making the stitches more visible. It looked like it was going to need future attention.

The left side of Zach's face, along with his neck, began to change from the time we first arrived at the hospital. Originally, we had thought that his face wasn't affected, but that was not the case. As it turned out, the heat from the flames on his shoulder caused third degree burns on his face, and the skin started turning bright red. It wept and bled as time went along. The nurses applied white ointment regularly to help with the pain and healing.

The doctor also continued to be very concerned about Zach's left arm, unsure whether it was going to mend and be salvageable. It was wrapped up, but we could see around the edges of the bandages that the skin underneath was blackened and charred. His left thumb looked bad too. The skin and fingernail looked as though they were barely hanging on.

Thoughts of Zach losing his arm scared us. Seeing him without his legs was hard enough—the loss of his arm would be even worse. The thought of him being disassembled limb by limb was torturous. We were concerned that Zach would not want to accept living without three of his limbs. It was all too much to think about.

Dwelling on issues we didn't have answers to only opened the door wider to fear. One thing I regularly practiced during the times that fear overwhelmed me was to turn everything over to God. It's true that a person can't help what they feel emotionally, but they *can* control their thoughts, so I chose to make myself *know* that God had the situation handled. It was a battle, but eventually I taught myself to trust that no matter what, God would take care of Zach and all of us as well. Believing that with all my heart was the best way to relieve the tension and stress and the only way for me to have peace of mind. Jodi and I held each other up so many times, reminding each other of this. We kept telling each other that because Zach survived, God must have plans of a future for him.

I also found comfort in spending time with Zach in his room. He was never left alone for long, and I was hoping that he somehow knew we were always around. Dr. Bingaman mentioned once that people who are burned and then put into comas usually have traumatic dreams while in the comatose state. It bothered me that Zach might be experiencing nightmares on top of everything else he was dealing with, so I hoped that having family around him would alleviate that possibility. I also did a lot of praying that he would not be tortured by nightmares. Whenever I went into Zach's room, I talked to him as if he could hear me, telling him that I was wishing him good dreams. I loved watching him sleep and listening to him breathe. I'd put my hand on his chest so that I could feel his heart beating, making me feel so grateful that he was alive. And then I'd pray over him: "Lord please surround Zach with your angels. Be with him and give him the strength to heal.

Comfort him with good dreams and help him to know that we are here with him and he's loved."

My nephew, Nic came for the first time to see Zach after a few weeks. The two of them grew up together and were close. Nic had worked for us during several harvests, but a new full-time job took him away, and he missed out on being part of our last one. When he entered Zach's room, he only held it together for a short period of time before breaking down in tears. Seeing his cousin lying in bed unconscious, hooked up to monitors and without his legs, was more than he could stand.

"I should have been there that day to help," he sobbed. "Maybe this wouldn't have happened if I...." Before he could finish, I cut him off. Astonished that he had been carrying remorse, I wanted to relieve him of the guilt he seemed to be harboring. "Nic, you have nothing to do with what's happened here! Don't blame yourself. Nobody is blaming you." His breathing relaxed and he calmed down, as if he had just heard something he must have needed to hear.

I felt badly that Nic even had thoughts like that. It seems that we all tend to go through feelings of guilt and blame when it comes to accidents. We try to figure out why and how things happened and how we could have made a difference in preventing them from happening. "If only I'd..." seems to start most of those types of conversations.

With the multitude of heart-breaking accidents that I've seen in my life time and after reading many books on near-death experiences, I've drawn some personal conclusions. I've opened my mind to the possibility that these events were destined to take place before we were even conceived. I don't believe that God causes terrible things to happen. He gives us our own free will, so we come into the world with a life plan of our own choosing—a type of roadmap that's intended to take us through all the ups, downs, and curves that life offers, teaching us lessons and presenting us with experiences. We love, hurt, learn, and grow with each of our experiences, and after achieving what we came here for, we leave this life and return to eternity, where we become more evolved spirits because of what we've been through in our lifetime on Earth. Along the way, our lives also impact and help others' lives in their journey back to God. This idea just seems to make sense to me.

I've even been contemplating the theory that the amount of time we spend on this planet is predetermined before we come to this life. I used to believe that when it's our time to go, there is nothing we can do to prevent it, although after what we went through with Zach, I now question that thought. I wrestle with the idea that God heard the pleading prayers and gave Zach more time, or whether it was the plan all along for Zach's accident to bring us to our knees and help us find or stretch our faith by witnessing the miracles God granted. No matter what one believes, a life taken or nearly taken causes us to question those beliefs.

I'm reminded of a Biblical story when I think of Zach's situation. John 9:3 seems so fitting. It tells the story of how Jesus saw a blind man passing by. His disciples asked him, "Rabbi, who sinned, this man or his parents, that he was born blind?" Jesus answered, "Neither this man nor his parents sinned, but this happened so that the works of God might be displayed in him."

8

SIGNS FROM GOD

It wasn't until Nic and a few of Zach's friends visited that I took the time to think more about how Zach was rescued from being electrocuted to death. All of us were standing around Zach's bed talking about the events of that day, hashing out the details, when something came to light that blew us away. Everyone knew it was a shovel that Les used to free Zach from the electrical currents, but what we learned about that shovel gave me chills!

A few days into harvest, a friend of ours, Tyler, had seen a shovel lying along the roadside as he was driving near where our crew had been harvesting just a few days before. He assumed our crew had lost it since it was near where they had been working, so he tossed it in his pickup and carried it around with him for several days. When Zach and Les were in town having lunch, Tyler saw them and mentioned that he'd found the shovel. Les looked it over and said it wasn't ours but told Tyler to throw it into the back of the service pickup because we'd probably use it.

That shovel had a wooden shaft with a plastic scoop and handle. Had it not been in the service vehicle the day of Zach's accident, Les would not have been able to detach Zach from the grain cart ladder! There would have been nothing to use that wasn't made of metal.

I'm a firm believer that there are no such things as coincidences. God works in mysterious ways, and learning the story of that shovel was yet another sign that He was looking out for Zach. What are the chances that a shovel would magically appear on the roadside? How amazing it was that the shovel was made of plastic and wood, a rarity in our inventory of tools. I don't think I've ever even seen a full-sized shovel that wasn't partly made of metal. To go even further, we own two service trucks. The one that contained the shovel was the one that happened to be out in the field that day, and moreover, Les was probably able to act faster since he was familiar with the shovel. He would have known the second he spotted it that it would be safe to use. Amazing! Just amazing!

Two weeks at the hospital had gone by when someone wished Chris and me a happy anniversary. We had lost all sense of time and weren't even aware of what day of the week it was, let alone that it was our anniversary. I read all the Facebook good wishes along with the comments regarding our family having strength for what we were going through, and then made use of time to post my thoughts:

> We've come through three surgeries. With each one we felt incredible fear for Zach's life, so we prayed, and we waited. Each time Zach rallied through, and we were able to breathe more freely. You all say we are so strong. Believe me, I have not always felt strong. My insides feel like sickening mush at times. That's when I pray for God to give me strength. And then I use all my strength to *believe* He hears me and will take care of our needs. I ask myself what good it is to ask God to act on something I need, if I don't believe in what He can or will do? I completely trust that He knows what's best for Zach and all of us—He has a plan, but in my selfish heart, I want His plan to be what I want...... for Zach to live. Because I don't know God's plan, that's when the fear sets in. So, I tend to go around and around with this battle in my heart. I do think God is working through all of you to help calm our fears, hold us up and give us strength and hope. There are so many ways God's shown us he loves us through all of you. Thank you! And thank God!

I had to concentrate on my own words when Zach had surgery number four. Infection had set in at the amputation sight of one of his legs and needed immediate attention. Doctors also planned on skin grafting Zach's side and back, and then wanted to explore the left arm some more.

To be able to graft skin is an amazing procedure but it is also, in my opinion, so harsh. A tool is used (makes me think of a potato peeler) to remove the top layer of skin (the epidermis) as well as a portion of the second layer of skin (the dermis) from an area of the patient's body (the donor site) that has healthy skin. To make the donor skin go further and allow fluid to drain under the graft, it is run through a machine that cuts small slits in it, creating a mesh-like appearance. Then the skin is stapled in place to cover the damaged area. In Zach's case, because he was burned on over 54% of his body and his legs were amputated, there wasn't much healthy skin area from which to harvest. It also meant that not only would he be tender in the burned places, but also in the places that were perfectly healthy and unharmed until they became donor sites. We were told that the donor sites are more painful than the areas that are grafted, and moreover, skin gets harvested from the very same donor sites in as little as two weeks if there aren't many places from which to utilize healthy skin!

Before skin is grafted by using the patient's own skin, cadaver skin is first applied to see if the area is ready to accept a covering. If the area immediately rejects the cadaver skin, it will reject the patient's skin as well, which would be a terrible waste. It would be wonderful if the cadaver skin would last permanently, but it doesn't—eventually it deteriorates because the body will not accept it as its own. Besides acting as a temporary covering, though, cadaver skin works wonderfully to relieve pain, prevent infection, and help maintain body temperature.

Surgery number four was yet again another time to sit on pins and needles and wait, praying and hoping that the reports would be what we wanted to hear. We were back on that rollercoaster of ups and downs—another scary ride.

Having Brynlee with us was a blessing. She kept us busy running after her and tending to her needs. Much of the time, it was hard to have the energy to keep up with her; she was energetic and constantly on the move, always getting into things she shouldn't (as a thirteen-month-old does), but looking back, I believe it was good for us to have her there keeping us distracted from the negative thoughts that lead to fearful thinking. One nice afternoon, I took her for a stroll outdoors around the hospital to get some fresh air. The pulsating sound of a Life Watch helicopter flew right over our heads. I pointed up to the sky, "Look, Bryn, that's what your daddy rode in to get here." Squinting and straining to see past the sun, she looked up at the sky just in time to see the helicopter fly through a small snippet of a rainbow. Immediately a thought came to my mind: "A rainbow is the sign of a promise from God." Yes, it's a promise that He won't ever flood the entire Earth again, but still, it's a promise sign. Since the Life Watch helicopter (just like the one Zach flew in) flew right through the middle of that rainbow while we were watching, the thought immediately came to my mind that it was a sign from God that Zach was going to be okay. That revelation gave me chills, and a sense of peace came over me.

Jodi had a similar experience one night as she was praying for Zach not long after we first arrived in Wichita. She said that during her prayer, her legs took on a tingly, warm sensation that felt like nothing she had ever experienced before. She promptly sat up and asked her mom, Staci, who had been lying on the floor next to her in a hospital waiting room, to feel her legs. Staci looked at her as if she were crazy but did as Jodi asked and didn't discover anything unusual. "Mom…Zach's going to be okay! God's telling me that, right now!" Jodi felt certain that God was speaking to her in this way. She too, had a sense of calmness afterward, just as I had.

Once surgery number four was completed, Dr. Bingaman gave us the depressing news that it was not looking good for Zach's arm. Another specialist agreed with him, but they still wanted to give it a little more time. They also reported that Zach had infection in his blood. They were hoping it was due to wounds and not something internal. They ordered CT scans to find out. With that news, my insides were shaking, and I felt sick. I needed to cry and I needed to pray. I also needed to ask everyone I knew if they would again pray for us, so I did just that.

On a more positive note, while we were waiting on Zach's surgery, a man visiting the hospital caught our attention. He had prosthetic legs that were exactly like how Zach's would be. His left leg was amputated above the knee and his right leg was amputated below the knee. He also had a prosthetic left arm! He was tall, over six feet, and walked with confidence and grace as he headed down the hall in front of us sitting behind the glass windows of the waiting room. Matthew, Jodi, and her parents, as well as myself, all looked up and watched in amazement as he strolled past the windows and then disappeared out of sight. We asked ourselves if we had really seen what we thought we saw, or if it was an angelic apparition? Jodi's mom, Staci, decided she was going to watch for him to come back and when or if he did, she was going to flag him down.

Later he appeared again! There he was, walking swiftly toward the other end of the hall. We were so excited! Staci promptly ran out of the waiting room to catch him. They talked outside the door and then he walked away. Staci reported that she explained to the man about Zach, then asked him if we could please talk to him about his life with prosthetics. He explained that he was on his way to get his son who was about to be released from the hospital.

Apparently, his son had been ill and was on the same floor as Zach and now was well enough to go home. The man told Staci that he would come back to talk with us as soon as he had a chance.

We gained so much positive energy from our visit with Dave, the man with the prosthetics. He was a very compassionate man who took the time to answer our many questions about how he lived his life since the loss of his limbs. He told us his story—he was in his early twenties, just like Zach, when he became ill from complications of Meningitis. He suffered such a high fever that his body lost circulation in his limbs, which then had to be amputated. He told us he had a rough time at first adapting to his new way of life. He was single at the time and thought that no one would want to have a relationship with a disabled person like himself. He spiraled into severe depression and nearly committed suicide when he heard a voice in his head that stopped him from driving off a bridge. He began to find his faith, and that's when his life turned around. Today he is married with four children and has a successful engineering career.

Dave gave us such a gift when he shared his personal story. He lifted us up and gave us hope. Like I said before, I believe there are no such things as coincidences. God puts people and situations in our paths on purpose and at the right time. He put Dave in our path that day to relieve our fears and to help us see that Zach could still be productive and live a quality life. God was showing us that he had not deserted us.

We knew that the situation could change in a heartbeat and that Zach was still in critical condition, but we finally began to feel like there was more hope than before. When we received the very good news that the CT scan showed no visual damage to Zach's internal organs, what a blessing and a relief that was! His temperature and vital signs began to look a little better, as did his wounds and his fight against infections. We were in for a long stay in Wichita, which might sound grueling to some, but to us, that was an exciting feeling. It meant that we were moving toward recovery and rehabilitation instead of worrying as much about life and death. The prayers were working, and I experienced a sense of calmness and contentment that I hadn't known since the beginning.

While driving from Wichita to Salina for a dental appointment, I wasn't just thinking about Zach; I was also thinking of my son Matthew. Matt hadn't left the hospital since Zach was admitted. He had worked daily with Zach at the farm for years, and it was difficult for Matt to leave him. I was seeing the hurt and worry in Matt's face and it broke my heart. All moms know that when any of our kids hurt, we hurt. Chris and I could see that we needed to help Matthew allow himself to go home. Chris finally told Matt that he needed to get away for a while and go back home to the farm and to work, as that would be good for him. Zach was better, Chris explained, and he promised to keep Matthew posted, just as we were doing for Kelsey, who needed to be home with her family.

As I drove northward on I-135 and reflected on Zach's healing, I apologized to God that I was so weak. I was still worrying, instead of trusting that He had everything in His hands. I imagined God speaking to me. I heard Him say, "Did I not spare Zach's life in the field that day? Did I not send him back to you when his body failed? Whenever there was a threat of infection or internal damage, weren't you given the news that all was well or under control? Where is your patience, Lisa? Be still and know that I am here!"

A black and yellow colored bird flew straight toward my windshield, stealing my breath away and startling me out of my deep thoughts. I nearly hit him, but he swiftly swooped sideways just in time to avoid getting hit. I looked in my rearview mirror, saw him fly away safely, and sighed a breath of relief, whispering "That was close. I'm so glad he made it!" Instantly, a revelation came to mind. Isn't that what God had been trying to tell me all along?

The dentist found that the pain in my jaw and teeth was caused by stress, from clenching and grinding them together. God was pointing out to me that the worry was worthless; it was just causing me unnecessary pain. "Thanks for the reminder and the lesson, God," I murmured out-loud to myself as I drove back to Wichita.

9

WAKING UP

The only way the doctors could know how to move forward with Zach's left arm was to see if he could move it; they would have to bring him out of his coma. On the morning of November eleventh, the nurses turned the sedation down. It was so exciting to think that we would see Zach become conscience again! It had been seventeen days since we had seen him with his eyes open—we could hardly wait.

Jodi's thoughts immediately flashed to the prayer warriors on Facebook. She solicited all the prayers she could muster, as it was so very important that Zach could move his arm—there would be little hope for saving it if he couldn't.

When the doctors were ready, they asked Jodi to wait outside Zach's room so that he wouldn't get distracted while they quizzed him. Anxiously, she stood watching from the doorway. She could see that his eyes were open and that he was moving his right arm and his legs, but sadly, he was not moving the left arm at all. But when the doctors squeezed his left finger, he grimaced—he could feel it! That pain was a spot of light in the darkness. At least he had feeling in that finger.

The doctor told Jodi that they would try again the next day after allowing more time for the drugs in his system to wear off. They put him back under sedation for his comfort and so he could rest. Jodi stepped in to be with Zach who moved his head toward her voice and opened his unfocused eyes but was still too groggy and out of it to respond.

As if it weren't discouraging enough that Zach didn't move his arm, we had more disheartening news added to the morning when a nurse informed us that the Cat-Scan revealed the presence of a fluid-filled pocket in Zach's abdomen. They told us that either the fluid had accumulated due to his organs being stressed in the accident, which could be a normal reaction, or it was possible that he was having some internal bleeding. The medical team needed to see which it was by drawing off some of the fluid to test.

Internal bleeding?! Just when things seemed to be leveling out and moving forward, a new threat came along to knock the wind right out of our sails. Having vital signs that appeared normal was reassuring but didn't always mean that everything was perfect inside Zach's body. Doctors couldn't be certain there was no damage by the vital readings alone. Only time would tell if everything was operating normally. The presence of fluid worried us that maybe something was going on that was just beginning to show up—Aaaaarghh! First Zach didn't move his arm, and now came this! Sometimes the stress was unbelievable!

We waited through a very long afternoon before finally getting the results of the test. The fluid came back clear—no blood. Hallelujah! Thank you, God! We could relax and breathe freely again.

The next day came, and again, Jodi and I waited on pins and needles, this time because doctors were running behind and couldn't get around to lowering Zach's sedation. It was hard to be patient when we were so anxious for him to wake up and communicate with us. We had so many questions for him. What was he experiencing in his mind while in that coma? What could he remember about the accident? Did he have a near death experience and possibly see God? Would he be the same Zach we had always known?

Finally, by midafternoon, the sedation was turned down and we eagerly stood by as doctors tried again to get him to move his left arm. Unfortunately, our eagerness quickly turned to despair. Even though his eyes were open, it was as if he weren't awake inside. There was no response—not from just his arm, but no response at all! He did nothing to show he could move the arm or even show that he was able to comprehend what the doctors asked. He just laid there as if he were sleeping with his eyes open.

Jodi needed to release some of her disappointment and frustration, so she turned to her phone and posted on Facebook:

> Sometimes I just break down. And I know that IS okay! Especially when I am talking to him and get no response. I want him to know who I am, and I want him to be able to see us and talk like he did before. I am impatient, and I know God is testing that. I know day by day, he gets stronger but gosh dang it, I miss him so much! I hate seeing him in pain! Sometimes I feel I want to give up, but I remember that God wouldn't give up on me, so I can't give up on Him. Especially after all the miracles He's given us. It will get easier, but right now it's so hard to watch. Today I'm asking for prayers for both of us.

The medical staff tried to lessen our worries by explaining how it can take days for the drugs to wear off, that Zach wouldn't just wake up and be back to normal—recovery can be a slow process. I, however, wasn't sure that even they knew what to make of him at this point. Zach's ability to speak cognitive sentences right after his accident offered hope that his mind hadn't been affected, but after the sedation was turned off and there was no response from him, I was uncertain. I hoped it meant that he needed more time to wake up, but for the first time, I feared that maybe his mind was more damaged than we had suspected. Nobody voiced that thought out loud, but we were all thinking it.

As we stood around the bed, I noticed that Zach's face, which had been looking better, was showing more redness and irritation. It appeared that conditions were going backward instead of forward. The day that we had been waiting for just didn't go as we had hoped and expected, and it left us deeply anxious.

I was restless and unable to sleep that night. I was afraid that Zach was slipping away, and I couldn't stop the blizzard of negative emotions swirling around in my head. My stomach began to knot up. After all, powerful electricity had exited out of the top of his head! How could there not be repercussions from something so violent like that?

No! I had to stop thinking like that! I had to remind myself to hand over my fears to God and stop worrying. Worrying was wasted energy that only made myself miserable. I needed to trust that whatever happened, God had Zach's best interests covered. "He wants the best for all of us," I whispered to myself, "and things would go according to *His* plan and in *His* own time. He brought us this far for some purpose, and was not going to desert us now." Reminding myself of this was the only way I could get any rest.

John 10:10 says, "The Devil comes to kill, steal and destroy." He was doing just that by putting fear in my head at a vulnerable time, always making attempts to shake my beliefs. I'm sure it drove the Devil mad to see the unity of so many people bonding in prayer and faith.

The night was long. It was in the early hours of morning when it occurred to me that today was my birthday. Obviously, it wasn't like all the past years, a day carved out for activities that brought me joy, so I laid there contemplating what would give me peace. Most people, including myself, would have assumed the obvious—that I wanted Zachary to heal and come home. That was what I had wished and prayed for all along, but that morning, that's not what came to my mind. For some reason, it felt selfish for me to wish for that.

Tears filled my eyes, and a thought welled up from the deepest place in my heart—an overwhelming truth. I realized for the first time that what I wanted was possibly not what would make Zach happiest. I loved him so much that I would fight tooth and nail for him for however long it took to get him through this hellish battle, but I know Zach—he is a people pleaser. If he was fighting only to please us, then I loved him too much to ask that from him. I thought long and hard about whether he would want to go on living as a handicapped person. Would he truly be happy that way? I wasn't giving up on him—I was realizing that I had come to a place in my heart and soul where I had to let go of my own wants and desires and think of his. Of course, nobody had control over any of it anyway—nobody except God. But as much as I wanted for Zach to heal and return home, it felt right in my heart to ask God for His will to be done, not mine.

Literally, as I released my requests in my thoughts, the phone rang at 6:45 am. It was the hospital calling Jodi. They didn't usually call so early, which alerted us that maybe something was wrong. My heart sunk as I strained to hear the one-sided conversation from my room upstairs.

Waking Up

The doctor phoned to say that early that morning, he was paged to Zach's room. He said that the respiratory therapist had been there to work with Zach—who turned his head to look at her! He was awake and responding! The doctor added that Zach nodded and shook his head to answer questions, and he tracked with his eyes. What fantastic news! But then came some bad news—Zach was able to move everything except for his left arm. He tried really hard—his face reflected the pain—but he just couldn't move it.

After that information, Jodi and I dressed and got Brynlee ready as fast as we could. We rushed to the hospital, anxious to see Zach, anxious to talk to him knowing that he would finally see that we were there with him. We parked the car, grabbed the stroller, and raced through the hospital to the elevator, carrying Brynlee and all the paraphernalia that accompanied her needs for the day. At the nurse's station at the entryway of the ICU, we learned that when Zach was having his dressings changed, the pain was so overwhelming, and he tried to pull out his ventilator, so they put him back under sedation.

What a disappointment! We missed our chance to see Zach awake. But we still had the great news that he was responding! Our fears of mind damage had been put to rest. What a relief! What a blessing!

We soon met with Dr. Bingaman, who updated us with what he had learned after spending the morning assessing Zach, and he reassured us that Zach was mentally cognitive. Dr. Bingham explained that Zach simply had needed time to wake up and respond. He went on to say that he felt Zach was strong enough to soon have the ventilator removed! Then he turned to Jodi and said that while he was quizzing Zach, he asked the newly awakened young man if he'd like to see his wife, and Zach nodded his head.

That bit of information made Jodi even more anxious for Zach to wake up again. She and I, with Brynlee, waited impatiently for hours, but Zach slept for most of the afternoon. It wasn't until early evening when a nurse finally approached Jodi in the waiting room and delivered the words she was waiting to hear: "Zach is awake, and he's asking for you." Jodi's face lit up. She rushed to his room.

Sadly, their visit wasn't exactly the fairy tale moment one sees in the movies. Zach wasn't the Zombie we had seen before, but he still wasn't very alert, and he was a very sleepy guy. His face showed his struggle with pain, and he couldn't speak because of the ventilator. As much as she longed to have more time with him, Jodi couldn't bear to see him hurting, so she asked the nurse to give him medication to make him more comfortable, which put him back to sleep. Before he drifted off, though, I briefly got to see Zach while his eyes were still open. I'll never forget how moved I was to see him actually looking back at me. It so warmed my heart.

Jodi was happier than she had been in a long time after seeing Zach's eyes open and confirming he was still there inside. She reached for her phone to update everyone about the latest on Zach, and typed this message out:

> He is THERE! Praise the Lord! Zach will get his vent taken out soon! That means he is strong enough for no sedation!!! He remembers me! That was one of my biggest fears. I cannot wait to hear him talk! God is good!! Now, keep praying that I can get him to move that left arm. God has given us many miracles and I know He will keep giving if we keep believing and accepting! PRAISE THE LORD! GOD BLESS YOU ALL!!

Waking Up

What a great birthday! It may sound horrific to say that I spent the entire day in the hospital with my son, burned and broken and helplessly lying in a bed, but it will be the most remembered and heartfelt birthday of my life. I finally saw Zach's eyes focusing on mine. I could finally see that he knew I was there. This was the most precious gift I could ever receive.

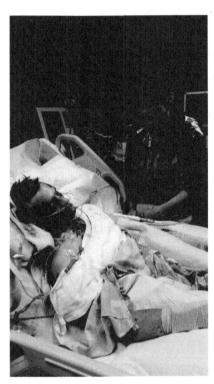
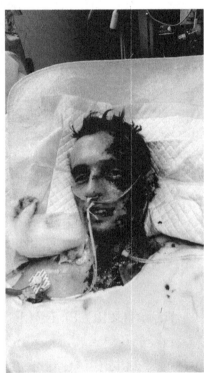

10

THE HOBBIT

Three weeks after it went in, Zach was strong enough to breathe without the ventilator and it was removed! We were informed ahead of time that he had a lot of pain killers and residual sedation in his system and that he wouldn't be able to speak or even make sense for a few days after being extubated. He would be "out of it" for a while, doctors said. That was normal procedure and we were prepared to wait it out—but that is not what happened.

Early the next morning, seven or eight nurses surrounded Zach's bed, staring at him in joyful disbelief. They had called each other into his room because they could hardly believe that he woke up so coherent and able to talk! Everyone, including the doctors and nurses, were amazed! They had never seen someone recover so quickly in all the years any of them had worked there. One of the nurses laughingly told us that Zach stared back at them with an expression that asked, "Who are you and why are you all staring at me?"

Learning the news that Zach was talking, Jodi could hardly wait to hear what he had to say. Her face was beaming with exhilaration when she entered his room. "Why are you looking at me like that?" Zach croaked, puzzled. He had seen her happy to see him before, but this time she was glowing and excited and he didn't understand why.

Surprised by his reaction she said, "You were in a bad accident—I wondered if you would even remember me."

"Why wouldn't I remember you?" he said as if she were being ridiculous. "I would never forget you and Brynlee. I love you." Jodi's eyes filled with tears and she began to cry. She was so relieved that he knew who she was. That had been one of her biggest fears, that he would not remember her and Brynlee.

Zach paused, trying to get a handle on what Jodi had said—*a bad accident*. He slightly recalled an incident in the harvest field, but until then, it hadn't been in his mind. He didn't remember the details and it didn't even seem important to him. He dismissed the confusion and asked, "Where is Matt?"

The doctor had warned Jodi that Zach had been under the influence of powerful drugs and might not remember or comprehend much about his situation. At this point in her visit, it was clear to her what the doctor was talking about. She played along, letting Zach lead their conversation to wherever he wanted to take it and answered: "Matt went back home to the farm to get work done, but he's going to be back here today. Do you want me to call him?"

"Yeah," Zach muttered. Knowing that Matt would be surprised, Jodi dialed his phone and put him on speaker so she and Zach could both hear. When Matt answered, he expected to hear Jodi's voice since the call was made from her phone. Instead he heard Zach, "Hey, Matt."

Matthew recognized Zach's voice immediately, and excitedly asked, "Is this really Zach?!" He could hardly believe he was hearing his brother.

Zach lowered his voice to a whisper, as if he were going to get in trouble if someone overheard what he was about to say. "Can you bring me a Samuel Adams? I'm really thirsty."

Both Jodi and Matt burst out laughing. Zach had been comatose for three weeks, and when he could finally speak, his first words to Matt were, *Can you bring me a beer*?! Zach had never even drunk Samuel Adams beer!

After the short phone conversation with Matt, Jodi broached the question that she and everyone had been curious about. She hesitated for a moment, then put it into words: "Zach, did you see God?" Even though she knew that Zach was still not back to clear thinking, she was too anxious to wait any longer. He answered slowly: "Yea...He told me to go back."

To this day, we still don't know what Zach really experienced. He was under the influence of so many drugs he doesn't know if what he said actually happened or if he was still a little loopy. So many things were hard for him to recall. He couldn't decipher what was real or what was hallucinations or dreams. If he did see God, it was erased from his memory because to this day, he doesn't recall much after seeing a white light at the scene of the accident. He did mention later down the road that he distinctly remembered seeing my dad with him at some point. He said my dad, his grandpa, looked younger than when he passed away. We had really hoped he would have a story to share with us, but that's alright—we were just happy to have Zach. That was all that mattered.

After Jodi had time alone with Zach, Chris and I went in, where the first words that Zach spoke to me as we entered his room were, "Happy Birthday." Wow! Music to my ears! What an exciting moment—to hear Zach's voice again! I suspected it wasn't possible that he could know what date it was. I had to ask the nurse, who let me in on the surprise that she had coached him. She knew it would make my day for him to wish me a happy birthday. It was a day late, but it did make my day! Zach was talking—he was back!

It was extremely exhilarating to see that he recognized us and showed that his personality was still the same! We kept our conversation light, knowing he was not completely coherent. We weren't sure how much he was aware of, concerning his health and situation. He didn't exhibit any signs of anger or sadness; we were surprised at how good-natured he was. When he talked to the nurses, he was so polite. Whenever he needed something from them, he'd ask as if he was worried that he was disturbing them, as if he didn't want to be a bother or wasn't deserving of their time and attention. After they fulfilled his requests, he'd always let them know how appreciative he was. He was an ideal patient—the nurses loved him.

Those nurses were the greatest. They cared so much about Zach and our family. One nurse, Elizabeth, was the most competent, proficient nurse I had ever seen. She was the head nurse and took her job very seriously. With perfection and professionalism, she did everything in her power to make sure Zach had the best care. Any time she was on duty, we rested easier knowing that she was watching him closely. Elizabeth was like our guardian angel—so beautiful, too, with her green eyes, long auburn hair, and peaches and cream skin. She was just as beautiful on the inside, the way she cared for Zach and the rest of us. All of the nurses who attended Zach were exceptional. After so much time spent with them, they became like family and we were grateful beyond words for all that they and the medical staff had done to help us on this journey.

That day when Zach first spoke reminded me of the movie, *The Wizard of Oz*, where Dorothy awakens to find her family surrounding her bed. They had been worried about her and were relieved when she woke up, and they saw she was okay. Just like that movie, our whole family was around Zach's bed, and we were elated to be talking to him. We were laughing and crying happy tears and loaded with questions. At times Zach was humorous. Because of the drugs in his system, he sometimes spouted out things that were a bit off the wall. He had requested a beer and later a Shasta cola, which was another odd request, because he never drinks Shasta either. I was surprised he had even heard of Shasta.

It caught us off guard, but we all laughed because of his quick wit and funny attitude when he blurted out, "I'm the Hobbit." Did he subconsciously know what he was saying? We didn't know for sure, but it was almost morbidly funny. I guess that's because we were so happy to be talking to him that we were almost giddy. With that comment, I couldn't help but wonder if he was aware that his legs were amputated. Surely he couldn't be joking about something so tragic. It had to be the drugs. None of us mentioned his legs in the time we were with him. Actually, Jodi informed us that the doctors requested we not bring it up. There would be time for that later once he was fully sober. Talking to Zach about the tough issues was something that Jodi prayed over. She asked God for the strength to answer Zach's questions when the time came.

That day when Zach woke up and we saw that he was the same guy we all knew and loved was the day that life was breathed back into us! And if that wasn't enough, something else happened that made the day even more miraculous—Zach moved his left hand, fingers, and left arm! The movement was so minute that it was hard to tell, but when doctors examined him once again, he was able to move those appendages! Dr. Bingaman said that because Zach did respond positively, he wanted to see what could be done to save that left arm, and he ordered a MRI. He knew that it was going to take a lot of planning and extremely gifted hands to repair

Zach's arm. So much of the upper arm and shoulder, including the bones, was damaged and contained dead tissue. It was going to take very complicated and delicate procedures to repair and reconnect muscle and arteries. We figured we might have to seek other surgical experts; most surgeons would not want to risk the undertaking.

On the second day after Zach was extubated, his voice softened and wasn't as clear as day one—it took a lot of effort for him to speak. His speech was faint, as if he were winded. At times we had to ask him to repeat what he'd said. He had probably strained his vocal cords the day before with all the chattering we'd done. We had to remind ourselves not to wear him out by spending too much time in his room, which was hard because of our eagerness to visit with him.

The fact that he was so dehydrated with thirst was another reason Zach couldn't talk as easily. He had to pass a swallow test before he would be allowed to eat or drink. He begged over and over to be given something to quench his thirst, but had to wait for the therapist to come to his room to do the exam. We were informed that normally patients don't pass the swallow test on their first try, but when the therapist finally made it to his room, Zach did! Passing the swallow test so quickly was another thing that surprised the medical staff. His incredible ability to overcome obstacles in his path was displayed every time anything was put before him! He never ceased to amaze us with his efforts to get back to life. We didn't know if that was because God was always behind everything, or if Zach had an incredible will to survive. I'm sure it was both.

Something else that made a difference were the prayers from literally hundreds of people. The news had spread through

Facebook, television, and word-of-mouth about Zach's story. People everywhere were concerned and praying for him. I was constantly impressed at the number of people who didn't even know us but were taking such an interest in how Zach was doing. Why did they care about him so much? I could never figure out why they were holding on to our every move and wanting to know the latest on him. Some told us that it was because his story was giving them faith in God and in miracles. They never stopped caring and wanted to know how they could help him and his family. The cards and monetary donations came daily in the mail. It was the most generous outpouring and display of love that I have ever seen!

Back home there were plans in the making for a fundraiser at our local city building. We hadn't even hinted that we were in financial need, yet our whole community was working hard to make sure our expenses were met. They had already done so much up to that point, yet still more was in the making.

Friends and neighbors organized a soup supper that was donated by our local Wendy's restaurant, and neighborhood ladies made desserts to be served as well. It was freezing wintery weather the night of the supper, yet over six hundred people showed up in our little town (whose population is around four hundred) to support the cause. People stood in long lines that wrapped around the building, waiting to go inside to eat. When the volunteers serving the food thought they were going to run out of chili, they called another restaurant, Jim's Chicken, who donated more soup to feed the remaining crowd. It turned out that there was exactly the amount needed to feed every person, with nothing left over.

We feel so fortunate to live in a community where kind people still care enough to take care of one another. Zach's accident surely did draw the best out of people and pulled them together in a wonderful way.

11

FACING FACTS

It snowed on November sixteenth and it looked so peaceful and calm outside. That's a good way to describe how I felt on the inside—peaceful and calm. The previous three weeks were like a blustery storm, blowing nonstop, but finally things were calming down—we could breathe easily again.

I must have had snow on the mind. I was lying in bed that morning at the loft, thinking of how Zach reminded me of Frosty the Snowman. Everyone knows how Frosty was silent until the magic hat brought him to life. I was comparing that to the way Zach was silent until the nurses removed the sedation and vent, and then the Zach that his family knows and loves came back to us. Maybe the reason I put Frosty and Zach together was because the first words they each spoke were, "Happy Birthday."

Zach became more alert as the coma drugs wore off, and he had many visitors wanting to talk to him, hoping to learn more about what he had experienced in the past weeks. How could it be true he was alive and speaking to us again? His mind was functional, his personality was the same, even his memory was good. He recalled the entire accident; he vividly remembered how the electricity crackled and surged around him and he couldn't get free. He remembered his ears ringing, and he saw a white light before blacking out. He couldn't breathe when he became conscious again, then told us that he knew he was on fire and that Les freed him from the electricity's grip with something that hit him hard across his shoulder and neck.

Zach also knew, by that day, his losses. He had seen that the bed sheets laid flat where his legs should have been. Jodi explained to him that he would've died from infection and that there was no other choice. She was relieved when he didn't fall apart after her explanation, but we all knew that because of the pain meds, the fact that his legs were amputated didn't hit him as hard as it would without the drugs.

Jodi couldn't bring herself to tell him that there was a possibility he might also lose his arm. Not yet, not at that moment. He'd already been given enough devastating news for the time being. He would have to face reality soon enough.

The MRI report showed that the joint on Zach's shoulder was still intact—news that gave doctors something to work with. There were no promises made that the arm could be saved, and we knew it would be a massive undertaking for the right surgeon, but at least we had hope.

Dr. Bingaman was using all his resources to find the best procedures and people to help Zach. He was bringing in an orthopedic specialist to assess whether Zach's arm could be salvaged. It just HAD to be possible! We could not imagine having to tell Zach he would lose his arm—it might break him, as would it us.

By that time, Zach was encountering new problems. After twenty days of sleeping in a drug induced coma, he soon had the opposite problem—he couldn't fall back to sleep. He was taken off some of the narcotics, and he slipped into a sort of twilight zone.

We were told that when patients are weaned off the high-powered drugs, they often hallucinate, become restless, and have difficulty sleeping. Zach was in and out of reality for several days. Many times while we were having a conversation with him, he would drift off into a world of his own and say something that didn't make any sense, or mumble gibberish that sounded like a foreign language. Sometimes he would reach out in the air with his right hand as if to grab something, then realize what he was reaching for wasn't there and come back to reality. It frustrated him that he couldn't differentiate between what was real and what was his imagination or a hallucination.

Dressings needed to be changed every day for his burns and wounds, which was so extremely painful that Zach had to be put back under sedation during that time. That led to more drugs at the same time they were trying to decrease what they had to give him. The vicious cycle went on and on, but we were told he would eventually overcome the effects of the opioids and would get better. It would just take time.

Time—it was so hard to be patient. Once conditions started to look up, anxiety took me on a fast track of wanting Zach to heal and come home. People posted words of wisdom for us to read on Facebook about having patience and waiting on God's timing. That was something I needed to be reminded of. Sitting in a hospital all day long for twenty-four days in a row was indeed trying.

We saw many people come and go in the waiting room on those days, including homeless people who would show up under the false pretense of being a visitor of a patient. They would come inside to warm themselves and look for food left out on the counters. One morning we came back to the hospital to find the refrigerator in the waiting room had been robbed of everything we had stored inside. Sub sandwiches, fruit and cheese trays, bottled drinks, casseroles—all gone. There was quite a lot of food in there marked with our names, as the hospital requested. The cleaning staff hadn't thrown it out—it was taken. The theft was disturbing at first, but after some discussion, we decided that if someone was desperate enough to steal it, then maybe they needed it more than we did. After that, a hospital social worker made sure that the room and visitors were monitored a bit closer. Vagrancy and theft were problems they dealt with more often than one might suppose.

Not only was it hard to be patient waiting for Zach to make progress each day, but it was also exhausting. We often felt like we were on a rollercoaster that never came to a stop. Some days were extreme highs, with good news and big mile markers, and other days we plummeted with terrifying news of infection setting in, or the threat of Zach losing his arm—or his life. Other days were spent just waiting—not high nor low, but similar to the parts of the coaster track that go straight along, without a hint of what's ahead. That was the part of the ride we were on next.

It was the morning when the orthopedic specialist, Dr. Pollock, would join forces with Dr. Bingaman to examine Zach's shoulder during dressing changes. Together, they would assess whether or not his shoulder could be repaired. If they found the shoulder to be salvageable, they would let us know if they could conduct the surgery themselves, or if Zach would need someone more qualified. If they decided the shoulder was beyond repair, the arm—even though there was movement—would have to be removed. A person cannot have a functional arm without a viable shoulder to attach it to. We had already made up our minds that if the latter were the case, we would seek another opinion.

So, there we were again, putting our faith and trust in God and the doctors. I knew that if it was God's plan to save Zach's arm, then He would see to it that Zach's needs would be provided for. And if Zach's arm could not be saved, only God would understand why, and we would have to accept that.

"Ask and you shall receive. Knock and the door will be open," is the verse that came to my mind, and I took advantage of believing in that promising part of the Bible. We're told that God already knows our needs before we ask, but He wants us to invite Him to intervene... so we prayed a lot. But we couldn't sit idly by and wait for God to do all the work—we needed to do our part as well. We needed to pray, but also be proactive in finding the doctor with the knowledge and gifted hands to do what was needed if there was a chance Zach's arm could be saved. I drew strength from our family, friends, and community, knowing they were supporting us in this way.

Jodi and I were walking down a hospital hall when we were met unexpectedly by Dr. Bingaman and Dr. Pollock. We weren't aware until then that they had completed their examination. Knowing we were about to hear the much-anticipated results of their findings, our hearts started racing. There in the hall way, still dressed in their white lab coats, both doctors stopped in front of our paths to deliver the news. With serious looks on both of their faces, Dr. Bingaman looked at us and said, "Dr. Pollock and myself strongly believe...." he paused, keeping us in suspense, "that Zach's arm has too much function to consider taking it off." Jodi and I both inhaled sharply, then gasped as tears came to our eyes. Praise God!

They told us that Zach would need to see someone who was more experienced with injuries as complicated as his—someone who did those types of surgeries repeatedly. And this qualified surgeon would need to be located where there was a good burn unit. Dr. Bingaman added that in his experience, most surgeons don't like to do such risky one-shot surgeries on sick patients, so we needed to get Zach well and strong.

Even though Zach needed more skin grafts, plans to do them that week were canceled to allow his burns, wounds, and infections time to heal in preparation for the difficult surgery ahead. Dr. Bingaman felt Zach's body would benefit from the rest. The search for a qualified surgeon began.

How does one go about finding the perfect qualified surgeon? Would that surgeon consider coming to Via Christi for Zach, since he was so fragile to transport? If we found the right surgeon to do the job, would he/she be located at a hospital with a good burn unit? How much longer could Zach wait before it was too late? Afterall, his shoulder was exposed to the bone, and his arm had no flesh covering it. It had been nearly four weeks, and nothing had been done beyond keeping those areas clean and covered. We had so many questions and so many obstacles in our path. We put our needs and concerns out on Facebook, hoping the public could assist us with finding answers.

It was the twenty first of November when the mind-numbing effects of the drugs wore off and Zach finally came out of the hazy fog that had messed with his mind. Jodi walked into his room, expecting to find him as he had been, somewhat "out of it," when she was caught off guard.

"Jodi, I didn't know I was this bad! I didn't know that I lost my legs!" Zach wailed as Jodi entered his room. Her first inclination was to run and get help. How was she going to tell him, knowing that this time he was coherent and upset? She had rehearsed the moment in her mind several times. It appeared that the day had arrived. She grabbed a chair, along with her courage, and sat down next to him. "Do you remember telling the paramedic that you couldn't feel your feet the day of the accident?"

"Yes," he stammered.

"Well, they had to take them, because if they wouldn't have, you wouldn't be here today. They were THAT bad." She bravely continued: "It was so hard for me to have to be the one to give the permission for doctors to do that, but I wanted to do everything I could to keep you here."

Tears welled up in Zach's eyes and ran down his cheeks.

"It's okay to cry, Zach," she said, trying to console him. "I've had twenty days since that surgery for it to sink in with me; this is all new to you."

It took everything she had to not break down, "I didn't marry you for your legs," she said, with assurance in her voice, "I married you because you have a heart of gold. I will be by your side every step of the way—no matter what. We'll find someone to get you new legs—it's just going to take time." Then, afraid of an answer she didn't want to hear, Jodi asked the question that she needed to know: "Are you glad you are here—that you survived?"

Without even hesitating, Zach answered, "Of course!"

That was the answer we'd all been hoping to hear. It had been hanging over us—the possibility that he might rather have not survived than live with the damage to his body. It was still early, however, and he had more to learn. Jodi was relieved to see that Zach wasn't as devastated as she had imagined. She was also thankful that his attitude seemed positive.

The two had only a short visit before the physical therapy team arrived in Zach's room to work with him. They planned to have him sit up for the first time on the side of the bed. They called it "dangling."

When they asked him to try to move his left arm, he wanted to know why it hurt so badly. He had a lot of questions about himself. Jodi told him that we were in the process of finding a surgeon to help with it, but she didn't let him know how bad it really was.

As the physical therapists prepared Zach to sit up for the first time, Jodi and I watched with anticipation. It took two therapists to lift him from a reclining position and maneuver him upright to the side of the bed. One supported his back and the other stood in front of him.

Everywhere they held on to him caused intense pain from their touch on his raw burns. He winced continuously, the expressions on his face showing the hurt. It was exciting to see him in an upright position, but at the same time, it was evidence of how fragile and weak he was and how much his body had wasted away.

My young son who had once been a strong, agile athlete resembled a man who looked to be in his eighties. He was so thin, willowy, and weak he could barely support the weight of his own body sitting up. It was the first time for us to see the back of his head where the pillow had worn a large bald spot in his hair. It was quite emotional for us to watch him try to move his damaged body, making us again realize he had a long way to go, but he was trying hard to find the strength to do what the physical therapists asked. His body was weak but his will was strong, and that meant the world to us.

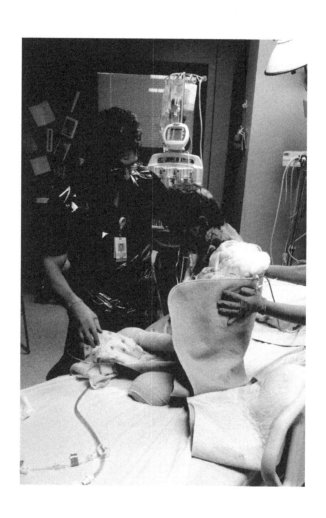

12

BELIEVE

Once the public knew we needed recommendations for a surgeon, they were hot on the trail to help us find someone, and suggestions flooded in. However, it seemed that every time we followed up on a reputable name, we were told, "This surgeon is good, but here's the name of one that might suit your needs better." It was as if nobody wanted to touch Zach's situation.

Other times, when a good surgeon was recommended, it turned out that they weren't located in a hospital with a burn unit. Or the burn units wouldn't have a qualified surgeon with the experience we needed.

Several days went by and we were growing more frustrated, pleading to God to lead us where we needed to go. We hadn't accomplished anything regarding a surgeon, and we felt time was wasting. And speaking of wasting, Zach's arm was beginning to emit an odor of dead flesh, which made us worry all the more. The smell nauseated Zach because of his keen sensitivity to unpleasant odors. He was ready to move on with his recovery and was tired of waiting and not knowing what was going to happen—we all were.

After researching surgeons all over the country and being overwhelmed with the lack of a positive match, the thought crossed my mind that the situation would come together when the time was right. If God had brought us *to* this, He would get us *through* this. We just had to hold on to that and believe. We *had* to believe, or we would drive ourselves crazy.

Our family and community made sure we remembered that they were consistently there. They found a beautiful way to show how they were united with us—they had purple tee shirts printed with the words, "Believe in Miracles" on the front. Orders went out by the dozens—additional fundraisers for Zach, and we'd see people wearing them everywhere—even people we didn't know! Lots of our friends and family were taking pictures of themselves wearing the shirts and posting them on Facebook to let us know they were behind us all the way. How incredible was that?

On November twenty-second, Dr. Bingaman met with us to say that he had come to the end of his time with us. He had been diagnosed with the early stages of melanoma skin cancer and was going to need to take time off for his own care.

That didn't stop him from diligently working to find a surgeon for Zach, though. On his days away from the hospital, he continued the search, informing us that he was looking into someone in St. Louis. He told us that he was following up on Drew, a former patient of his from two years ago, who was burned in an electrical accident which caused him to need extensive surgery to save his hands. Dr. Bingaman went on to say that Drew went to St. Louis to see a surgeon, Dr. Amy Moore, and until he had made a call for Zach, Dr. Bingaman hadn't known the results of Drew's outcome. What he learned was that Drew still had his hands and was making progress little by little. Dr. Bingaman wanted to get Zach hooked up with Dr. Moore, but first he needed to research the hospital some more, and there were a lot of hoops to jump through.

It was a bittersweet moment saying good-bye to our beloved Dr. Bingaman. He had become a hero to us for saving Zach's life and keeping him on the path to recovery. We intensely appreciated his professional care and loving manner and told him that we would never forget what he'd done for us. We would miss him, but at the same time, we were also ready to move on.

Before he left, Dr. Bingaman filled us in with what to expect for Zach's care. He told us that later in the week, another doctor would finish the rest of the skin grafts on Zach and redo the ones that didn't take; he'd treat the grafts everywhere except for Zach's left arm. After the Thanksgiving holiday, we could expect to move to the hospital that would take over. However, we would have to wait a little longer until we knew for certain where that would be.

Time dragged on. While waiting to leave Wichita we saw many patients come and go, including Sally's husband and son. We were extremely happy that Scott and Alex recovered and healed enough to move on to rehab. It gave us hope that recoveries do finally get to that point. We were so looking forward to the day Zach would get to move on to rehab as well.

In spite of the long days lying in bed, and regardless of his pain, Zach's attitude couldn't have been better. He chose to be positive. Jodi overheard him tell a friend who came to visit, that he truly felt lucky to be alive, and that he thought he would be able to handle prosthetic legs.

Life in the hospital was beginning to be more tolerable for him as he healed. Changes in his diet plan allowed him to eat soft foods and drink whatever he wanted, which improved his situation immensely. Another change that made his life more pleasant and helped to pass the time was when he could watch his favorite team, Kansas State, play football on TV. The KSU Wildcats coach, Bill Snyder, even sent Zach a get-well card with a personal letter inside! That did a lot to lift his spirits.

Basketball Coach Bill Self of Kansas University must have caught wind of Mr. Snyder's personal gesture because he followed suit and did the same thing. Mr. Self's card and letter thrilled not only Zach but Jodi, who has been a faithful KU fan of K State's rival team.

Cards came in such abundance for Zach that Jodi and I decided to decorate his room by hanging them on the walls. We also hung up all the get-well pictures that kids from his former grade school colored for him, making his surroundings look more cheerful.

Since Zach was talking and awake more of the time, it seemed like a good idea to leave Jodi to sit with him through the day while I took Brynlee back to the loft where she could sleep in a bed. The stroller had been her napping place for an entire month. I don't know how many laps I and other family members made around the hospital corridors trying to lull her asleep. The loft would be a nice reprieve for the two of us.

Spending every day of one month in a hospital waiting room offered enough drama to last a lifetime, and I was ready to be out of there. We thought we had front row seats to a Jerry Springer show one day when a group of people started arguing and nearly fist fighting over who was the real father of a child patient in the ICU.

There was another time when we were pretty sure we were sharing the room with Honey Boo Boo's relatives. They loudly blurted out profanities to one another while telling obnoxious stories regarding the drama in their lives, competing to draw attention to themselves. One of them, dressed in leopard print pajama pants and furry slippers, moseyed over to our cooler where she helped herself to a Gatorade, then chugged it down and let loose a long, loud belch. This group trashed the room, leaving cellophane wrappings from vendor machine honey buns, broken chips, and plastic soda bottles strewn on the chairs and floor. I'm not sure if they knew a patient in the hospital or were just passing through. They didn't appear to be worried about anyone, which was much unlike the family that showed up later and broke our hearts. We witnessed the profound sorrow of family members huddling together and embracing, all the while profusely sobbing. After a week-long struggle, their loved one died. She had been beaten, raped, set on fire, then left for dead in a Wichita park.

Yes, it was wonderful to get to where I felt comfortable leaving the hospital waiting room. The loft offered a peaceful change where I could spend time with little Brynlee, yet wouldn't be too far away if a crisis occurred. Besides, Jodi needed time alone with Zach.

The Thanksgiving holiday was near, and the atmosphere in the hospital was changing. Dr. Bingaman was no longer there, and the nurses we had come to know were taking time off from work, leaving us with unfamiliar faces. Even the ICU was quiet. Before then, the hospital was constantly buzzing, and Zach had regular activity in his room.

The doctor who took over for Dr. Bingaman finished Zach's grafts as planned, and Zach's feeding tube was removed. The nurses had previously told us the feeding tube was absolutely necessary because Zach couldn't possibly eat enough calories to satisfy his body's needs to heal. Removing it was a sign that he was making important progress, although at that point he was still considered to be in critical condition.

After further researching St. Louis, Dr. Bingaman called to recommend that we take Zach there. Since we weren't offered many other options, St. Louis's Barnes Jewish Hospital sounded like the best choice. It would be four hundred and forty miles from home, but we were willing to go anywhere that could help Zach. We trusted Dr. Bingaman's advice and felt he knew best, so we decided to go with his recommendation. Along with a promising surgeon, a large bonus was that Barnes Hospital had a highly progressive burn unit.

It was a relief to have settled on a decision, and it felt right. Calls were made to St. Louis to see if Zach would be accepted as a patient, and after several days, Barnes Hospital responded back with the answer we had prayed for—that they would indeed take him in. There was just one problem—racial rioting was underway in the city of Ferguson, a suburb of St. Louis.

In August, two months before Zach's accident, a black man was shot by a white police officer. The incident sparked unrest and furious debate over the abusive relationship between law enforcement and African Americans, and centered around the use-of-force law in Missouri and the rest of the nation.

A second wave of protests was right in its climax in the city of Ferguson, which is near Barnes Jewish Hospital. Beginning on November twenty fourth, rioters were looting, vandalizing, and causing major destruction after the announcement was made that the officer involved would not be indicted for the August shooting. This was a concern for us and for the medical staff of Barnes Hospital. It meant that Barnes would need to be prepared for possible numerous injuries coming in to the ICU. It also meant that if the hospital were to fill with many patients, Zach might be put on the back burner and not receive the immediate care he needed. Dr. Bingaman didn't feel confident about sending Zach until the situation settled down, but his arm couldn't wait any longer.

13

THE EMERALD CITY

As fate would have it, everything worked out in our favor. Rioting came to an end right at the time Zach was scheduled to be moved to St. Louis. Thank God!

The last week of November in Wichita gave Zach's body time to rest and continue healing from all the surgeries before he would be moved. It also turned out to be the perfect time to celebrate with family—Thanksgiving week.

When I reflected on how far we'd come, I felt like every day was Thanksgiving. God had spared our son's life and seen to it that he and his family were cared for. We had never experienced so much love and compassion as we had received, from so many caring and generous people throughout the whole journey of the tragedy. We had more to be thankful for than ever before.

We celebrated together with family, filling every spot and corner in Zach's room. Since a Samuel Adams was the first thing Zach asked for when his ventilator was removed, the doctor approved of a beer for him on Thanksgiving Day. Every one of us filled our white Styrofoam cups and held them up high while we toasted Zach. It was a happy and memorable moment.

Dave, the mysterious man with prosthetics who had walked down the hall and was mentioned earlier, came to see Zach on Thanksgiving Day. He wanted to visit before leaving town to spend the holiday with his family. After first greeting Jodi and me in the waiting room, he took a detour to the restroom where he changed out of his dress slacks and into shorts so that he could better demonstrate to Zach how his prosthetics worked.

The two of them bonded right off the bat as Dave sat on a chair beside Zach's bed and answered his many questions. One thing Zach wanted to learn from Dave was if he would be able to run again. It concerned him that he might not be able to keep up with Brynlee. Dave reassured Zach that he would be able to do many of the things he had always done before, including hunting. Zach loved hunting, and he felt better hearing that Dave regularly participated.

Dave reassured Zach that his prosthetics had served him well. Employed as an engineer, he was able to explain the mechanics of how they worked as he demonstrated how the legs came off, and then he reattached them. He also removed his left hand to let Zach examine it closer. Talk about giving the guy a hand up!

On Sunday, November 30, thirty-six days from the time he first arrived in the Wichita ICU, Zach was stable enough to move out. The first responders from Salina who transported him the day of the accident offered to accommodate the move to St. Louis, and they were ready and waiting with the ambulance when it was time to go. They invited Jodi to ride along to help keep Zach comfortable, but unfortunately, he was in pain the entire way. He was used to lying in a special bed that relieved the pressure on his sores, so the conventional ambulance cot was really painful to endure for the six-hour journey. However, they made it without mishap, and Zach was admitted into the ICU by evening.

The day before Zach was to leave, I loaded up a month's worth of accumulation at the Wichita loft and gave the place a thorough cleaning. Next, I headed home to Assaria to do some office work at the farm, run some laundry and clean house with help from my mom and mother-in-law, then did plenty of packing. I was exhausted, and it was wonderful when I could sleep again in my own bed. I didn't realize how much I had missed it until I laid down. I thought about how much easier life was in a normal routine, and I longed to get back to it again.

Going home to reunite with Chris was also nice. He had been driving back and forth to Wichita as often as he could—especially at times when conditions were shaky, but we were apart much more than we were together. Activities at the farm demanded Chris's time; he needed to be there in spite of how hard it was to be away. He knew that Zach had Jodi and me with him and that we would call if any problems came up.

As much as I would've loved having more time at home, I was also eager to get to St. Louis to meet Zach's new surgeon and check out the hospital. Chris and I had been to that city only one other time, to catch a plane to Jamaica on a vacation, so we weren't familiar with the area much at all.

We took two vehicles to St. Louis so that we could leave one there and use the other for family to get home in. Matt rode with Chris in his pickup, and Kelsey and I had Brynlee with us in Jodi and Zach's car. Kelsey was great help with keeping Brynlee occupied for the long trip. Forcing a thirteen-month-old to stay in a car seat for six hours is grueling.

Matthew planned to stay with Jodi and me for a period of time while we became accustomed to the new city. It put our minds

The Emerald City

more at ease to have him with us, plus we would need his help after Chris and Kelsey returned home.

It was dark when we reached St. Louis. Traffic was heavy and somehow Kelsey and I ended up getting separated from Chris and Matthew. We took a different route, but we eventually arrived. I'll never forget my first glimpse of Barnes Hospital as we approached the top of the exit ramp, where it became visible. The vision of the hospital reminded me again of the Wizard of Oz—the part when Dorothy and her friends finally reach the Emerald City. Out of nowhere, it appeared right in front of them, and it was huge and lit up a like castle. Just like Dorothy, we'd traveled a long journey, not knowing exactly what we would find at the end of our destination but optimistic that this new place would be Zach's cure, hope, and salvation. We had followed long lines of red tail lights for miles and miles, then came around a curve and up a hill, and there it was—Barnes Jewish Hospital—all aglow with emerald green lights and looking like a small city sitting on top of a hill.

The hotel we chose to stay in was conveniently located right next to the hospital—in fact, it was attached to the hospital. Only one room was available when we arrived late that night and there were six of us, but we decided to take it and make it work, hoping more rooms would be available the following nights. The advantage of staying at that particular place was its convenience, and we could park at the hotel and avoid the fifteen-dollar-a-day hospital parking fees. Since we had two vehicles, that was a small but significant savings.

We checked in, piling our belongings on one of those luggage racks on wheels. We had several large suitcases, a stroller, Zach's wheelchair, and the special pad he needed for sitting on. There were tote bags filled with Brynlee's toys and baby care items—blankets, bottles, diapers, food—even an electric fan that Jodi brought for white noise to aid with sleeping. We probably over packed, but we were far from home and wanted to make sure we had what we needed. We didn't know how long we would be staying there.

Chris looked less than thrilled when I got back from parking the car. Not only was he stressed about the bumper to bumper traffic and the long drive, he was worn out, and he was not excited about all the "stuff" we chose to bring along that he had to load onto the cart. He piled it as high as possible with bags falling off every so often as we wheeled our way to our rooms. He couldn't understand why in the world we needed so much stuff. I chuckled as I took a picture of him straining to push the rack down the hall. "Remind me to never travel again with four females!" he growled.

Monday came early after our late-night arrival, and the medical team did not waste any time. Doctors had scheduled Zach for surgery to clean up the dead tissue on his arm and then planned to devise a game plan. The left arm had not had any treatment up until that point other than keeping it clean. We had worried about the repercussions of putting repairs off, but finally his arm was going to receive the much-needed attention. Our hope was that it was not too late.

When the surgery was over, we were introduced to the surgeon whom we'd searched high and low for, the one in whom we had put all our faith and trust. She was not at all the way I had pictured her in my mind. She was much younger. Much, much younger. All my life I had pictured an experienced surgeon as someone middle-aged or older—usually a man who had been practicing for years. How could this woman, who looked to be in her thirties and reminded me of a young Meg Ryan, be qualified and experienced enough to do the surgery we had been told would be extremely complicated?

Well, it goes to show that you can't judge a book by its cover. It didn't take long after visiting with her to sense that we had chosen the right person. We connected with Dr. Amy Moore right off the bat. Her compassion and competence were easily apparent as she sat with us and explained what she saw and felt about Zach and his situation.

Up until that point, we thought that Zach was improving—and he had been—but it wasn't until then that we'd learned he wasn't yet out of the woods—he was still very, very critically sick. I remember the serious look on Dr. Moore's face when she spoke to all of us: Chris, Jodi, Matthew, Kelsey, and me. The more she talked about all the issues she found during her exploratory surgery, the more my heart ached for Zach, and uncontrollable tears rolled down my face. I looked up and saw Kelsey and Jodi crying as well. All I could think was, "God bless my son for what he was enduring."

Dr. Moore listed out what she found and explained the things she did:

- Zach's blood had bacteria present. She was concerned that it could be in the bone as well.
- He had a bad fungus in his system that would need to be sent to the lab for identification in order to configure the correct medication to treat it.
- He was severely malnourished and in desperate need of more calories and nutrition.
- The gaping hole in his head was a potential source of entry for infection, so she cut out dead tissue and attached a wound-vac, just as they did on his leg in Wichita.
- She cut a part of Zach's left ear away because it also had dead tissue.

Next, Dr. Moore told us that his grafts needed more time to heal and that her team went in and thoroughly scrubbed his entire body to make everything as clean as possible.

The good news was that Zach's amputations looked like they were healing, and the great news was that she believed his arm could still be salvaged! She explained that it would not have full function or full range of motion; he would only be able to lift his arm from the elbow and not the shoulder, but it would be better than having a prosthetic. She concluded with the statement that it was her goal to make it possible for him to hold his baby girl again—and that warmed our hearts.

Dr. Moore ordered a different bed for Zach that would help with his bed sores, and then told us he would be back in surgery the next day and again on Friday. He would have multiple surgeries ahead of him with lots of repairs in lots of places, but she felt confident that she could get him where she wanted him to be, which included saving his left arm and hand.

That is what I loved most about Dr. Moore—her confidence. When I asked questions about the seriousness of bacteria and fungus in Zach's blood, she answered with reassuring positivity in a way that lifted the heaviness from my heart. With a matter-of-fact tone in her voice she said, "That is the reason we have specialists. It's their job to figure out the right formula for medications to treat those issues, and that is exactly what they will do."

We weren't accustomed to hearing news about Zach's issues in such an optimistic way. The Wichita team usually delivered information gloomily about all that could be wrong or go wrong. In the beginning I'm sure that the doctors wanted to cover all the bases and eliminate surprises, plus the survival issues they were dealing with were different back in Wichita. But this new assuring confidence made us feel that Zach was going to be okay and that we were in the right place. Dr. Bingaman and the Wichita team had done all that was possible to bring Zach to this point—they had saved his life, and Dr. Moore gave them credit for that. From this point on, it was going to be about restoring his health and strength and repairing his injuries to give him back a quality life.

Barnes Hospital was amazing—and also massive! It employed around ten thousand people, including nearly two thousand physicians. Because it was ten blocks long, it took us over twelve minutes to walk from the entrance of the hospital where our hotel was connected to the surgery waiting room. Needless to say, we got lost quite frequently.

I was so impressed with the way the staff worked together. Tuesday morning while we were visiting in Zach's room, a nurse told me that I could go out into the hall where the medical team was making rounds. There were ten professionals standing outside his doorway with their computers on rolling stands, reviewing Zach's status and working together to create a plan for his health. I went out to see if I could learn anything from what they were saying, but I failed to comprehend anything they were talking about. I felt I was surrounded by geniuses who were speaking a foreign language. Their medical terminology was so far above me that I stood there dumbfounded, without a clue as to what they were coordinating together. And they were all so young! I suppose that the fact that Barnes Hospital is a teaching hospital for Washington University School of Medicine had something to do with that. The campus is surrounded with specialized medical buildings and colleges. We had entered a whole different medical realm.

That same day, Zach spiked a fever and was in a lot of pain. He was taken to a holding room where he was to wait until his surgery. Jodi stayed with him and tried to comfort him as much as possible, but the wait was hard on him. Of course, he couldn't have anything to drink, so that made it even harder.

The plan for surgery that day was for Dr. Moore to do more work on his shoulder. She mentioned that his arm and hand had gone too long without attention and acknowledged it might be tough to reverse the damage, but she still projected a positive attitude about doing whatever she had to do to make the arm work.

Zach's surgery lasted four and a half hours that Tuesday afternoon. We didn't get to talk to the doctor in person, but she made a phone call to Jodi saying that it went well. Zach was recovering and she would update us in the morning. She went on to say that he would get a day off to rest and then another surgery would be scheduled for Thursday rather than Friday as previously planned. Three surgeries in one week. They sure didn't waste any time.

14

TESTING OUR PATIENCE

Two steps forward and one step back. That's what the doctors told us to expect and that's exactly how it worked. We hadn't yet heard from Dr. Moore about details from the previous day's surgery and were eager to know what took place and what her next step was.

The medical team arrived and informed us that Zach had bacteria in three of his wounds. A fungus from the field dirt from the day of the accident also remained in his system. They had to get those dangers addressed before they could graft or move ahead on his arm.

In the meantime, it was hard to watch Zach suffer the pain he was so tired of dealing with. He was hurting in so many places due to the surgeries, burns, donor sites, and bed sores—he was miserable and uncomfortable. He still had to be sedated when it came time for them to do his daily dressing changes. The pain made it unbearable for him to be awake during those times. "How many times can he be put under sedation? That can't possibly be good for him," I thought. Between the surgeries and dressing changes, he had been put under sedation over and over again.

Something that added to our stress that day was that Brynlee came down with an illness. Her eyes were matted and her nose was gunky. We had hoped we could get her doctor back home to order something over the phone. We didn't have the slightest idea of where to take her in St. Louis; we hadn't even ventured outside the hospital yet. Then there was the worry that her illness would spread to the rest of us, making it impossible to be around Zach.

Moreover, within the same day, a hospital employee informed us that children under twelve were not allowed to be in the patient's room or the waiting room. That meant we would have to take turns staying with Brynlee at the hotel, which was okay while she was ill—we would have to do that regardless, but none of us liked the idea that Zach wouldn't get to see his daughter for so long. He was already disappointed that she was changing so much and he was missing out. We never had to confront that issue in Wichita, where we were fortunate that Brynlee could be with us each day. "Oh Lord, I pray for strength and good health to stay the course. I can't get sick now. Please send mercy and favor to see us through all of this," I prayed.

Jodi was not only worried about her sick toddler, but also worried about catching whatever Bryn was suffering. She couldn't stand the idea of having to stay away from Zach. She said she could just scream—scream and cry. Some days were just more than a person could handle. She turned to her Facebook prayer warriors again and asked them to pray for her and Zach.

We decided it would be best to take Brynlee to the Children's Hospital emergency room. It was connected to Barnes Hospital and even though it wasn't an emergency, it would be the easiest solution at that point. Brynlee was diagnosed with pink eye in both her eyes and she had a virus causing the congestion in her nose. Poor little girl. She was miserable with her watery eyes and constricted air passages.

Our next issue was that we needed to find a long-term place to stay near the hospital, knowing that we couldn't afford to stay for weeks in the hotel where we first arrived. Someone mentioned a place called Barnes Lodge, which was affiliated with the hospital and located not far away. It was available for families of patients to stay at a reasonable rate. The amenities it offered sounded ideal: free parking, laundry facilities, kitchen, and shuttle service to and from the hospital. Only problem was, it had no vacancy; we had to be put on a waiting list.

That's what we had learned to do after so much time—wait. Waiting and being patient were two virtues that were required and tested again and again since the beginning of the whole journey.

Dr. Moore sat with all of us, including Zach, to describe her plan to operate on his left shoulder Thursday, the next morning. It would be very involved and take around four to five hours, she told us. She explained that she would remove the Latissimus muscle in Zach's back while it was still connected to an artery and place it over the exposed bone on his shoulder. Her concern was if the muscle would be large enough to cover. She then would remove full thickness tissue from his thigh to cover the hole left from where she took the muscle.

"Poor Zach," I thought to myself. "He won't hardly have anywhere left on his body that hasn't been burned, grafted, cut on, or cut out of. Plus, much of his skin, including some of his body parts, has been removed or is not in its original place anymore." It all sounded so cruel, but at the same time it made us aware of how amazing modern medicine is today. Zach had survived as a result of advances in medical technology and procedures, and for that we were thankful!

Dr. Moore also explained her plans for Zach's left hand in upcoming surgeries. She showed us a graphic photo of his arm and hand, then told us it would be necessary to remove two of his fingers. She would use the skin from the first and fourth fingers (which she thought were too damaged to be of any use to Zach) to cover his palm where the damaged tendons were exposed and where the nerves were missing, due to the fact that electricity had burned them away. She would later need to go in and insert new tendons into that hand—probably from a cadaver. Normally, she said, she would use nerves and tendons from the toes as donors for this type of repair, but Zach had no toes. In fact, because his legs were amputated, he didn't have many donor sites to take from. Dr. Moore convinced us that Zach would be surprised at how well he could get along without his pinky and index finger. She said that as long as he could use his thumb and one of the remaining fingers, he would do quite well with day to day tasks.

Zach was crushed. He looked at Dr. Moore with a mournful face and tear-filled eyes. "But I am a mechanic and need my fingers to be able to work." My heart ached for his emotional pain and tears blurred my vision. The sorrow in his eyes showed how he felt about losing something that was so valuable to him. Reluctantly, his face glum, he conceded. With resignation in his voice, he looked down at his hand, then raised his eyes to her face. "I understand. At least I will keep my arm. I am thankful for that."

Dr. Moore understood the pained look on Zach's face. It hit her as hard as it did us. She paused without saying a word, compassionately studying his eyes as if she were reading his soul, then said, "I can see how important this is to you. You are right, you do need your fingers. I'll think about this some more. We'll see how things go tomorrow." Before leaving, she told us that we could expect one or two surgeries a week for the next six weeks.

Jodi broke down in tears when she was alone with Zach. It upset her to see him so devastated over losing his fingers. It seemed that he mourned the loss of his fingers more than the loss of his legs. Inside she screamed, "Why us? Why my sweet family?" Then a calming thought soothed her angry cries: "God gave Zach back to us that day the doctors told us he wouldn't make it. He *can* and *will* live through this! He is still the same Zach mentally, and I should be thankful for what we have." Then she wrote in Facebook, "I know God won't give us more than we can handle, but please keep praying that we'll have enough strength to get through this journey!"

We *were* granted the strength and our prayers were answered. In the same week, Dr. Moore reported to us after a long six-hour surgery on Zach's shoulder that it was "a big win!" She told us that the Latissimus muscle she used to cover the shoulder turned out to be a perfect fit! She said that Zach was in recovery and doing well, and that she would plan for surgery on his forearm and hand on Monday. Halleluiah!! That was truly great news! The rollercoaster ride continued, but we had just ridden the exhilarating part of the track. We shared smiles and collectively breathed a deep sigh of relief.

More good news came when we received a call saying that we were finally accepted into the Barnes Lodge. It would be so much more economical to stay there. We could buy groceries to stock our own cabinet and make our own meals in the kitchen—a break from the expensive cafeteria food. The fact that the lodge was located only two blocks away and had a free shuttle that ran back and forth all day up until ten-thirty at night was a plus too.

Zach was in a lot of pain and had some issues with swelling while recovering from his shoulder surgery—his eighth surgery in St. Louis—but he handled it fairly well. He called Jodi when he finally awoke, asking her, "When are you coming over here?"

"Oh, here in a bit. I'm trying to get Bryn around, but Kelsey is on her way. Do you need something?" Jodi asked.

"Yeah! I have a *leach* on my arm and no nurse to be found!" Zach's voice quivered with panic.

Jodi laughed. She was aware that the doctors had applied leaches to his shoulder and she had wondered what his reaction would be once he woke up and saw them. Apparently, one had left its post. The leaches sucked the excess blood to the surface of the newly placed muscle flap, which caused the blood to coagulate. They also carried antibodies that helped the wound heal.

"I'll be there soon," Jodi said, still chuckling.

"It's not funny! I'm serious! I think I feel one that got lost somewhere under my gown!" Zach exclaimed, trying to convince Jodi of the urgency of the situation.

"Well, call your nurse," Jodi recommended, "and I'll be there soon to help if they haven't been in by the time I get there."

The day arrived for Chris and Kelsey to head back home. Chris helped get Jodi, Brynlee, Matthew, and me situated at Barnes Lodge before leaving. This would be the first of many trips between home and St. Louis for Chris. Jodi and I were pleased that Matthew would stay longer. We felt more secure and happy to have him with us, and of course, he was glad to spend time with Zach.

I hadn't realized up until that point how easy my life had been before. Having a normal, daily routine can be monotonous, but I longed to have it back again. Never again will I take normalcy and peace for granted. There was no place on Earth that I wanted to be more than there with my son as he healed, but the anxiousness of knowing that life at home was going on as usual without my being there crossed my mind whenever I had time to think about it. The bill paying and bookkeeping for our farm and two businesses needed my attention. It was getting close to the end of the year when I would need to prepare records and paper work for taxes and our accountant. I preferred not to rely on outside help—that is just not my way—but I pictured the mail piling up on my desk and I realized I couldn't do it all on my own. Thank goodness my friend Rhonda stepped in and offered to take care of payroll and necessary accounting. I coached her over the phone so that she could be my hands in the office—her help was a huge relief for me.

When crisis happens, it feels like the entire world should stop revolving, but then you realize at some point, life goes on with or without you. I needed to take one day at a time and stop letting anxiety get the best of me. It helped to have the backing of our family and friends, knowing they would contribute however they could, and I took comfort in the fact that they remained with us daily, providing prayers and supportive comments along the way.

Dr. Moore dropped in on dressing changes to examine Zach's shoulder from the surgery done three days prior. She said that he still had infections in some of the skin grafts done on his back in Wichita, and he also continued to have the stubborn fungus that they were trying to find treatment for. She felt several grafts would have to be redone. That was unfortunate, considering he had so few places from which to take skin. She planned to give the previous donor sites time to heal and then harvest from them again. She also said that the new skin flap on his shoulder was looking good, but about ten percent of the skin graft would need to be redone.

Next, Dr. Moore explained her plans for surgery the following day. At ten-o-clock in the morning, he would have a skin release performed on his neck.

The term "skin release" was new to us. When skin is grafted, it tightens up with time, which causes it to shrink and pull. In Zach's case, his left cheek and eye were being drawn down because of the graft under his chin on his neck. A skin release would involve making an incision under his jawline and then inserting skin taken from his collarbone to fill the gap where the incision pulled apart. That procedure was to be performed by Dr. Snyder-Warwick, a head and face plastic surgeon who specialized in skin releases, primarily on children. Along with the release, she also planned to graft sores that weren't healing on Zach's left upper eyelid by using skin from his right lid.

Working alongside Dr. Snyder-Warwick, Dr. Moore would clean Zach's inflamed lower left arm and cover it with cadaver skin. Lastly, she would remove his pinky finger and close the open wound on his left palm. She decided to wait on the procedure of removing his index finger until she could brainstorm another idea that might prevent her from having to use it. We were so thankful she cared enough about Zach's concerns for keeping his fingers. She's such a loving person and caring doctor.

Just as Jodi feared, she began running a fever and showing symptoms she was catching whatever bug Brynlee was sick with. It frustrated her that she couldn't be with Zach and had to be content visiting with him on the phone until she was back to good health.

With Jodi and Brynlee stuck at the lodge, I spent the day in the waiting room alone while Zach had his next surgery. I sat looking at my phone, catching up on people's lives on Facebook. It was December eighth. The pictures and ads that popped up on my phone screen made me realize that Christmas would soon be upon us. It was easy to forget, seeing that we spent every day at Barnes Jewish Hospital. Of course, there were no Christmas decorations there.

Since Christmas was on my mind and I had several hours to sit in the waiting room, I decided to share my thoughts on Facebook:

> While sitting here waiting on Zach's surgery, I am thinking about how it will be such a different Christmas this year. There will be no Christmas tree put up, no baking or cards to send, no shopping to do. I'm not complaining by ANY means. I could still bake for the people in the lodge and might still if I find time, or write a letter to send in cards. Shopping isn't really an option as there's no place to store things and I simply don't have the desire to leave the hospital and venture out in the heavy traffic of a strange city with a baby—especially when I'd rather be with Zach. No, I don't feel the need for any of it this year and I'm not down about it—it's okay. Our family has already received the biggest gift we could want. Of course, you know what that is. The gift of Zach's life! AND the complete love and generous support of our friends, family and many good and kind-hearted people out there. When I went to church yesterday, the priest said something that resonated with me. He said, "In

preparing for the spirit of Christmas, so many people seem to have their hands full and their hearts empty." We get so busy with all the preparation that Christmas becomes a list of tasks, and we lose the real meaning of the season. Usually, I love doing all the things to get ready for Christmas, but even though it won't be that way this year, my heart is full, our family is still our WHOLE family, we feel the presence of our Lord Jesus every day and not just at Christmas, and it feels like Christmas every day because of all the love and gifts you all have generously provided us with throughout this journey. We have received so much more than we could possibly ever give back.

It wasn't long after posting that when my phone rang. It was Jodi. Her voice was frantic: "Lisa, Brynlee is having a seizure!"

This was the third time in Brynlee's young life to experience seizures. When her temperature rose too high, she went into a febrile seizure. It scared the wits out of Zach and Jodi the first two times. Brynlee's eyes rolled back in her head and her body stiffened up; she did not respond to anything her parents did or said. She looked as if she weren't breathing. The young couple zoomed to the hospital with Brynlee but were told that there was nothing the medical staff could do but let the seizure run its course. They'd checked her to make sure she was okay afterward and sent her home.

Jodi went on, "I think she's starting to come out of it, but she's acting strange and she has a high fever. Can you come and get us? I want to take her to the hospital."

I had walked to Barnes Hospital that morning, so I sprinted the two-and-a-half blocks back to the lodge to get there as fast as I could. The seizure had lasted about ten minutes and Brynlee was listless by the time I got there. She looked very pale.

We loaded Brynlee into the car and drove to Children's Hospital where she had been checked over for her illness just a few days prior. She went from being limp and listless to crying nonstop during the time we were there in the emergency room. Jodi, looking pale herself, did her best to calm her down.

After waiting for what seemed like hours, the doctor there told us the same thing that Jodi had heard in Salina and in Topeka where the other seizures took place—that the seizure had to run its course, and Brynlee was not harmed from it. The staff told us that Brynlee had a nasty virus and then they sent us on our way. At the very least, Jodi felt that because each hospital had the same diagnosis, it must be true that there was nothing to worry about.

I had never experienced this with any of my kids—a seizure was new to me. I could certainly understand why Zach and Jodi were frantic the previous times that had happened. It was scary, and it makes one feel so helpless.

Between Zach's four-and-a-half-hour surgery and Brynlee's seizure episode, it was a long and stressful day. Dr. Moore and Dr. Snyder-Warwick gave us a report when Zach was in recovery. Along with what they told us they were going to do, they ended up removing infected cartilage on his left ear. Dr. Moore said that she fully covered his left arm in cadaver skin so he would no longer be in pain from the exposed nerves. He would be able to tolerate dressing changes without having to be sedated (Halleluiah!). Once signs showed that the cadaver skin was taking well, she would go back and recover the entire arm using Zach's own skin.

Lastly, Dr. Moore offered us some exciting news. She covered the exposed, damaged tendons of Zach's left palm with a temporary material called Integra (similar to silicone) instead of using his fingers! She said that she wanted to do an angiogram to see the blood flow in his fingers and determine if they might still function more than she originally thought before deciding to use them as permanent cover. It was possible they might not have much function any more, she said, but there was still hope. More nerve and tendon repair would be required for his hand in the future, but for now, the open area on his palm finally had a protective covering.

More good news was that Zach's infections were showing definite signs of improvement and the correct antibiotics to combat the fungus were finally discovered and working! Music to our ears! Even the ulcers on his back from lying in bed for so long were looking better. Dr. Moore said that the skin flap on his shoulder was serving the intended purpose and looked great! She mentioned that we turned a corner that day. We were two steps forward!

Two days later, Jodi, Brynlee and I ventured out to shop for a room humidifier and stopped for lunch at a Mexican restaurant. Brynlee started fussing nonstop. Her face felt warm and she had no appetite. It was obvious she was miserable. We were going to have to do something about her worsening health issues. She was getting sicker, not better, from the virus. A green goo was oozing constantly from her nose.

At that point, I recalled a text from a lady named Tiana who lived in Western Kansas. She didn't personally know us, but she knew of Zach's accident, and that we were in St. Louis in the hospital. Tiana had a sister who was a pediatrician located not far from Barnes Hospital, and Tiana mentioned in her text that her sister would see Brynlee if ever we needed her. What a God send! We did need this doctor. I texted Tiana and told her about our situation. I don't think it was even thirty minutes before I received a text back saying that we could head right over to her sister's clinic. Talk about answered prayers! It seemed that any time we had a need, God came through for us. He worked through people to take care of us.

We found our way to the clinic with no problem. Once inside, we approached the receptionist who was expecting us. The waiting room was a very kid-friendly environment with bright colors and children's toys neatly arranged. It was a busy office, but we didn't have to wait very long before Brynlee was called back to see the doctor. I went along with Jodi and Brynlee. I wanted to meet this wonderful lady who so kindly offered her services to perfect strangers. Her name was Jan Mueller. She was familiar with all we were going through with Zach, and she had nothing but empathy for us, wanting to help in any way she could to ease our troubles. I could see how much she cared by the compassion in her eyes. She had a busy day with all her other patients yet wanted to hear the details of our journey and took the time to listen. After examining Brynlee, she checked Jodi over as well, looking into her ears and throat. Dr. Mueller diagnosed both Brynlee and Jodi with ear infections and influenza A. She prescribed antibiotics for the two of them, along with Tamiflu for me and for Matthew since we both had been exposed. On top of all that, Dr. Mueller let Jodi know that she wouldn't charge any more than what insurance would cover, so there would be no bill to pay.

I felt like crying. It's indescribable to experience someone's generosity in that capacity, especially when that person doesn't even know you, yet comes to your aid. "Thank you, Lord, for putting kind people in our path." There truly are good people in this world. Our hearts were filled with gratitude for what Dr. Mueller did. We will never forget her or Tiana for stepping in to help us get a handle on our health issues. We were exhausted from being awakened three or four times a night from the crying baby in the room we shared. Our immune systems were weakened by the constant stress caused by worrying about Zach's condition, not to mention the multitude of germs we were exposed to in the hospital setting.

I too was beginning to feel a scratchy throat and achy muscles that night after our day with Dr. Mueller. Thank goodness the Tamiflu kicked in and I didn't end up getting worse, nor did Matthew. Jodi, however, was wiped out. Her body was in pain and she felt weak and looked white as a sheet. She needed to rest.

After making one last visit with Zach, Matthew decided to head home the next day. He had business to take care of and was feeling the need to remove himself from the illness that was spreading. He's a bit of a germaphobe at times and doesn't much like baby slobber, let alone gooey green stuff and sneezes.

Matthew was such a trooper to stay with us girls for as long as he did. He slept on an air mattress on the floor and became Brynlee's trampoline and launching pad early each morning. She loved to cuddle up to his back while he laid there trying to sleep. Uncle Matt was special to her, and even though he didn't feel comfortable showing it, it was obvious that his only little niece was special to him too. However, he'd had enough "quality" time with her and was ready to move out, knowing that Jodi and I would get along fine in his absence. He also knew that Zach was stable enough that he would see him again later.

I never thought I would see the day that Matthew would be such a caring nurse mate to Zach. Because Zach's right hand had lost all its strength, due to the radial nerves being fried, it dangled limply from the wrist. And, of course his left hand was completely useless, so he was unable to do anything for himself. Matt helped Zach with his meals, feeding him and holding the glass for Zach to drink. Matt applied Chapstick to Zach's lips, something Zach wanted done often as his lips were constantly dry and cracked from the burns to his face. I'd often see Matt adjust Zach's bed and pillow when Zach needed to reposition himself, and he made sure the nurses were answering Zach's calls for what Zach needed. Another comfort for me was knowing Matthew was sitting up with Zach to keep him company late into the night after the rest of us left.

These acts warmed my heart. Seeing that brotherly love meant the world to me. More and more I was beginning to find that in all the tragedy we'd experienced, there were beautiful happenings as well—things we'd never experienced before—beauty in the ashes, so to speak. There truly are silver linings in the clouds, rainbows after the storm.

The rainbow in Wichita that the helicopter had flown through became my promise from God that all would be okay. It later occurred to me that we were near another rainbow, one that was larger than life—the St. Louis Arch. I couldn't look at it and not think of a rainbow. We'd made the right decision in choosing St. Louis, and to me, that was yet another powerful sign.

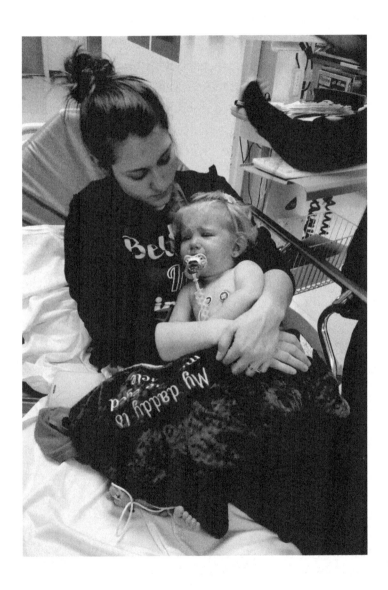

15

BREAKING DOWN

In the several weeks that Jodi and I lived together, our focus was on Zach and his healing. Our lives were put on hold for the time being, and we had no idea how much longer we were going to be staying in St. Louis. It didn't really matter—we were just grateful to have Zach alive and were willing to do whatever it took to stay with him.

Jodi and I got along well, considering how much time we spent together. It wasn't always easy cohabitating in such close quarters. Our accommodations at the lodge were similar to a college dorm room. It was nice to have a place to stay that saved us money, but it definitely was not the Holiday Inn. We shared a tiny bathroom and slept on narrow twin beds with mattresses wrapped in plastic, which caused us to sweat when we slept—and they made annoying crackling noises whenever we'd roll over at night.

Brynlee slept in a pack-n-play, and because she could see us in the room, she wouldn't lay down and go to sleep at bedtime. As a result, we couldn't stay up and read or watch tv because the lights and noise kept her awake. So just about e very night, Jodi and I spent time on our phones in the dark until we fell asleep.

Several nights, Brynlee woke up crying and wanting out of the pack-n-play, and Jodi put her in the twin bed so Brynlee wouldn't cry and wake the other residents. That practice soon led to a regular routine of Brynlee sleeping with Jodi, which made it hard for Jodi to rest since the bed was too small for the two of them. One night, Brynlee fell out onto the floor, so the blowup air mattress that Matt had used became their new bed, which took up even more of the limited room space.

After only a couple of weeks in St Louis, Jodi and I were wearing thin, which contributed to Jodi catching the flu. The stress of what we were going through was catching up to us, plus we were just plain tired—partly from lack of quality sleep, but also from chasing after a toddler all day after nights of interrupted rest. I had thought those days were past for me. I loved having Brynlee with us, but she did make life more challenging. One of us had to stay with her either at the lodge or in the lobby of the hospital. Neither place was fun for her or easy for us. Our room in the lodge was confining, and I'd get cabin fever after a while. The lodge had a living room, but other residents watched tv there, and our very active baby was a disruptive force in that place. She'd steal the remote, knock over drinks, or disappear into the foyer or kitchen before we even knew it. We'd have to chase her and bring her back again and again. She was at that curious age and into everything. If we could have gone outside to let her run around, she would have been easier to entertain, but it was wintertime.

Most times when Jodi was with Zach in his room, I spent the hours pushing Brynlee around the huge hospital in her stroller, and we'd visit the gift shops. Some people thought she was my daughter, which was flattering considering I was fifty-three. They'd say, "Your little girl is so cute!" or they'd watch Brynlee run down the hall and say to her, "You're sure keeping Mommy on the run." It was special for me to have her all to myself so often, but it took so much energy to keep up with her. Many times I just wanted to sit!

With Jodi and I spending a lot of time together, I got to know her on a deeper level. She certainly proved that she loved her husband through all the unfortunate circumstances. She was there to stand by him come hell or high water, and she did an incredible job. Zach's accident was so hard on her, but she constantly relied on her faith and stayed the fight. What a blessing that Zach found this young woman who was willing to hold onto him and their marriage, no matter what. She made sure Zach knew that she would always be there for him.

I did often worry about what life would be like for Jodi once we finally got home and she had to resume daily responsibilities. Her life certainly wouldn't be the same as before the accident. Not only would she not have Zach's help, but she would have to take care of him as well. Of course, Chris and I would lend a hand whenever possible, but we couldn't always be available. I just hoped and prayed that she'd be able to cope with their changed situation. A nagging thought in the back of my mind kept telling me that their lives from here on out were not always going to be smooth sailing. In fact, one afternoon the thought took a strong hold in my mind, and I had a bit of a meltdown. An accumulation of several things brought me to that point. It began with me feeling smothered by the clutter that was accumulating in our small room at the lodge. I couldn't stand dealing with the chaos anymore. The room was slowly closing in on me.

I'll admit that I'm almost neurotic about organizing and cleaning—Chris calls me Mrs. Spick and Span. It's my way of having peace and order in my life, and at that point, there was no order. I felt like I was losing control—not just of the situation in our lodge room, but of everything going on in my life at the time. The uncertainty was starting to overwhelm me. The cluttered room was the catalyst that added to the weight of the larger anxieties that had been preying on my mind. Along with the obvious—concerns about Zach—I'd also been worried about not taking care of affairs at my own home. I was feeling disconnected with Chris, and at that point, I worried about what the future held for Zach and Jodi once they returned to their home. I felt that I had no control anywhere—including something as minor as the environment around me!

It always helps get my mind off my worries when I'm busy and productive, so while we were in St. Louis, I relieved stress by cleaning and organizing our lodge room, and a few times I cooked meals in the kitchen. That kept things more normal for myself, plus I wanted to make Jodi's, Brynlee's, and my stay as much like home as possible. I also helped take care of Brynlee around the clock. Most mornings I woke up early to get ready for the day so that I was alert and prepared when Brynlee woke up. I much preferred to greet her with a happy smile than have her wake me and have to care for her when I was still groggy. I enjoyed getting her dressed and feeding her breakfast. It had been a long time since my kids were so young, and I was grateful to have that time with Brynlee, plus it allowed Jodi time to sleep a little longer in the mornings, which I knew she could use.

The day that I came unraveled happened after I'd been sitting in the waiting room during Zach's surgery and then went back to the lodge where Jodi and Brynlee were recovering from the flu. Jodi was beginning to feel better, but wasn't one-hundred percent, so I brought soup for her to eat in her bed.

Looking about the room, I saw that it was a disaster since Brynlee had been free to rummage around while Jodi was in bed. Toys and clothes were everywhere. We hadn't brought much from home for Brynlee to play with; we didn't have room in the car to transport the extra things, nor the space in our lodge to store them, but it wasn't long before compassionate people wanted to make life more fun for little Brynlee, so they mailed presents—lots of toys.

Lending to the problem of the mess in the room was Jodi's heaping laundry pile on the floor. She was still living out of suitcases in the closet, always having to dig through piles to find something to wear, and that began to grate on my nerves. She could never find what she wanted when we needed to leave, which frustrated me because I felt that her lack of organization was the problem. I had pointed out that there were drawers still empty for her use in the dresser, but she hadn't utilized them. After a week or so of living there, I was tired of not being able to find matching outfits or socks to get Brynlee dressed each day, so I took it upon myself to unpack Brynlee's clothes and put them away.

As I grabbed clothing and toys up from the floor, I glanced at Jodi, who was on her bed looking at her phone. One of those thoughts that had been bothering me popped into my mind: "How is she going to manage once she gets home with Zach?" It appeared to me that she hadn't done anything constructive all day long. Frustrated, I gathered things up, when it hit me—maybe I had been "feathering the nest" a little too much. Maybe I was acting as an enabler who might make it harder for Jodi to transition to all she was going to have to do once she got home with Zach.

With that revelation, I felt my anxiety rise another notch. I looked over at the desk that sat at the foot of my bed. Piles of mail spilled over its surface onto the floor. Most were cards sent to Zach and Jodi, but other pieces looked like bills. Some envelopes were opened, and others weren't. "What if Jodi isn't paying attention to her bills? Should I ask her? It's really not my business, but should I be doing something about this?" Those thoughts added fuel to the fires of my stress—I didn't know what to do. It didn't seem like her to be taking this lackadaisical approach to life, but then again, I'd never lived with her before, and after all, she was just getting over the flu. I tried hard to give her the benefit of the doubt, but with all the negative thoughts going through my mind, I couldn't seem to get a handle on my frustration, and anxieties continued to build. I knelt to sort laundry piles while trying to hide my emotions from Jodi. "How is she going to take care of Zach and Brynlee, the bills, the house, the laundry, and everything else waiting for them at home? It seems that all she wants to do these days is spend time on her phone."

It was at that moment that Jodi looked over at me and said, "Why don't you relax?"

That question did not set well with me. It didn't come across as concern for my wellbeing—instead it was a way of saying, "You're driving me nuts!" Even though I don't often lose my temper, that remark sent me off into a tailspin, releasing the frustration, anxiety, and anger that had built up. I immediately went into a pity party inside my head: "Jodi isn't the only one tired and hurting, I'm mourning too. I'm Zach's mother, for God's sake. Nobody is taking care of me. I'm expected to be strong...." The pot boiled over.

For a few more moments I continued to plop clothes into separate piles, then I lashed out at Jodi: "I'm not here to be your nanny and maid. I'm here for Zach. I feel like you are content with me doing everything around here!"

That wasn't completely true. I was there for Zach *and* I was there to help Jodi—I wanted to. I was just spewing out angry words because I was upset. This was a mother-in-law Jodi had never met. It took her by surprise, and she defended herself by saying, "But I've been sick."

I didn't feel any compassion at that moment. Instead I preached at her as I continued to sort clothes on the floor. "I know that and I understand, but you're feeling better now, and it seems that you're relying on me pretty heavily." I went on explaining the main reason for my outburst. "I'm just worried about how you're going to manage once you get home. You've got a lot ahead of you; I'm not going to be able to take care of everything for you." She listened as I added, "I know it's not easy to keep going when you're not up to it, but when I was your age, I had a job and *three* kids, and I still had to manage the house, the meals, and go to work on the days I didn't feel well. Sometimes you have to make yourself do things, even when you don't feel like it."

Jodi didn't say a word—she sat there on the bed, tears rolling down her face, crying. I grabbed a pile of clothes and left the room.

Looking back, I see how harsh I was to Jodi. I had to be overwhelmed with anxiety to speak to her like that because it is not my character to act that way. I had made myself look like "Super Woman" for having managed so much on my own at her age. Being married to a man who put long hours into farming, leaving me to manage the kids by myself, had toughened me up, and I felt no compassion at that moment for this young mother. I expected her to toughen up as well. I hadn't intended to compare my life to hers. It just came out once I started to give voice to my frustrations. I should not have compared my life to Jodi's. She was going through a whole different set of circumstances. She needed all the help she could get, but I needed help myself. It later became clear to me that I was trying to give what I no longer had. I'm not talking about physical energy. I was depleted emotionally.

God has perfect timing. When I left our room after unloading on Jodi, a woman about my age approached me in the lobby. Her name was Chris and she had come to visit me at Barnes Lodge. Her timing couldn't have been any better—I needed someone to talk to. She brought homemade soups bottled in canning jars along with several flavorful loaves of bread. Chris had learned about our family's tragedy through her niece, who was a classmate of Kelsey's. Since Chris lived in the St. Louis area, she felt compelled to help make Jodi and me feel more comfortable and cared for, knowing that we were out of our element in the large city.

Chris and I visited for quite a while. We talked about our families and our jobs, and of course I shared about Zach. Before long, the conversation gravitated toward my worries and concerns over what was taking place at the moment. It's odd how easy it is to share personal feelings with a perfect stranger, but she made me feel safe as she patiently listened, extending empathy right at the time I needed it most.

Voicing my troubles out loud made me realize that I needed time away—I needed to recharge. I had not even talked to my husband since I'd last seen him, which was several days. My husband and I had become so separated—and I don't mean in miles. It almost seemed as if we had become estranged. He tried to drive the five-and-a-half-hour trek once a week if he could, but sometimes it was longer between visits. And when he'd arrive in St. Louis, he wasn't the man I was used to. His mind was distracted and far away, and he acted angry and impatient. I really looked forward to seeing him, but he didn't seem to share the same feelings for me. The situation made us both out of sorts with each other. Life was changing and uncertain. We were both going through intense emotions that we had never dealt with before, and they were beginning to interfere in our relationship.

I didn't acknowledge it at the time, but looking back, it's now obvious that we were caught in the aftermath of stress and depression—Chris perhaps more so than myself. He wasn't dealing well with his emotional pain and wasn't talking to anyone about it. Actually, neither was I, but while I was turning inward for strength through spiritual guidance, he was turning to alcohol to relieve the gut-wrenching pain of his worry and sorrow.

Back in Wichita, there were times I couldn't find Chris in the hospital. I assumed he was in the cafeteria or on another part of the campus. Several times he told me he was leaving to look at farm machinery in the area, which he sometimes did, but frequently he'd gone to visit a bar instead. I can't believe I never picked up on that—mainly because I wasn't paying attention to him. I was in my own world—we both were.

It wasn't until I was writing this book that Chris revealed to me his reliance on alcohol to take the edge off his anxiety. I had begun to suspect that he'd been drinking when he'd visit us in St. Louis, but he was good at hiding it, and I sure didn't want to bring it up—that would've been like poking a bear. I didn't know what to do about it, and I was too wrapped up in what was going on in Missouri to deal with more issues from Kansas. At times when he'd arrive for a visit, I felt so hurt and disappointed by his attitude that I was relieved when it was time for him to leave. After a while we didn't even phone each other the entire time he was away.

I have heard of couples divorcing after the loss of a child, and I understand why. It took over three years for Chris and me to get back on track with our relationship after Zach's accident. He harbored pain, and I harbored resentment, and we didn't ever talk to each other about it. We both knew things didn't feel normal between us, but we didn't know what to say or how to make it better, so we avoided the subject. I guess we didn't want to trouble each other with more problems and hoped the issue would go away with time, but it truly felt like I was married to a man I didn't recognize anymore.

It all makes sense to me now. Chris is the type who never shows weakness. He doesn't complain when he's tired or ill or in pain. He sucks up his troubles and doesn't let anyone know what's going on inside him. He is the one whom everyone else turns to, because he is a pillar of strength and knowledge. I know him well enough to see that he was struggling tremendously because he couldn't *fix* our situation. Our son was changed for life, our family was hurting and living apart from each other, and there was absolutely nothing he could do to change what had happened. Reality was eating him like a cancer.

I didn't understand what we were going through at the time—that Chris's behavior had nothing to do with me. I took everything personally, which weighed me down even more. So often I'd lie in bed at the lodge unable to sleep. I cried to God in prayer. I told Him I needed His help to handle all that I was dealing with. I prayed that He would help Chris, and that He would give me the strength and patience to hang in there.

I also didn't want to open up to anyone about the pain I was feeling, so I was in prayer with God more in those few months after Zach's accident than I'd ever been in my life. It kept me sane and level headed and helped me feel peace. I felt like God was holding my hand and feeling my sorrow as I gave all my worries to Him. He was my friend, my confidant whom I could tell all my troubles to without feeling judged or pitied. I felt heard and understood and cared for whenever I prayed. I believed that He was looking after me and my family, and I worked hard to trust that eventually we would be okay.

I sure don't know how people who haven't included God in their lives deal with tough times. I can't imagine how much harder it would have been for me if I didn't know God. I didn't want to tell anyone else what was going on inside of me, so I didn't—I just kept talking to God.

Our situation began to make more sense to me when I Googled "depression in men." It hadn't occurred to me that depression could be the problem with Chris until the thought popped into my head one night when I was lying in bed looking at my phone. I'd hit the nail on the head with my suspicions when I read the description:

"anger, frustration, irritability, distant, tired"—and there it was—"sometimes turns to the use of alcohol to self-medicate."

Learning this information helped me but didn't fix anything. When I finally woke up to what was going on—that depression was more than likely the problem—I was better able to tolerate some of Chris's behaviors towards me. I tried to brush off some of the things that offended me and did my best not to cause a rift, but sometimes I had a tough time finding the heart to handle his behaviors. I was his safe place to fall, and unknowingly, he took out his anxieties and anger on me as if I were his punching bag.

After all we had been through, it's no wonder we weren't ourselves! We had not lost a child to death, but we were constantly threatened with it. Zach survived by the grace of God, but we had just experienced the scariest ride of our lives, and conditions were still uncertain. For nearly two months we had witnessed, felt, and lived every single detail of what Zach was experiencing, and it hurt us to the core and consumed our thoughts. Our entire focus was on helping Zach to live, to mend his body so he'd have a quality life—to overcome the pain, the infections, the amputations—and to instill the strength to push on.

Chris, Jodi, and myself were all going through a post-traumatic stress period once the situation finally looked more promising for Zach. We had been dog paddling in a swift current, trying to keep our heads above water, trying not to drown in fear or lose faith. When it finally looked like Zach was truly going to make it and also keep his arm, we could breathe more freely again, but we were exhausted from the struggle. The worst of the battle appeared to be over, but living with the casualties was just beginning.

Breaking Down

My time spent with the lady from St. Louis, Chris, was medicine to my soul. Our visit gave me a way to gather my emotions and gain a better perspective. After she left, I was ready to go back to our room to make amends with Jodi. I had been hard on her and needed to explain why.

Jodi's face was wet with tears and she was still lying on her bed. I felt badly and was hoping she'd forgive me and understand my breakdown. She didn't look angry—more like a sad puppy that had been punished.

"Jodi, I've been thinking about things. We've been living together in this small room and having to deal with so many hard issues for such a long time. I didn't mean to make you feel bad, and I'm not mad at you. I just sort of lost it with all I've been worried about."

"Your way of doing things isn't wrong and neither is mine," I continued. "We are just two people who deal with situations differently, and we got tossed together under stressful circumstances. Maybe God wants me to learn to relax a little more and you to step up a bit, so he put us together to work that out."

Jodi didn't say anything but she listened. "I've been thinking about something else," I said. "When was the last time that you and I had any fun? We have not had one day since the beginning of all this that we have enjoyed ourselves! What do you think about finding that place we heard about on the radio as we were on our way here—the place we can drive through with all the Christmas lights? Brynlee would love that! Afterwards maybe we could get some ice-cream and just have a good time." Jodi wiped her eyes and nodded in agreement.

That evening, we found the place with the lights. Thousands of colorful, twinkling animations all aglow were situated around a large park with a lake. As I drove slowly through the display with the car radio playing Christmas music synchronized to the rhythmic lights, Brynlee stood on Jodi's lap squealing and dancing. Jodi and I laughed joyfully, entertained more by Brynlee than the lights.

The two of us had better dispositions after that day. I was more relaxed, and Jodi started taking on more responsibilities, starting with her laundry. The atmosphere was cleared, as was our room, and our relationship felt better.

We were on our way out of the lodge one afternoon when a woman from Alaska who was also staying there approached us in the foyer. After visiting for a while, the woman said, "How wonderful that you two can live so well together and spend time with each other."

I answered back, "Yes, you really don't know someone well until you've lived with them." Jodi didn't say a word, but her face fell. She thought I was implying that she was hard to live with. But she broke into a smile when I followed with, "NOBODY should ever have to live with their mother-in-law!"

Although hard on Jodi, my breakdown was essentially healthy for me. It was a tension release that brought to a head matters I was not dealing with but needed to. It opened my eyes to my subconscious anger and allowed me a better understanding of what Jodi needed. Before, I felt that through her phone, she was living in a sort of "cyber world"—a realm that gave her escape from reality. I knew that once she got home with Zach and my support lessened, the reality of dealing with a toddler and a handicapped husband would be difficult for her to face—and that worried me. I'm sure that Jodi was going through some depression herself. I recalled later that she had been exhibiting behavioral signs before she became ill with the flu. She had mentioned to me that she might be experiencing PTSD (post-traumatic stress disorder) when we were still in Wichita. That made sense to me with what she had gone through, but I didn't really notice any changes then like I did once we were in St. Louis. That's when I started to see symptoms. She became extremely paranoid of the people and places surrounding us and had a lot of anxiety whenever we left the hospital. Her interest and energy for taking care of daily tasks slowed, and she began spending more time attached to her phone.

What I learned, though, was that Jodi was drawing strength from the comments and prayers people were sending her via Facebook. Friends, family and even strangers gave her hope by sending inspiring songs, poems, and videos to keep her focused on the positive and prevent her thoughts from growing dark. Maybe that's exactly what she needed. Maybe that was the perfect medicine for a scared twenty-three-year old wife and mother unsure of the future. I needed order and organization for my sanity—Jodi needed positive reinforcement for hers. Our lives collided when we were exhausted and worn thin, although we had both been doing the best we could to get through each challenging day.

Again, God came through at the perfect time. Jodi's aunt called to say that she would be happy to take a week's vacation and come stay with Jodi and Brynlee in St. Louis. Her offer would allow me a chance to go home.

Jodi asked if she should tell her aunt it was okay to come and take my place. I looked at her with a big smile on my face: "Don't just tell her yes. Tell her HELL YES!" Jodi's expression of surprise gave way to giggles. It was probably the first time she'd ever heard me swear.

What a gift it was for Jodi's aunt to offer her time. Besides needing a break, I needed to go home and take care of business, and there was no way Jodi could manage with Brynlee alone—nor did I want her to. Hospital rules would not allow her to take

Brynlee along to Zach's room, and Jodi definitely would've been uneasy staying in the lodge without another adult. Even though the surrounding neighborhood was clean and mostly safe, it was not Assaria, Kansas. We didn't venture too far from the hospital if we didn't have to, especially since the Ferguson riots were still fresh news.

Telling Zach goodbye when I was ready to leave was awfully hard. Even though he was twenty-four years old, I felt like I was deserting my child. I cried all the way to the lodge as I walked back from the hospital. He was in good care and would be okay, but I couldn't get my mind off how sad he appeared. It wasn't because I was leaving—it was because his days were so much longer. His left eye was bandaged shut after another graft surgery, and he couldn't wear his glasses to watch tv or read. He had too much time to think, and there was little to distract him from the pain and discomfort.

I so wished the healing process didn't have to take so long. It just seemed like more than he should have to bear. Sometimes I asked God, "Why? Why does he have to suffer so much for so long?" I know there is a time and purpose for everything, but it was hard to be patient while waiting for him to heal and have relief from the incessant hurting. But I also ran into residents staying at the lodge who shared their horror stories. Some had children in the hospital with long term conditions that had been dragging on for years! Those children had never even known a normal life outside of their illness. It just mortified me! "How did those parents do it?" We had been going through heart ache for just under two months, yet it felt like an eternity. Meeting those people and hearing their stories made me realize that there is always someone else out there worse off.

Jodi and Zach were so happy to see each other after four days apart while Jodi was recovering from the flu. They talked about how lonely life was without being together every day. Jodi was quick to let him know that she was not complaining, however, because God didn't take him away. "Yeah," Zach agreed. "They tell me I'm lucky to be alive." He went on, "I really missed you. I promise I will take care of you and Bryn when I get better."

"I know you will," Jodi said, choking back tears. "I am so glad I have you, no matter how long it takes to get you home. I feel like the luckiest girl in the world!"

16

FEELING THE LOVE

Chris drove to St. Louis on December twelfth, visited Zach that evening, and then took me back with him on the thirteenth. It felt so good to be home, to sleep in my own bed again! It was surreal to see where time had clearly stopped in my life. An unread newspaper with the date of October 25 was lying on the coffee table. The lunch cooler I took with me to work in the tractor was still sitting on the kitchen table, packed with my sun glasses and a MP3 player inside. Strangest of all was that the Halloween decorations were still up around the house and yet it was Christmas time! All the neighbors had their trees and lights up. Someone had posted a little Christmas flag in our yard that was waving in the wind. It had a picture of Santa and the words "Believe in Miracles" written across it.

Seeing all these remnants from the past made me feel like I had wandered back in time. Oh how I'd wished that I could open my eyes and find that the last several weeks had not really happened, but instead had been a bad dream. But that was not the case. Our family would have a new normal to adjust to, and that would take time. Still, I was unbelievably grateful that we had been given more time at all!

It felt so good to be surrounded with familiarity for a change; such a contrast to the first time I'd made a mad dash home to get clothes, and fell apart over seeing anything that reminded me of Zach. I was so anxious to see the rest of my family, especially my grandson Liam. I was also eager to connect with friends and acquaintances at church who are like extended family. There, Chris and I were greeted with welcome hugs and joyful faces; the congregation had consistently prayed for us and wanted us to know that we had their support. Everywhere Chris and I went, we were greeted like that, not only at church. Even complete strangers approached us to say how much they cared about what we were going through.

The timing was perfect for me to come home. The annual Christmas Cantata was planned for that Sunday and little did we know, the church had dedicated it to Zach and our family. The choir decided that our story fit with the theme of the Cantata, "*Celebrate the Joy!*" The music was joyful, and it *did* feel like a celebration. We listened to our pastor narrate Bible stories that went along with the songs the choir sang, and I felt so thankful to be celebrating life and miracles and all that God had given us.

As I looked over the congregation, my heart overflowing with the warmth of our welcome, I spotted a family sitting toward the front of the church. Instantly, my bliss turned to sorrow. I knew what that family had recently gone through. For them it was a Christmastime without their mother and wife. She had been my age but had lost her battle with ovarian cancer. I remembered her friendly smile and how outgoing and beautiful she was.

"Our family could have been in the very same situation" I thought to myself. "We could so easily have been sitting in this church suffering an emptiness and loss, just as that family surely is experiencing." An immediate sense of gratitude came over me that we still had Zach. How fortunate we were that he was alive.

As I continued to look around the sanctuary, I realized that there were several individuals who probably didn't feel the joy of Christmas. Some had lost loved ones who used to sit in our congregation but were no longer with us. We want to believe that those people are celebrating with Jesus, but that hope doesn't take away the pain from those who are left behind. I had never really been as keenly aware of others' losses as much as I was since our experience with Zach.

One of the reasons a church family is so valuable is that we need each other in those tough times. We hurt along with those who hurt and we celebrate together in times of joy. A good example is our church choir, whose director had texted me for Zach's favorite Christmas song before I left to come home from St. Louis. I chuckled when Zach told me his answer, but I passed it along to the director. The choir wanted to create a video of themselves singing the song to Zach. They thought they'd need to practice for something beautiful like *Silent Night* or *The First Noel*, but nope— nothing like that. Zach made it simple for them. after a couple of Christmas carols and shoutouts of get-well wishes to Zach, the choir wrapped it all up with his requested song—*We Wish You A Merry Christmas*. "Yeah," someone said later when I told that story. "That sounds like Zach."

Days later when I returned to St. Louis, I watched Jodi adjust the iPad so Zach could see the video the choir had made. We were all totally absorbed in the moment. What a thoughtful and powerful gift they had given to lift Zach's spirits and help him see the faces of people who cared about him. The whole episode warmed my heart, and I again became strongly aware of how fortunate I was to have God's love, a beautiful family, a caring community to live in, and a church family with which to celebrate life.

And speaking of a caring community! The next day after the Cantata emphasized that fact more than we could ever have imagined! The clouds were heavy with moisture on that cool December afternoon, the day our community scheduled a big fundraiser for Zach. We heard bits and pieces about people putting together an auction, but we didn't know the details and were anxious to see what it entailed.

I was heading to my daughter Kelsey's house to deliver a stack of T-shirts my neighbor had given me for our family when I was distracted by something that caught my eye. It was a beautiful double rainbow. The colors glowed vibrantly, emitting bright light against the background of the foggy gray sky. Both arches were visible from one end to the other, with nothing obstructing the view in-between. I'd never seen a rainbow so close and so perfect. The fact that we rarely see double rainbows made it even more spectacular.

Kelsey stepped out of her doorway as I approached the porch of her house. She had noticed the rainbow before I arrived and like me, was eager to talk about it: "Mom," she said as she looked northward, "this is so strange—it always bothers me to look out that direction because all I can picture is the black smoke from the fire the day of Zach's accident. And now, there in that very same spot, is the end of that rainbow!"

I knew what she was talking about—I'd realized the very same thing. "And look how the other end stretches over to Zach's house at the farm," I said, as we stood marveling at the sight. It was like a message straight from Heaven!

I handed Kelsey three red T-shirts for her, Broc, and Liam to wear to the auction. They were printed with a clever phrase on the front that Kelsey had come up with—*Nothing 'SHORT' of a Miracle*—the word *SHORT* referring to our last name. The community was selling them as an additional fund raiser for Zach and had generously donated them to our family members.

That double rainbow remained visible for a long time. Even as Chris and I drove to the auction held at the rural high school, it was still vibrant. It was another sign from God, just like the first rainbow I saw the Life Watch helicopter fly though in Wichita. It was as if God wanted everyone attending the auction to know that He was in control of the whole event.

We weren't the only ones who felt that way. Many people talked about it at the auction, and several posted their comments on Facebook along with rainbow photos that they captured:

"Benefit dinner.... God was there with us!!"

"Zach's rainbow!"

"This picture was taken on our farm looking toward Southeast of Saline High School where the benefit auction is about to be held. I think God is trying to say something!"

"We all saw it as we came to the auction. A beautiful sign from God!"

"I looked out and saw that one end was at the accident site, just north of us. The other end had a white glow. I have never seen anything like it before. It was amazing!

"Huge double rainbow at SES High, walking into the Zach Short fundraiser. It was the brightest rainbow I'd ever seen... coincidence? I think not!"

Feeling the Love

Driving down the highway to the auction, I felt God speaking to me through my heart saying, "I am here, I love you, and I'll show you so," and that's exactly what He did!

The parking lot was full of cars when Chris and I turned into the school. We were surprised to see that so many people would take the time to attend. Until we entered the school, we had no idea what we were about to walk in to.

Chris opened the door, then followed behind me to go inside. What we saw was mind blowing! The building was as full as if it were a big game day against a rival team back in our high school days. People were visiting and buzzing around everywhere. Some were browsing over tables covered with items; others stood in a line where workers were seated behind one side of a long table, assigning numbers to auction bidders. Another long line led into the kitchen where people were placing money in a large jar before being served a meal. Looking in the kitchen, we saw several volunteers busy dishing up spaghetti with all the fixings.

Chris and I knew some of the people who were working, but there were many we didn't recognize. We were awestruck! We absolutely had no idea that the community had come together to put on something so big! And oh my! The work it must have been to plan it all! We were blown away!

Chris and I tried to make our way into the gym where the auction was being held but were unable to get past the foyer for quite some time because of all the people who approached us, wanting to visit and hear the latest on Zach. They wanted us to know they had been praying for him and keeping up on his progress through the newspaper, TV and Facebook.

When we finally made our way to the gymnasium, the sight was overwhelming. Chattering crowds were sitting on the bleachers while volunteers, wearing the same red t-shirts we had on, were down on the floor preparing numerous auction items.

I had brought along with me a draft of a "Thankyou" speech which I jotted down at home just before we left, not knowing I'd be delivering it to so many people. The thought of speaking to such a large crowd made me quite nervous, but Chris and I wanted to express our appreciation for all that people had done for Zach and our family, and this was the perfect time and place to do it.

We worked our way down to the gym floor where I was handed a microphone. The noisy crowd quieted down, but many continued to visit, not realizing I was going to speak, which gave me some relief that not all the attention was focused on me. When I pulled the paper out of my pocket and began to read, my voice choked and my heart pounded; what I wanted to say about the gratitude we felt for the generous acts of our community seemed impossible to express with words. It felt so inadequate, yet somehow, I managed to say most of what was in my heart. Chris had told me earlier that he preferred for me to do the speaking, but his face expressed what was in his heart through the tears that trickled down his cheeks.

The crowd applauded when I finished and then the auction began. There was a plethora of items that people donated: handcrafted toys, gift baskets, contributions from people's businesses, donated services—a whole cornucopia of treasures.

A master woodworker built and donated a child-sized wooden rocking horse. A friend of ours who works in house construction built a beautiful doll house that stood over four feet tall. It had three separate levels of rooms, little windows and doors, a porch adorned with tiny working Christmas lights, and even real tiles on the roof. A neighboring farmer donated his hay tub grinding service; another donated a side of beef from his cattle operation.

Moreover, people were paying outlandish prices for the auction items and then many donated the items they won back to our family! We saw two men battle it out for the rocking horse and when one of them finally won the bid, he said loudly, "Give it to Zach's little girl!" The beautiful doll house ended up in Brynlee's possession the same way.

A vacation package to a lake house was auctioned, then gifted to Chris and me, which we passed on to Jodi and Zach. They also gave us wreaths made out of gift cards that came in useful when we were back in St. Louis.

Another very special item was auctioned from a well-known local artist and friend of ours who paints the sunrise every morning to celebrate life after surviving a brain tumor. She painted the sunrise on the day of Zach's accident and beautifully framed it, then awarded a certificate to paint any day's sunrise for the highest bidder of Zach's sunrise painting, which also ended up being gifted to us.

One of the auction volunteers shared some information with Chris and me when he saw us sitting on the bleachers shaking our heads in disbelief. He told us that the auction committee had to eventually turn away donated items because the event would've gone on too long into the evening had they accepted them all.

We had never in our lives seen so much generosity from people as we did that day. I took pictures with my phone throughout the evening and forwarded them on to Jodi and Zach, who had no idea, any more than Chris and I did, that so many people had gone to so much effort. We could barely comprehend what motivated people to care as much as they did. No words could adequately express the overwhelming gratitude we felt in our hearts. It was as if God squeezed us with his loving arms through hundreds and hundreds of benevolent people to show us how much He cares. If someone had told me thirty-five years ago, when I graduated from that very same high school, that I'd be giving a speech in front of several hundred people, thanking them for donating their time, talents, and gifts for something that would help my family, I would never have believed it. We were moved to tears again and again to see so many people supporting us in such a selfless way. It was almost incomprehensible!

The crazy thing is, we never expressed a need financially. People just took it upon themselves to take care of us. Occasionally, someone would ask if we had a specific need, or they would inquire as to what we were facing financially, but we couldn't give them an answer. We had no idea what Zach's medical insurance would ultimately cover, and we had no way of knowing how long he would need to receive medical care. We also were not clear at the time as to whether Zach's insurance would pay for the type of prosthetic leg he would need if he chose to continue farming. If insurance didn't cover the expense, some legs could cost him as much as one hundred and twenty-five thousand dollars, and the leg only had a life span of ten years!

Then there was the worry about Zach's financial future. What would the situation look like for him down the road? We chose to take one day at a time and not stress over what we couldn't begin to know, but we also were aware that he wouldn't receive workers compensation because he was self-employed and not covered for it. He would probably qualify for disability pay, but Zach didn't like the thought of that. How much of the medical bills would that even take care of? How long would he be laid up and unable to work? Would he even be *able* to work? Those were all questions that couldn't yet be answered.

Zach normally earned an income working on machinery in the shop in the winter, but that was not happening for now. Chris and Matthew could help out while he recovered by taking over his farming responsibilities once farm season resumed. That's one of the benefits of farming together as a family unit. Any one of us would help out the others as long as possible. For Zach's sake, we had hoped that covering for him would only be temporary, and he would be back to pursue the career of his dreams.

As it turned out, people's contributions were a huge blessing to Zach and his family. The expenses accumulated quickly. Every bit of the money raised was slated to removing financial burdens. Between the medical fees that insurance didn't cover, costs incurred by living away from home, and the need to renovate Zach's entire house to make it handicap accessible, expenses proliferated.

Chris and I had financial issues also. We had to hire extra help to cover our positions while we were absent from our jobs, and the expenses of traveling back and forth to St. Louis, including the lodging and meal expenses, hit our pocket books as well.

We had never been in a position to receive charity before and were at first uncomfortable accepting it. Someone counseled us to let go of our pride and allow others to help, because rejecting people's gifts takes away their opportunity to feel like they are making a difference. That made sense. Chris and I had never looked at it quite that way before, and the new perspective relieved some of the guilt we felt for accepting help.

I was so thankful for the opportunity to have gone home! Not only was it a refreshing break to recharge my soul, but my stress was lessened after I took care of business I had put off. Plus, I got to witness the fantastic fundraiser and the Cantata at our church. I wished that Jodi and Zach could have been there for those events. They missed out on our hired man Jason's wedding as well. Zach was supposed to stand up with his lifelong friend, but since he couldn't, Matthew took his place. I was moved to tears when the pastor offered a special prayer for Zach, at Jason's request during the wedding ceremony.

Driving back to St. Louis, I had time to reflect on the events of the past several weeks, and I felt immeasurable gratitude for what we had experienced. Christmas was coming, and my heart swelled to think that we would be spending the celebration of Christ's birth with *all* our children.

The situation was really beginning to turn around. Miracles were turning up everywhere: from the sparing of Zach's life, to providing him with successful surgeries—from finding knowledgeable, compassionate, and talented medical care, to surrounding us with the loving support system of our community—from helping people find their faith, to beautiful signs like double rainbows—from all of these instances, evidence abounded that God's light had shone through in every aspect of Zach's healing process. God is most definitely present in our lives. I sincerely believe that we would all see that if we took the time to notice.

17

ONE MOMENT IN TIME

During the time I went home to Kansas, Zach had his twelfth surgery. Dr. Moore removed a football shaped flap of skin containing arteries and veins from his upper right arm and used it to cover the exposed, burned area on his left wrist. She spent hours painstakingly reconnecting the arteries and veins. That area of Zach's arm was considered "high-risk" for two weeks and had to be monitored every half hour. Nurses used a sonogram instrument to listen for a pulse in each of those newly attached blood vessels. If a pulse was still detectable after two weeks, the sound would be confirmation that the transferred skin flap was successful.

Chris, Jodi, and I met up with Dr. Moore, who approached us carrying an apple she'd been munching. She was always on the go and snacked to sustain herself until she had time for a real meal. Updating us with the latest on Zach's progress, she said that the muscle flap reconstruction she performed on his shoulder was healing beautifully, was serving its purpose, and was infection free! She described it as "a big success."

"He won't be able to lift his arm using his shoulder; it will only be able to lift from the elbow," she explained as she demonstrated with her own arm, bending it at the elbow, "but at least he will have some use of his arm."

I didn't understand and asked, "Since you covered his shoulder with a muscle, why won't he be able to use the muscle to lift his arm?"

"It doesn't work like that," she answered. "The muscle flap on his shoulder is merely used as a covering. It cannot physically operate as a working muscle."

That information was disappointing but made sense. At least he still had his arm and would be able to use it, even if movement was limited. That was enough in itself, considering the alternative. We had prayed he'd get to keep his arm and our prayers were answered. Dr. Moore added that the pressure sores on Zach's back and the back of his head were healing nicely and the white count in his blood was finally normal. The fungus in his system was still a problem but would hopefully get better with time. She stressed that when Zach first arrived in St. Louis, he was nearly septic and was in very poor shape nutritionally—he was very critically sick. Improvements had taken time, but he was finally turning the corner. They had found the right antibiotics to allow recovery to happen.

Even more great news came when Dr. Moore said that she wanted to give Zach a week of no surgeries to allow his body time to rest over the holidays. She was impressed with Zach's progress, and the whole time she was speaking, I was impressed with her—I mean absolutely impressed! Thank God for leading us to this woman and this hospital!

Chris and I made our way up to the ICU, eager to see Zach. He was awake and sitting alone in his room as we entered to tell him good night. When he raised his chin to look at us, I noticed that his eyes looked watery and assumed that the nurse had administered salve for the dryness. Then I noticed a streak of blood trickling down his neck. I started to ask him about it, but realized almost as soon as the words formed in my mouth that he had been crying. Tears rolling over the raw skin on his face picked up blood as they ran down his neck and made it look like he was bleeding.

What's wrong, Zach?" I asked as both Chris and I searched his eyes for telling signs.

"My phone rang," he mumbled. "It was my friend, Alex. I tried to pick it up, but I couldn't answer before it stopped ringing." We could see the frustration on Zach's face. His left hand was useless, and his right hand still hung limply at the wrist, making it almost impossible for him to do anything without help. I felt a stab in my heart, picturing him fumbling around trying to use his taped-up hands and wrists to pick up the phone.

"I'm so tired of all this. I want to go home," he sobbed as the tears fell more freely. It was the first time Chris and I had seen him break down. Ever since he had become conscious, he'd kept his chin up, always trying to be strong and accept what was in front of him. We had wondered when this moment would come. It had been an ongoing concern for Chris and me to know what he was feeling inside, but the timing had not been right to ask him. We decided it was better to wait for him to tell us when he was ready. At last, the opportunity was here.

Seeing him break down was all it took for the pent-up emotions and tears just below the surface to come bursting out. In a way, it was a release for all three of us. Chris and I drew close to the bed and listened to what Zach needed to say.

"Why did this have to happen to me?" Zach implored, defeat in his voice. "I've always tried to do things right in my life. Why did God let this happen to me?" The tears came faster.

"Oh, Zach," I sobbed, overcome with what I'd been waiting to say, "you have every right to be frustrated, and we've cried out to

God with the same question." Chris chimed in, backing my every word with the same empathy.

"We've been right there with you hurting for your pain and frustrations. It's okay to let it all out—nobody expects you to always keep your chin up." Zach wiped his eyes with the back of his wrist, his head down, while I continued. "You've been through so much already, and there are going to be more frustrating days ahead, but you've got your entire family to lean on. We're here to help however you need us." I went on: "We don't understand why things happened this way—it doesn't make sense. It just has to all be a part of a plan that God has for you. He spared your life for some reason—and we're so thankful he did!"

Zach seemed a little more resolved as he said, "I'm glad to be alive—I don't mean to sound like I'm not grateful. It's just that I've always been the one that others came to for help. Now I have to have help with everything I do." Chris and I could see that helplessness tore him up.

"It's alright, Zach," Chris said. "We just have to take things one day at a time. You're going to get better and we're going to help you. We'll get through this."

Zach then revealed what had brought him to this point: "Things were just beginning to build up inside of me." His mood subtly shifted from sadness to worry. "How am I ever going to thank all those people for what they've done for me?" I understood his feelings, as I had fretted about the same thing.

"From what I've seen," I told him, "those people want to thank YOU! You've brought them back to their faith."

Zach had no idea of the inspiration he had been to so many people and how he had touched their lives. We spoke on that subject a little bit more, but I knew he wouldn't grasp the impact he had made until he was out of the hospital and able to talk to those who were following his journey.

We could see the physical and emotional progress of Zach's healing, but it was hard to watch him suffer with so much pain—he was always dealing with pain. Chris and I wished we could trade places with him. We so wanted to give him a break. My mind went back to that statue in Wichita of Mary holding a broken and bloodied Jesus, not because of the physical pain that Mary saw her son suffer, but because of the emotional pain. I could relate to the way she looked at him with her eyes, and in my heart, I understood exactly how she felt.

Dr. Moore did as she said and gave Zach a full week to recover before any more surgery. Christmas was only a few days away and just like at Thanksgiving, it was the perfect time to give his body rest.

Matthew, Kelsey, and her family made the trip to St. Louis to spend Christmas with Zach, Jodi, Brynlee, Chris and me. It was so great to have all our kids and grandkids together again. Jodi was excited that her parents would make the trip as well. She missed not seeing them for so long. They had used all their vacation time off from their jobs when we were in Wichita and weren't able to spend as much time in St. Louis as they would've liked. All of us had some celebrating to do and were excited about the opportunity. It was even more special and meaningful to be celebrating life with our whole family. Zach's spirits lifted to see the familiar faces again.

Chris rented several rooms at an upscale hotel near the hospital to make everyone's stay more special, a welcome change from the lodge where Jodi and I had been living for the last several weeks. The families spent much of the time taking turns to visit

Zach, but also toured the beautiful Arch and ate at a couple of classy restaurants.

At that time of year the winter weather was chilly, but it was refreshing to get outside and breathe the crisp air as we meandered down the city streets, admiring the Christmas decorations while pushing Brynlee and Liam in their strollers. "Such a huge shift from the last time we were all together," I reflected as we snapped photos of our group posing in front of the Arch. Life was returning to normal, a feeling that in the crises felt like it would never come again.

Zach was recuperating steadily and for the first time was moved from the ICU to a regular room. The nurses removed his catheter and detached him from the various monitors, checking his vital signs every four hours instead of continuously.

Because it was no longer the ICU, Brynlee was able to make visits to Zach's room. His face brightened to see her, and after weeks of only face timing with her daddy on the iPad, Brynlee was tickled to be with him too. As usual, she was a little ball of energy, constantly on the move—running around Zach's bed, climbing on and under chairs, and chasing her toys around the room. She brought life to any space she occupied and was such an entertainer. Jodi pulled out her phone and played Brynlee's favorite song, *All About that Bass* by Meghan Trainor, knowing it would get Brynlee excited enough to dance for Zach. When Brynlee heard the song, she jumped up and down and wiggled with enthusiasm, just as we'd hoped. I joined in, waving my arms and shaking my hips, all while dressed in a yellow paper hospital gown. Jodi laughed while Zach just shook his head as we held our hospital dance party.

Zach's morale and our moods were boosted even more when a couple of strong male staff members of the hospital entered and carefully lifted him into a padded recliner chair. Something as simple as sitting upright in a chair rather than lying in bed seemed like such a milestone—Zach was one step closer to regaining his strength. I again marveled at how much we take for granted until we lose it.

And then on December 24th, something wonderful happened—a miracle really. Zach raised his straightened left arm several inches off the bed, using his shoulder muscle! This was the arm Dr. Moore told us would not be capable of doing such an act. He defied the prognosis! Miracles do happen, something we already knew with what we had been through. We were excited by the prospect that there might be even more miracles ahead for Zach as he healed. In the process of discussing that possibility, it occurred to us that his kidneys had also defied medical science.

By now, it was fairly safe to assume that he would not need a transplant or even dialysis like the medical experts had predicted in Wichita. After what his kidneys had endured, the doctors were certain one or both of those procedures would be necessary, yet now the kidneys were functioning efficiently. God is good! Zach was living proof of His goodness and power.

Zach's recovery was going so well until he started getting sick at night when he had to take his meds. We worried about all the potent drugs he'd been taking for so long. Especially the pain narcotics. He had a few hallucinatory episodes that made us plainly aware of how the chemicals were playing havoc with his mind.

A couple of times he tried to convince us that he had bolts moving around in his wrist. He was so afraid something was terribly wrong. He was frustrated that we couldn't see what he was imagining. He would sit staring intensely at his left wrist for long periods of time, waiting to catch the "bolts" moving, and then he'd croak, "See that?! Did you see that happen?!" We'd look at each other like he was crazy and then tell *him* he was too.

The doctors talked about weaning him off several of the drugs to get him ready for rehab. The talk about rehab was so exciting! It meant that we were seeing a light at the end of the very long and dark tunnel. First, though, Zach was scheduled to have surgery on the Monday following Christmas to finish grafting his left arm, and then again on Tuesday to graft the left side of his face. The doctors also wanted to work on the large exit wound on his head—the one they placed a wound-vac on. Plans were to wait for those sites to heal and then decide if Zach was ready to move on for rehab. We weren't sure where rehab would be but hoped for closer to home. We also knew that the surgeries done before his release from the St. Louis hospital would not be his last. Zach would return for tendon transfers and nerve repair in his left arm and hand and possibly his right hand if it didn't come around on its own. There would also be more skin releases, but by that point, the surgeries would be performed after first getting him home!

Jodi posted on Facebook, as she usually did, to solicit prayers for Zach's final two surgeries. Such a trooper she was, always believing and hoping for the best. She was his head cheerleader and lead prayer warrior. She made a special request online, mentioning that the doctor was concerned about a blood clot in the right side of Zach's groin. For that reason, he was put on blood thinners administered through injections into his abdomen. His condition was always a rollercoaster no matter how well things seemed to be going. We learned to never take anything for granted.

In addition to the request for prayers, Jodi posted a list she titled, "The ten things I have learned since Zach's accident":

1. Farming is a super dangerous job!
2. I never, ever, EVER knew I was capable of being so strong.
3. I feel like a sixty-year-old in a twenty-three-year old's body.
4. Never take a kiss or hug for granted. It's been sixty-four days!
5. Hospitals are NO place to raise a fifteen-month old!
6. Always know the doctors are giving you the worst possible scenario first.
7. Zach is the strongest, most determined person I know!
8. I have had to make decisions that no twenty-three-year-old should ever have to make.
9. I could NOT raise Brynlee on my own, ever!
10. Without God I wouldn't have my husband anymore.

By this time, Jodi had a large following on Facebook. People were so willing to hold her and her family up with prayer and to provide loving support. They truly were her lifeline.

Zach's four-hour surgery to finish grafting his arm went well on that Monday following Christmas. Dr. Moore told Jodi he would be "pretty sore" because she had to take skin from his back and his behind to do the grafts. He was readmitted back into the intensive care unit.

Due to the OR scheduling conflicts, surgery to graft his face and work on his head wound was put off until later in the week. As eager as we were to see the final surgery—number sixteen in St. Louis—it was good that more trauma wasn't added to the pain Zach was suffering. He was already putting up with more than most humans could stand.

I don't know how he tolerated the pain of so many extensive and invasive procedures. Chunks of flesh and muscle were cut off, cut out, and moved to different locations. His skin was shaved off almost every part of his body and grafted somewhere else. He had to endure painful dressing changes daily where the bandages stuck to his raw wounds and had to be peeled off to clean the newly grafted skin and donor sites. Simply lying in bed was excruciating to his skin and body. A special bed filled with sand plus air circulating through the mattress alleviated some of the pressure, but he was never comfortable. His face showed the hurt, but he rarely complained and his attitude and pain tolerance was incredible.

Zach and I had a heart-to-heart talk on the Tuesday his surgery was postponed. He wanted to talk about the accident and explore what the future held, which made me believe that he was making progress mentally. Before then, his focus was only on the present day and what was being done to help him through the moment.

My heart ached for him. It took every bit of faith I could muster to help him come to terms with what had happened. I had rehearsed those conversations in my head so many times, and the only way I could even begin to formulate an answer was to draw on my faith in God that there is a purpose beyond our understanding. I don't believe that God *caused* the accident, but believing that there is a purpose was the only answer that I could offer, because there *was* no other answer.

God makes no mistakes, so when it comes to why Zach's accident happened, we'll never know the answer in this lifetime. But I do know that He intended for Zach to live—otherwise things would've turned out differently. God could have put some obstacle in Zach's path to stop him from going to the grain cart, or He could have taken his life right there and then. Instead, Zach was directed down a different path that was a drastic change. He was grieving for a life that would be no more, and the loss hurt him to the core.

Zach's entire physical being and independence had been stripped away. He had always been one to help others, but now he was having to accept being dependent. I pointed out to him that he was still helping others but in a new way, and that it was okay to receive help from them. I assured him that he would eventually get back his strength and ability to care for himself—he would, I promised him, work again. It would take some time, maybe a year or two, and he would have to practice patience. I continually stressed how grateful we all were to have him with us, and he let me know that he was aware of that. It was just so hard for him to keep from going back to that place in his mind that kept saying *if:* "If only I had run around to the other side of the tractor and not jumped over the tongue....If only I hadn't been there to help that day at all!" *If, If, If!!!*

That's how these things work. One decision—one moment in time—can change the whole path of our entire life. We think these events happen to other people, not ourselves. We can't go back in time and change what happened. We have no choice but to accept our current condition, so it all boils down to attitude. Attitude is what will make or break us. At that period in Zach's life, he had every right to grieve and be angry. I had been angry too, as had Chris and Jodi. I'm quite sure that the rest of our family at some point struggled with anger. I anticipated that Zach would vacillate back and forth in his search for answers for some time as he learned to accept and adjust to the life ahead of him. I prayed that he would fall back on his relationship with God when the times got hard. I knew he might choose to be angry with God. If so, I believe God understands that human part of us. Even Jesus questioned God's will and grieved in the Garden of Gethsemane the night before he was crucified. But I also believed that If Zach would call on God in his times of need, God would listen and take care of him.

The final surgery on January second took less than the predicted three hours. Zach had to continue wearing the wound-vac on his head and remained in the ICU.

Dr. Moore met with us, as she usually did after surgery. By that time, she had become a close friend to our family. We had genuinely come to love and respect her and held onto every word she said, just as we had Dr. Bingaman. She told us that we would need to wait patiently for about ten more days to make sure all the grafts took and the incisions healed. if everything looked good, it would be the end of surgery for Zach for several months. She said that she wanted to give Zach's body time to "beef up," as she put it: "Time to repair and rebuild."

It didn't take a professional to know that Zach's body had deteriorated. He had taken on the appearance of a skinny old man. Generally, we had seen him wrapped in so much gauze covering his entire body to keep his burns clean, but when the time came that some of his wounds didn't have to be covered any longer with thick pads and bandages, it was shocking to see how much his body had withered away. His muscles had atrophied to the point that they didn't hardly exist. I couldn't believe how tiny the stumps of his legs were. They looked like they belonged on a small child. I could touch my middle finger to the end of my thumb when I wrapped my fingers around his bicep near the bend of his elbow. That was partly due to the fact he'd had so much muscle and flesh taken from that area to cover his wrist, but still, his arms were so thin that they were merely skin on bone, a flesh-covered skeleton. His hair was completely shaved off which changed his looks as well. The bareness of his head exposed multiple scars from pressure sores and exit wounds. It was painful to see all the signs of battle his body had endured. He looked so frazzled and wasted.

When Dr. Moore told us Zach would get a break from surgeries to rest, we all felt relieved. She wouldn't see him again for weeks, and when she did reconnect with him, she would bring a plan to deal with the nerves and tendons in his left arm and hand. She had successfully saved his arm from amputation, but much repairing was still necessary to make the arm and hand functional.

As for Zach's right hand that drooped limply at the wrist, Dr. Moore wanted to give the nerves six months from the time of the accident to heal on their own before deciding to intervene with other options.

And finally, Dr. Moore recommended that rehab be done conveniently close to our home. As much as we appreciated the care in St. Louis, we welcomed that recommendation immensely.

REHAB—that was the word we had longed to hear. Every day brought that part of the healing process closer! Zach was ready to move on too. We were anxious and hopeful that he would make great strides once he got in the hands of the therapists. He had always been strong willed about pushing himself to achieve a goal he wanted, so we hoped that his determination would serve him well in the future.

Knowing we were so close to the end of our time in the St. Louis hospital made those last days seem longer. Once the prospect of going home was in sight, thinking about anything else was difficult. Jodi especially grew more anxious. "I miss my house. I miss my dog. I miss my own bed! Can time please speed up?" she cried out while sitting in our lodge bedroom one evening. "I want to go home—but it isn't home unless Zach is there. Gahhh—70 days! Haven't I been patient long enough? Some days I want to just sit and cry! But then I get a little voice in my head that says, 'Jodi, be patient. It will happen.'"

Turning to her phone, she played a song for me that helped to keep her focused. She said that she had listened to it every night when Zach was in a coma. It was called *Angel by Your Side* by Francesca Battistelli. I had never heard it before, but when she played it, I could see why she felt connected to the song. The lyrics fit perfectly with Zach and Jodi's situation. The vocalist sings to her beloved that she can't promise to take the pain away, but she won't stop trying. She says that "she'll be the angel by his side, to get him through the night. She'll be the strength he can't provide on his own." The song was beautiful and made me tear up.

Jodi wanted Zach's rehab to be in Kansas City. The rehab center was right across the street from Kansas University Medical Center if Zach needed emergency care, and it also had a burn unit. Another plus was that it was located about an hour drive from where her parents lived. She could stay with them and commute back and forth, utilizing their help to watch Brynlee. It sounded ideal.

At Jodi's request, the St. Louis medical team applied for Zach to have rehab in Kansas City, but the process took days. Not hearing back or knowing, was a real test of Jodi's patience. It didn't help matters that Brynlee was unable to be in Zach's room since he was back in the ICU. Zach had not seen his precious little girl for a full week. Jodi knew how much they enjoyed time together and could hardly wait for him to be moved to a regular room. The hands on the clock just couldn't turn fast enough.

We received some good news on Monday, January fifth, after Zach had a dressing change that took two hours in the OR. Ninety percent of the grafts Dr. Moore had done during Zach's last surgery had taken and therefore would not have to be redone! About eight hundred staples were removed from his body. There were still some signs of infection on his arm, but the medical team assured us that the antibiotics would clear them up. So with that report, Zach's release for full range of motion rehab was scheduled for the following Monday or Tuesday! One more week! Seven or eight days yet to wait, but we had a date! Two of the plastic surgery doctors told us that Zach would probably be in rehab for a couple of months, and then he should get his new legs! We were so excited! And we wouldn't have to come back to St. Louis for six to nine months!

The next week at Barnes Jewish Hospital was spent slowly weaning Zach from the hospital equipment. The wound-vac was finally removed so he no longer looked like a character out of *Star Trek* with that hose attached to his head. The leads were removed from his chest because he didn't have to be monitored twenty-four/seven, and he was once again moved to a regular room.

After visiting in the afternoons, I kept Brynlee in the lodge with me each evening Jodi went to be with Zach. Jodi was on the verge of emotional exhaustion and the toughness she had exhibited was wearing thin. She missed their home. Ten weeks had passed since she had been there other than to get clothes one afternoon. "I hope you never get into another accident like this EVER again!" she blurted one night when she was alone with Zach.

"Jodi, when it's your time to go, it's your time to go," Zach responded. "You can't change that. It just wasn't my time to go." Reassuring her, he went on: "I will get to spend more time with you...with my family. We still have each other. I haven't been able to kiss you since October 24th. It's hard on me too."

Jodi broke down and cried. Through her tears she told him how thankful she was—even when she was having some rough days. Those days made her realize how much she needed Zach. He was her rock.

"I haven't seen this hand in seventy-five days," Jodi mused as she examined Zach's left hand, finally unwrapped and newly revealed. Considering how badly damaged it was, it looked pretty good. He was able to hold his hand out straight, and move his wrist a little bit.

Dr. Moore walked into the room just then and caught Zach raising his left arm slightly out from his side. "Didn't you say I wasn't supposed to be able to raise my arm like this using my shoulder?" Zach asked, pleased with himself.

Dr. Moore was speechless—she didn't know how to answer his question. There *were* no answers—not that science could explain anyway. She shook her head in disbelief then told him how happy she was with her decision to save his arm, especially after seeing how good it looked and what he was already able to do with it. She added that she was glad Zach was referred to her. Then she said something that she'd never given a hint of before, even in the slightest way. She told Zach and Jodi that she was not positive in the beginning that the surgeries would turn out as well as they had. She hadn't realized when she accepted him as a patient, how critically sick Zach was until he arrived in St. Louis.

Whether true or not, we had heard through the grapevine rumors that Dr. Moore was reprimanded for accepting such a high-risk patient. A hospital's reputation is put at risk when patients don't survive, which explains why we had such a difficult time finding a willing surgeon who would take a chance on Zach back when we were frantically searching for one. Whatever prompted Dr. Moore to do so, we'll never know—it had to be a God thing, and we were thankful beyond words that she did accept Zach! We were so fortunate to have found her. Without her, Zach most likely would have lost his arm. His survival would have been so much more difficult in so many ways had that been the case.

Dr. Moore let Zach and Jodi know that she would be leaving town for a few days and if everything kept going well, it looked as though Zach would be released for rehab in Kansas City the day before her return! She said that she wanted to see him again in a month for a check-up and also to observe how the nerves were growing back in his hands. Nerves naturally grow about an inch per month, she told them, and Dr. Moore was eager to see if his would heal on their own as she hoped they would.

A week after his last surgery, Zach was able to feed himself again. His limp wrist gained just enough strength to hold a utensil, and he managed to scoop up a bite of food from his plate and bring it to his mouth. He was making progress and remaining healthy. It was time to move on!

Five weeks in the Wichita Via Christi burn unit with twenty of those days spent in a coma—six weeks in St. Louis's Barnes Jewish Hospital with over a dozen surgeries. Finally, on January 13, 2015, eighty days after the accident, Zach was heading to the KU Acute Inpatient Rehabilitation Center in Kansas City!

18

REHAB

When the day finally came that Jodi and I would leave the hospital with Zach and part ways, the situation felt surreal. The daily routines we had developed sometimes seemed to be the way our lives would go on forever. It was as though time and place didn't exist anymore outside of the hospital campus. Walking long corridors, riding up and down in elevators, and sitting for hours in waiting and patient rooms had become our life.

After I cleaned up our lodge room and finished packing my things, I took the time to send a Face Book update to my friends and family:

> Chris is on his way here to St Louis to help Jodi and me get packed up and leave for home! We've finally reached the point that Zach is going to rehab. It just seems too good to be true. I've guarded my heart for so long trying to be ready for anything, but God has come through for us! It feels like an eternity has gone by in just two and a half months. So much has happened in

that time. It was as if God loaded us up on a ship and took us sailing through a sea raging with high waves and storms, but also along the way there was beautiful scenery and promising rainbows. Our prayers have been answered again and again. We've called on God and kept him close. From a personal perspective, I've always kept God close—not just in times of need. My life is much richer with Him in it. I've never been one to spill my personal life for the world to see on Facebook—strange how that has happened. It all began with a cry for help to as many people as could be reached to start praying for Zach that day of the accident. Facebook became a way for Jodi and me to keep people posted on his status which then grew into a conglomerated web of prayer and faith and support that spiritually moved people, including myself—amazing! I just want to thank everyone from the deepest place in my heart for holding us up through this whole journey. Your prayers and positive, encouraging comments have been a life line for my family and me. All the ways that you've supported us with fundraisers, donations, and gifts have been overwhelmingly generous. I've said it before and I'll say it again—God has wrapped his arms around us through all of you, and we feel the love. Thank You and thank God! Zach is being transported by ambulance to KU. They predict he'll be there a couple of months before he'll get to go home. He will return to St. Louis in a month to be seen by his doctors who anticipate he will need skin releases as his grafts *tighten. They will also check the nerves in his hands and arm to see if they've grown back any. No surgeries expected for months! Time to heal and rebuild. He has a lot of busy days filled with hard work ahead of him and he's ready for it!*

As I mentioned earlier, rainbows had been my sign throughout our journey that God was showing us He was with us. I was thrilled when I learned the address of the rehab center Zach was moving into: 3910 Rainbow Boulevard. Again, I took that as a sign we were right where we should be.

I had never been to a rehabilitation center before and really didn't know what to expect. When Chris and I made our first trip there to see Zach, it was like visiting another hospital, only not so large. Zach was in a room much like his room in St. Louis—private, with his own bathroom. The atmosphere in the rehab center felt so much different than when we visited Zach in the hospital. It was uplifting to see patients working to get stronger versus sick and weak in bed. The place felt progressive and more hopeful, like lives were getting back on track again.

There was a waiting room at the entrance of Zach's floor where guests could view patients through a glass window as they were doing exercises with physical therapists. Watching them work and seeing all the large colored rubber balls, exercise mats, workout equipment, and such filled me with excitement, especially knowing that Zach would be there participating as well.

Zach didn't know what to expect from a rehab center either. He called Jodi, who was happy that he made it there safely. It also pleased her that he was able to hold the phone on his own to make the call. "It's weird here," he observed. "The room is small, and I haven't seen hardly any doctors!"

Jodi laughed, then reminded him, "You're not in a hospital anymore!"

It was interesting to watch how therapists moved Zach around. He had very little strength and his body was dead weight, so they used a harness chair that was attached to the ceiling with cables as the method for lifting him from his bed to the wheelchair, then from the wheelchair to the work out table. It was exciting to see him use a wheelchair for the first time. He was mobile again!

Already on the second day, Zach was scheduled with four hours of therapy. He was eager to get to work. He looked at the harness and joked, "I could probably do a back flip with that here soon." His good humor hadn't changed.

Chris and I were so excited the first time we saw Zach headed to the workout area. We were eager to watch what they would do with him and how they would help him. I was happy that the therapists let us be in the room with them to observe. We followed Zach's wheelchair to the workout area where I sat on a table that was thigh high and covered with a soft, blue padding.

Zach, dressed in a green hospital gown, resembled a sheik—his head wrapped like a turban in white gauze. He was slowly lifted out of his wheelchair with the harness, swung over to the table I was sitting on, and then lowered with the use of a remote control until he was seated next to me. His shortened legs (I hated to call them stumps!) were barely visible under his gown. One had a plastic brace around it and protruded out a bit further.

After seating Zach, the therapist removed his harness and then turned to do something behind her when—KERPLUNK—he fell over onto his left side like a bowling pin. He laid there on the padded table unable to get up or help himself at all. My reaction and emotions were a complete conundrum. I felt like crying and laughing at the same time. I looked at Chris, and I could tell by his face that he was experiencing the same. One second Zach was sitting up next to me, and the next he was lying with his arms at his sides and his short legs sticking straight out like a Munchkin that fell over drunk.

It was funny—Chris and I both started to laugh, but the realization of how helpless Zach was stifled our giggles—laughing seemed so cruel. We wanted to chuckle and weep at the same time—it was one of those bittersweet moments we'll never forget.

The therapist reacted quickly to Zach's predicament and apologized for letting him topple over. It happened so fast. She wasn't aware that he was unstable and couldn't use his left arm to stop his fall.

Zach wasn't hurt physically or mentally or even set back by that incident. In fact, he pushed through the challenges put in front of him like a soldier. He started off moving around in a wheelchair, which was difficult because of his body weakness and the limited use of his hands to push the wheels, but he surprised the nurses with how quickly he figured out how to maneuver and soon wheeled himself right down the hall.

It wasn't long before the rehab center used a short, temporary prosthetic on Zach's right leg—the one with his natural knee still intact—and taught him to stand and step using the help of a walker. His left leg was still way too raw to be fitted with a prosthetic. The therapist stood behind Zach to aid his balance as he feebly hopped along on one leg while leaning his elbows on the walker to support the weight of his upper body. It was an intense moment. He looked so fragile and wobbly, and we could see that he was using all his strength and concentration to propel himself forward. "You're doing it, Zach. You're doing a great job. Keep it up!" I cheered as he inched his way a few more feet across the room with the therapist in tow. As sad as it was that Zach was forced to learn to walk again, it was also exhilarating that he was actually going to walk! He had several hours of rehabilitation therapy each day and with each session he grew stronger and more capable.

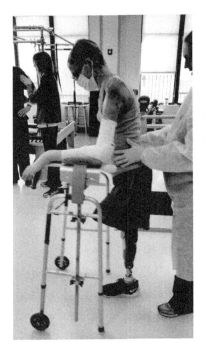
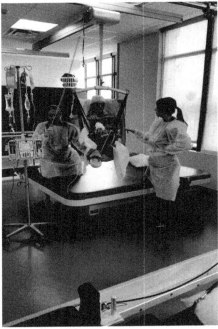

The first weekend that Chris and I came to visit, we asked the nurses if we could take Zach outside in his wheelchair for a stroll. It had been almost three months since he'd seen the outdoors, and the idea appealed to all of us. The air was chilly but not too cold, and the sun was getting ready to set. The nurses approved of our request, but with the stipulation that we didn't go any farther than the sidewalks around the building. We agreed and bundled him up with blankets, and then Chris and I took turns pushing him around the rehab center. It was funny to think that watching the traffic go by on a busy Kansas City street would be entertaining, but it felt wonderful to get Zach out of the hospital environment he'd been imprisoned in for so long—to let him breathe fresh air and see the sky. Afterwards we bought Zach's favorite meal—cheeseburgers and fries—at a nearby fast food place. Even though his stomach wouldn't let him fully enjoy his meal, he appreciated our efforts that evening to make him happy—which also included sitting in his room to watch football playoffs for the rest of the evening. Without the anxiety of life or death hospital stress, our existence was slowly returning to the routines of an ordinary family.

Jodi had been traveling back and forth from her parent's house each day to spend the hours with Zach. She stayed overnight on several occasions in Zach's room on a cot provided for her. After so many nights apart, she had looked forward to the time when she would be able to sleep in the same room again, but she quickly experienced what Zach's nights were like—a busy unrestful environment. "The nurses came in so many times to wake Zach for his meds," she complained. It reminded her of the nights when she had a newborn disrupting her sleep.

As Zach grew stronger, he was able to do more and more for himself. He was given special eating utensils that were easier for him to grip in order to feed himself better. He learned how to transfer himself from one location to another with use of a sliding board. With the aid of a shower chair, he was able to once again feel the sensation of water spraying on his skin: "It feels so good to wash myself clean after all those months of sponge baths!" And then there was the sweet moment when he was finally able to accomplish something he had long waited for, something Dr. Moore had made a goal—he once again got to hold his little girl.

The day that someone special came to meet Zach was another milestone. The visitor was Alex, the young man who lay in a bed of the ICU next to Zach's room in Wichita—the one who was about Zach's age and was burned with his father when the water heater in their house exploded.

Sally and I had prayed that our sons would heal and live to meet each other someday, and at last that day became a reality! Alex and Zach talked and talked, spending the afternoon comparing wounds, scars, and stories. That they were both alive was a miracle in itself. Seeing them together was proof of how far they each had come.

Since Chris and I visited Zach only on weekends, we were seeing positive, big advances each time we went to Kansas City. Zach's attitude remained good and he continued to demonstrate his determination by working hard at therapy. We could tell that he was beginning to put on a little more weight and regain muscle tone. He had lost fifty-five pounds at his lowest ebb—over one third of his normal weight. Getting some of that back was hugely significant.

Zach's hands still had limited use, but we were assured that time and future surgeries would help repair them. The skin wounds where donor sites were slow to heal on his back, head, and left leg remained tender. The doctors in St. Louis had covered most of them with a special dressing made of pig skin called biomembrane, so that he wouldn't have painful dressing changes while he was in rehab, but the KU nurses became concerned. The yellow colored coverings were stuck so tightly to Zach's skin that we all wondered how they would ever come off. However, knowing that he was going to go back to St. Louis for a checkup, the rehab nurses left that issue for the doctors at Barnes Hospital and didn't disturb them.

Our biggest concern was seeing the numerous drugs Zach was still taking. One day while Chris and I were visiting, I counted eighteen pills on his tray that he was expected to take before he had his lunch, and that was just one dose of several throughout the day and night. When Chris and I asked why he was still having to take all those pills, we were told that the various drugs were treating several different things. A lot of the pills were vitamins, some were for constipation, nerve pain, anxiety, or for the fungus that remained in his system, but he was also still taking pain pills.

The rehab doctor told us the narcotics were important because the human body can heal quicker if it's not stressed with pain.

Since the beginning of Zach's accident, he'd consistently been on opioid pain drugs as well as prescriptions for anxiety. Throughout his time in the hospital, he was on Percocet, Methadone, Fentanyl, Dilaudid, Hydrocodone, and Lorazepam—just to name the ones we were aware of. It very much concerned us because we knew all those drugs are highly addictive and he'd been on them for weeks. We asked the doctors if they could ween him down from the pain pills and other medications that weren't absolutely necessary, and they assured us that they planned to start working on that, and that they'd merely been following the regimen that St. Louis started.

Just when his recovery seemed to really be moving forward, Zach was transported to the hospital across the street after his pic line became infected. The doctors suspected that he had a blood infection. Cultures were taken and rehab was put on hold.

When the medical staff reported that Zach's blood platelets were critically high and his hemoglobin was low and they didn't really know why, we were anxious and worried for his life once again. At that point in the journey, we had hoped we were past life-threatening situations but were quickly reminded of how conditions can change in a heartbeat. Zach was treated with blood transfusions and high-powered antibiotics. Thank goodness the treatment worked! The infection gradually cleared up, and after a few days he was returned to rehab where he got back to work.

The doctors at KU anticipated that Zach would need to be in rehab for a good two months, but his time there was actually cut to half of their predictions. The therapists were astounded by how fast he regained stamina and strength, and picked up the routines so quickly. It was exhilarating for Chris and me to see that his coordination, balance, strength, and determination were just as evident as when he was a wrestler in his youth. He wanted to get back to life as he remembered, and he wasted no time in working to make that happen.

On a cold wintery day, a nurse wheeled Zach out the entrance of the rehab center to the curb where I had parked Zach and Jodi's car. We were headed back to St. Louis. Jodi followed behind the wheelchair, trying to keep blankets on Zach who was shivering in the frosty wind. I was glad of the decision to leave Brynlee with Jodi's mom, Staci, who offered to take care of her so Jodi and I could make the trip for Zach's checkup. It would only be for three days: a day to drive there, a day for three appointments, then the drive back to Kansas City. After that, on the next day, the destination was Assaria, Kansas—home! After thirty-one days of rehabilitation, Zach was finally strong enough to go home!

I got out of the car and hurried around, ready to assist however I could as Jodi opened the passenger door of the car. It was so cold that our breaths puffed out into the wind like thick smoke. The nurse wheeled Zach over and parked him as close as possible to the passenger seat, then locked the brake on his wheelchair. Jodi, the nurse, and I watched as Zach lifted his body up off the chair using the strength of his arms while his hands bore the weight, then transferred himself to the front seat of the car. He made it look fairly easy. It was impressive to witness how much strength he had gained back, yet I felt a heaviness in my heart. Seeing him achieve the maneuver without help was comparable to the fulfillment of watching a child accomplish something that helps them become independent, like using a spoon for the first time. But at the same time, it hurt so deeply to realize that this would be his new normal. The reality hit me hard.

Showing his sense of humor, Zach offered to drive. He was the one dealing with the pain and struggle, yet he kept the situation light and fun whenever he could.

After the three-and-a-half-hour drive to St. Louis, Zach, Jodi, and I checked into the hotel that was connected to Barnes Hospital. It was the one we had stayed in several times before we found the Barnes Lodge, so we knew our way around quite well by that time. We were tired and hungry, so we decided to grab a bite at the Applebee's restaurant that was conveniently attached to the hotel. We were excited to take Zach out into the public for the first time—somewhere other than a hospital or medical facility.

Jodi wheeled him up to the hostess counter to put our name on the waiting list, then pulled him back against a wall out of the way, as the front area was crowded and seating was limited.

The delay quickly turned uncomfortable. As we stood waiting for our turn to be seated, the three of us grew keenly aware that Zach had become the focus of people's attention. They looked at him with curious glances while trying not to stare. A couple of young children pointed and asked their parents what was wrong with him and why he had no legs. This kind of attention caught Jodi and I off guard. We knew that Zach would be noticed, but we didn't realize that it would feel the way that it did. Immediately Jodi and I both grew anxious about what Zach was feeling and how he would take it.

I'm sure we've all seen people in our lives who don't fit into the "normal" category and have drawn our attention in this same way, making us wonder what that person's story was. It's just so awkward to actually *be* that person. Obviously, I was not the focus of attention—Zach was—but I felt every bit of what he was feeling as if I were him. It was heart breaking.

It was easy to know exactly how Zach felt when I looked at his face. He was embarrassed and uncomfortable—like he felt he was a circus act that people were amused by. I so wished that I could make the awkwardness go away. But this was part of what his life was going to be like, and we all knew deep down inside that he would have to get used to that kind of attention. It would hopefully get better once his shortened legs wrapped in gauze and braces were replaced with prosthetic legs and his head, face, and neck were no longer covered with scabs and reddened sores. It was obvious that he had been badly hurt, and people were naturally curious.

That night after our outing to Applebee's, we headed straight to our hotel room where it was Jodi's first time to take on the role of Zach's care provider. She wanted my help, so I stayed with them in the same room, grateful to be asked. Jodi had reserved a handicap room. It was the first time we had ever made use of one—or needed to. It featured doorways wide enough for Zach's wheelchair and hand rails for him to use in the bathroom. Jodi and I quickly became appreciative of these details that made his life easier. The ramps, family restrooms, and handicap parking everywhere we went made our situation so much more convenient. They were factors we hadn't paid much attention to before but quickly appreciated how essential they are.

Zach was tired and hurting from sitting in the car for the long drive we had taken that day. He had a special cushion that we took along everywhere, but even it was not effective after so much time sitting. He needed his medications doled out and his bandages redone as some were beginning to fall off. His weariness showed as he grew impatient with Jodi and me—novices that we were—as we tried our best not to hurt him when we pulled off his clothes and redid his dressings. Before we could put his dressings back on, Jodi had to apply salve to his wounds, which made him wince and grumble from the pain. I had the gentler job of massaging lotion into the dry skin on the part of his back that wasn't covered with biomembrane.

We were overwhelmed by the effort it took to simply get Zach ready for bed. The evening was quite chaotic. Our room looked like a bomb had gone off with all the bags and boxes of cotton, gauze, special thick padded dressings, braces, ointments, and medications the rehab provided for us. It had been a real job transporting the materials up to our room along with our luggage, purses, coats, blankets, and a two and a half foot long sliding board which Zach needed for transferring himself from one seat to another. Poor Zach had most of it piled up on his lap; we used his wheelchair with him in it to transfer the baggage from the car through the hallway to our room.

After sorting and studying the multiple medications and then clearing the floor so Zach could navigate his way to the restroom during the night, we finally managed to collapse in our beds and close our eyes. The activity would begin at dawn, and we knew it would be another long day.

In the morning when Jodi's phone alarm went off, our feet hit the floor running. This was our first experience to get ourselves as well as Zach ready for the day, eat some breakfast, and be at his first appointment on time. We weren't certain how long the preparations would take us, so we made a plan and started early. Thank goodness we didn't also have Brynlee to worry about. While we missed her, we were so glad she was in her Mimi's care.

Zach had three appointments; the first was at eight am with an infectious disease doctor. We left our car parked in the hotel parking lot since all the offices were in the same general area and not far away. The appointments were located within walking distance but seemed like they were miles apart when we headed into the cold wind. Feeling like we were in a race, Jodi and I took turns wheeling Zach from the hotel to the first office, which was located close to the hospital. There, the staff informed us that the lab had formulated a special medication to treat the persistent fungus in Zach's system that he'd picked up from the field the day of the accident. The medication was extremely expensive—several hundred dollars—and would need to be refilled several times, so it was a relief when they told Zach that they were going to help find a way to cover the cost.

Next was the appointment for Zach's nerve test, which we only had minutes to get to in order to be on time. I felt like we resembled the bicycle scene in the movie *E.T.* as Jodi and I pushed him all bundled up with blankets in his wheelchair as fast as we could down the sidewalks. He was completely at our mercy and I knew he was feeling every bump and jolt along the way as his blankets came unfastened and blew in the wind. He had to trust us to not topple him over or throw him out of his seat when we hit the holes and cracks in our path—which nearly did happen once! The poor guy needed a seat belt—or more likely, better drivers!

When we arrived at the hospital, we continued to hurry down several long hallways which led to a lobby where we waited in a crowd of people for our turn to go up several floors in the elevator. We made it to the office on time and signed Zach in on the list. Of course, it's always the same—we'd hurry to make an appointment on time, and then sit and wait forever to be seen. That's what happened at our second appointment. And, after sitting in his wheelchair in the waiting room for a very long time, something he wasn't yet healed enough to do comfortably, Zach spent three hours—THREE HOURS—getting poked with needles!

Testing to see how Zach's nerves responded to electrical shocks, the technician watched a monitor and recorded data while poking Zach's arms and hands with needles that had long wires attached to them. Jodi and I sat there and observed the entire time. Although it wasn't easy for us to watch, Zach handled it all like a trooper.

Finally, running late, we found our way to Dr. Moore, who was as pleased to see us as we were her. She was happy that Zach was looking healthier and stronger. We sat down and visited awhile before she gave us some good news. She already had the results of Zach's nerve test, and it showed that the radial nerve in his right hand was repairing itself! The nerves were growing back and his hand wouldn't need surgery to correct his drooping wrist—it simply needed more time!

The left hand and arm, however, showed signs that all three main nerves were damaged. Time would tell her more, but Dr. Moore suspected that surgery would be necessary in a couple of months to repair tendons and nerves. We would also need to come back for skin releases on Zach's face and for another checkup in a month.

Next came more bad news. The biomembrane—the yellow dressing used to bandage Zach's back, and left leg—had become integrated with his skin but needed to come off. It was supposed to fall off naturally after two weeks, Dr. Moore told us, but instead Zach's own skin grew into it, incorporating the biomembrane skin within his own. Dr. Moore confessed that she had never seen anything like that happen before. The look on her face revealed that she was upset over the thought of what she knew she had to do. The covering was going to have to come off, and it was not going to be as simple as pulling a band-aid off a wound.

Jodi and I stayed in the room and wondered how Dr. Moore was going to go about removing the pig skin. We hoped she had some way of freeing it up before pulling it off, but sadly, that was not the case. Zach laid on his side on top of a table with Dr. Moore seated eye level to his back. It was gut wrenching to watch her carefully peel off the membrane, piece by piece, taking his own skin with it. The blood oozed down Zach's back as Dr. Moore tore away little pieces, continuously blotting the bleeding flesh with gauze as she worked. I saw Zach's back muscles tighten and flinch and his hand shake from the pain, so I went around to the other side of the table so I could see his face. Tears streamed down his cheeks and his nose was running. He made no sound other than an occasional sniffle as he laid there suffering. I could hardly stand it. Tears welled up in my eyes. I wanted so badly to scream at Dr. Moore to stop, but I bit my tongue. Jodi did her best to hold on to her composure as she paced the floor back and forth.

I still wonder if Dr. Moore read the terror in my expression when she looked up from what she was doing because she *did* stop. She put down her instruments and apologized, saying that she was sorry for putting Zach through such pain. She then decided that the procedure was something she could complete on a later date while he was under anesthesia.

The day was long and torturous for Zach. It was six in the evening before we finally finished with appointments, packed, and got back on the road to Kansas City where we planned to stop for the night. Because of the painful new sores on his back and the aches from riding in the car, Zach had a difficult night trying to sleep. The thought that kept him positive and motivated enough to endure the torment through the long night hours was knowing that with the dawning of the new day, he would be heading home!

19

GOING HOME

Jodi and I couldn't move fast enough to pack up our things at the hotel—we were so excited to get on the road. People were aware that Zach was coming home and had arranged for a large group to greet him as we arrived in our little town of Assaria. Knowing that a big welcome awaited, made it even more exciting to get there. Jodi and I had talked about our dreams of a homecoming several times while we were isolated in St. Louis. It was beyond exciting that our dreams were actually coming true! Zach was coming home! We visualized it in our minds.

Jodi wanted the homecoming to be a big surprise for Zach, so she worked hard to keep the whole celebration a secret from him. That was a bit challenging, since she needed to stay in touch with people back home to coordinate the timing of our arrival without Zach hearing or seeing her on her phone.

After we finished a quick breakfast at the hotel, Jodi texted one of the people who was heading up the greeting party to let them know we were about to leave Kansas City. We were on our way to checkout when we ran into a woman from our church who happened to be staying at the same hotel. Her husband was in the nearby rehab center, the same one Zach had been in, and in the room just above where Zach's was.

This lady was so excited to see us and wanted to talk about Zach. She wanted to hear about all the details of our journey, and also, because her husband was ill, she had a lot to share about what was going on with him. We sensed that she wanted us to stay and visit, so restraining our enthusiasm to leave, Jodi and I put off our departure a bit longer. Concerned for her and her husband, we didn't want to appear uncompassionate by cutting our encounter short, but at the same time, we were like horses ready to knock down the starting gates at the Kentucky Derby while we waited for her to wrap up the conversation. Zach had been absent from home for one hundred and twelve days, and we were anxious to get back there!

Finally, we were back on the road. Jodi and Zach were traveling in their car as I followed in mine. All I could think about while driving home was the excitement of seeing those happy faces gathered to welcome Zach back. People had been talking about his return for weeks. My heart raced with the thought, and I was extremely grateful that we had made it to this day. I wanted to post something about it on Facebook so I used the voice text function on my phone as I drove:

> This is the big day! Zach's homecoming! Isn't it just like God to open his heart and show his love on this most appropriate day...Valentine's Day! What a beautiful gift. Best Valentine's Day ever! My son is coming home!

About forty minutes from home while still on the interstate, we drove under an overpass where several people were gathered with big smiles on their faces—hollering and wildly waving their arms at us. It had started already! I wasn't expecting people to welcome us as soon as that far away from home, and it completely caught me by surprise. My heart skipped a beat, and I broke into tears of joy and appreciation. All that God and our loving community had done for us was overwhelming sometimes. It's a good thing I was in my own car. Zach would've seen my emotions and wondered what was going on. He had no idea that those people were out there for him, and Jodi didn't tell him.

About seven miles north of Assaria, I saw Jodi's car signal, then take the exit ramp off interstate. I was puzzled as to why she was leaving the highway at Salina but followed along behind. Sitting at the stop sign, I couldn't figure what the plan was. I didn't want to spoil the secret by calling Jodi on the phone and having her talk out loud, so I texted her: "Did you exit to get gas?"

She answered back quickly, "I'm almost to Assaria."

Perplexed, I studied the car ahead of me as I pulled closer and suddenly realized that I had been tailing the wrong car! I had no idea how or when I lost Jodi and Zach. It must have been clear back at the Topeka toll booth that I ended up behind a car that resembled theirs! All I could think was that I was going to miss out on the big moment that I had been dreaming of! I had to get back on to the interstate and catch up as fast as possible!

Naturally, I hit a red light after I hustled down the busy city street, weaving in and out around cars. While waiting for the light to change, I texted Jodi again: "I am in Salina! Got behind the wrong car. Please slow down and wait for me to catch up, will you? I don't want to miss anything!"

She answered back: "Yeah, I'll try."

At the first exit out of Salina, I headed back out onto the highway and put the gas pedal to the floor. The speedometer swung up to ninety-eight miles an hour, but I didn't care—I was determined to catch up. I wasn't going miss the homecoming!

After a fast few miles, I could see Jodi's car pulled over to the side of the road just before the Assaria exit. It didn't set well with Zach when Jodi told him that they had to wait on me to catch up. He was eager to get home and didn't understand why I wanted them to wait; he knew that we didn't need to stick together by that point. He didn't see any purpose for what Jodi was doing until his attention was diverted by what he saw ahead. Up by the stop sign of the Assaria off ramp, he noticed several police cars parked on the road who began flashing their patrol lights. The expression of his face when he looked at Jodi showed he suspected something fishy, and he asked, "Did you do something that has to do with this?"

Jodi just smiled and said, "I didn't do anything. Everyone knows you are coming home today."

Once I caught up to Jodi's car, we cruised up the off ramp together. Even I had no idea we were going to be met with a police escort!

One police car went ahead of us while three others followed behind. We turned left toward the entrance of our little city of Assaria that was a half mile down the road. We resembled a Fourth of July parade as the flashing lights of the police cars alerted the townspeople that we had finally made it back. It was an overwhelming sight. Zach sat speechless and awestruck as he witnessed scores of people and cars lining each side of the street as we drove into town. They were honking their horns, cheering and clapping, waving and yelling out, "Welcome home! Yay, Zach!"

Cars along the lane had ribbons tied to the mirrors, making me think of the way yellow ribbons are tied around trees when soldiers return home. I saw both of Zach's grandmas and so many of our friends and neighbors holding and waving signs that read, "We love you, Zach!" and, "Welcome home, Zach!" The smiling faces and loud cheers were nonstop as we drove slowly through town, taking it all in. I was laughing and crying so hard that I could barely see to drive. It was one of the happiest moments of my life. People were standing out in the cold wind, pouring their hearts out for Zach to see, and it was amazing!

Looking back on that moment makes me think of those scenes in movies I've seen where the crowd all stands up and cheers after the main character heroically prevails over some challenging feat. Our welcome home felt just like that. God is so good! Zach was finally home! We were all home—and so happy to call Assaria our home!

The farm was just a half mile more down the road after we drove through the crowd in town and was another welcoming sight. There, we were met with a camera crew from the same local news station that had covered Zach's story since its beginning. They knew that Zach was eager to be home, but they wanted to take a moment of his time do a short interview and update their viewers on this big day. Mostly they wanted to get some footage of him arriving and the community welcoming him back. He took the opportunity to thank everyone who had supported him with prayers and let them know how grateful he was to live in a community that cared so much.

Brynlee was thrilled to see her daddy again when a family member handed her over to Zach, who was seated in his wheelchair near the back-door entry to his house. Zach's face lit up as he squeezed her lovingly. He, and Jodi too, were happy to see their little girl after being apart for several days. Brynlee had enjoyed staying with Jodi's parents in Topeka and had recently travelled back with them so she would be at the house when we arrived.

The first thing Zach wanted to do was go out to the big shop where in the past he had spent so much of his time. He transferred from his wheelchair to an electric scooter that had been donated by a friend, then maneuvered his way out into the yard, the camera crew following. His big black Labrador, Milo, was so excited to see him that he launched his front paws onto Zach's lap, licking him in the face as Zach hugged the dog around the neck and grinned.

Les, our righthand man who used the plastic handled shovel to save Zach (and is a hero to us), had been doing some mechanical work out in the shop. He put down his tools and wiped his hands, then turned to greet everyone and have a few pictures taken next to Zach. We will forever be grateful for his brave act. Zach wouldn't be alive today had it not been for Les's quick thinking and willingness to risk his own life.

20

REALITY SETS IN

I had worried that reality was going to hit hard once Zach and Jodi arrived home, but I hadn't planned on it happening so fast. Things went sour rapidly after the spectacular homecoming.

After we unloaded the car from our trip, Zach and Jodi's house looked a lot like our hotel room in St. Louis the first night we arrived with Zach. *Stuff* lay everywhere. The carload that Chris had brought back from Barnes Lodge earlier that we no longer needed there, he left in a pile on the living room floor. That, along with the luggage, the medical equipment, the bags of medical dressings and bandages, as well as several smaller bags of prescription drugs which accompanied stacks of home care information papers, surrounded us like an invading army.

When Jodi looked around the room at the multitude of materials and tasks that demanded her attention, including the special bed she'd ordered for Zach that was sitting in the living room still unmade, her anxiety spilled over. She knew that her parents and Chris and I were soon leaving, and she was overcome by the chaos staring her in the face.

Walking over to where Chris and I were standing, she pointed down at the two steps that led from the living room to the kitchen and demanded, "How is Zach going to get from the living room to the kitchen? There's no ramp." She looked accusingly at Chris. "I thought you were going to build a ramp for him." Chris hastily explained that he had intended to make a ramp, but after further thought, he decided not to make any changes to the house until Zach came home to tell him exactly how he wanted the alterations done.

The house did not welcome Jodi with the warm feelings of home she had looked forward to for so long. Instead, the alien reality of a drastically different life assaulted her spirit. Overwhelmed by the realization, she cried out to her parents who were nearby, "How am I going to do all this?! This is my life now! This is my life!" She collapsed on the couch sobbing into her hands. George and Staci sat down on either side of Jodi and put their arms around her, trying their best to console her. I looked around and saw Zach on his electric scooter, shaken by what he'd just heard and seen, and my heart sank. I wanted to cry. What was he feeling? They had both been looking so forward to finally getting home, hoping that everything would be so much better once they got there, but instead, reality smacked them both in the face less than an hour after arriving. They were awakening to what must have felt like a life sentence in prison. In one fell swoop, they went from the highest of highs to the lowest of lows.

George and Staci had planned on driving back to their home in Topeka that evening, and after the long drive from Kansas City, I was looking forward to getting back to my home as well. We had thought that Zach and Jodi would want to be left alone, but it became obvious really quickly that being left to fend for themselves was not the best plan of action. They needed us to stay and help them settle in, so the four of us parents jumped right in to bring organization to the chaos. Staci tackled outfitting the new bed with sheets and blankets. We decided to leave it set up in the living room until a handicap accessible bathroom off of Zach and Jodi's bedroom was constructed. There was already a bathroom close to the area where the bed was set up, which made getting to it easier for Zach, but it was still difficult for him to use because the doorway was barely wide enough to squeeze his wheelchair through. Chris was right—the entire house needed a lot of revamping to make life easier for Zach, and Zach needed to be the central figure in making those decisions.

I looked around to see what I could do to be helpful, then drifted into the kitchen where bags of prescription drugs smothered the counter top. The white paper bags looked like fast food orders—enough for a harvest party! It was easy to understand why Jodi felt overwhelmed. It took me a lot of time to read the doctor's orders and sort into pill dividers the many medications that Zach had to take—and of course, it had to be done accurately. I felt rather overwhelmed myself before I was done with that task.

Next, I collected totes to sort the different bandages, dressings, creams, and ointments in a way that would be easier for Jodi to identify and access, while Staci helped Jodi put away the mountain of toys, clothing, and supplies that were piled on the floor and in the luggage. Chris and George retired to the shop and built a ramp. All of us were tired before we began—not just physically, but mentally too. We were absolutely exhausted by the time we finished. It had been a long day, and I was so thankful that George and Staci were able to stay a while longer to help.

After a day or two, the dust settled and Jodi adapted to her new routines at home. She just needed time to prove to herself that she could handle affairs on her own. Once she saw that she could, her fears dissipated and she managed just fine.

Reality Sets In

Jodi's situation was similar to the way I remember feeling years ago when I arrived home from the hospital with Kelsey, my first child. The responsibility of caring for a little baby who was totally dependent on me was really frightening. I was scared I might not remember the correct procedures without the help of the nurses to direct me. Even though I had Chris, he didn't know the first thing about babies, and besides, he had to be away at the farm a lot, leaving me to take care of our daughter on my own. My mom helped me for a few hours each day for the first week or so, but after that, I was on my own.

Those first couple of days that Jodi cared for Zach with his special needs might have felt a lot like my early childbearing years, but thank goodness, Home Health Care soon came into the picture. They gave Jodi much appreciated assistance in managing Zach's meds and dressing changes, along with scheduling his many appointments with medical providers.

Jodi quickly learned a lot about being a care provider and soon did a great job of it. She took over the role of Zach's personal nurse and was his chauffer too. It took a tremendous amount of time and energy to keep up with her expanded daily tasks. Again and again she loaded up his wheelchair in her car, drove to his scheduled appointments, unloaded the wheelchair and Zach, and then did it all over again to come home. That was in addition to caring for Brynlee and the regular household tasks. She had a lot going on. Thankfully, she also had the help of nearby family whenever she needed us.

Zach never took Jodi's help for granted and showed his appreciation often. One day when she was helping him remove his contacts, Zach confessed that he didn't know what he would have done without her and said that God knew what he was doing when He sent her to be his wife. His love was the motivation that kept her going. Even when times were tough and days were tiring, she was thankful for their little family, and prayed that their lives would only get better each day. Those first few days had been rough while establishing a routine, but they both were so thankful to have each other and be back in their own home.

For the first few weeks, Zach couldn't shower in his own home. Doctors wanted him to clean himself using chlorinated water rather than the well water at his house. That meant that Jodi had to load him up in her car and bring him to our house. Chris and I didn't have a ramp, so we would have to lift him in his wheelchair to get him up each of the three porch steps leading to our front door. Along with having chlorinated water, Chris and I had a large shower stall with a built-in bench where Jodi could sit to wash Zach while he sat on a shower stool. It became a daily routine. Jodi cleaned Zach in the shower while I entertained Brynlee. After showering, Jodi would carefully pat Zach dry, then Zach would transfer from his shower chair back to his wheelchair, and then from the wheelchair to my bed, where he'd have his bandages applied. Each day I cleaned up piles of blood-and-water-soaked gauze from the shower floor, as well as bloodied towels, and an old sheet I used to protect our bed from the blood and greasy salves left behind after doctoring Zach.

It was a grueling process for Zach. Quite often I heard him yelp in pain when Jodi was washing him in the shower. The only way to get his bandages off was to let them soak up the water, because they were stuck to his sores. Jodi would peel them off carefully, but it was extremely painful—the water burned. So often, Zach would come out of the bathroom with tears rolling down his face. Showers had always been punishment to his wounds, but after the biomembrane was removed from his back, they became tortuous.

Reality Sets In

It wasn't easy for Jodi to put Zach through what she had to do, but with time, it got better, and Jodi became so efficient at wrapping his wounds she no longer needed Home Health Care to assist her.

Throughout the next few months, Zach had issues that required Jodi to rush him to the hospital, many times in the middle of the night. On those nights when Chris and I were awakened from our sleep by calls from Jodi, we immediately went into a small panic, knowing that something was not good with Zach. I could always hear the urgency in her voice when she would call, usually explaining that Zach's temperature was way too high or his pain was unbearable. Then they would make their way to our house to drop off Brynlee and take off to the emergency room, leaving us to worry and wonder what the issue was all about.

High temperatures usually indicated infection. The Salina hospital was very aware of Zach's fragile condition and always treated him with priority, immediately working him in to be seen in the emergency room. He would most always be treated with high powered antibiotics which worked well to fight the infections, but they caused him to develop severe problems with C-Diff (a repercussion of taking antibiotics). The good bacteria in his digestive tract was killed along with the bad bacteria, which resulted in unrelenting diarrhea. Probiotics were usually the protocol but did little to help, so he ended up having to have a disturbing procedure done to bring him back to health. We had never even heard of such a thing before, but he had to have a fecal transplant. That is, he had to have *feces* from a donor infused into his intestines to make the good bacteria grow back! The thought of that procedure repulsed Zach, but it's what finally worked to make him physically well again. Oh, for the things that guy endured!

More issues continued to put Zach back in the hospital as time went on. His body had been through so much stress that it began to age. He had to have cataracts removed from his eyes; he developed painful kidney stones that had to be lasered and broken up; and then it was decided that he needed to have his gall bladder removed because it was full of sludge and stones.

We had hoped that some of those measures would correct the nausea he felt so often, causing him to lose his appetite, but they didn't. He learned that unless he took pain pills, he had no appetite at all. He tried to get along without the pills and force himself to eat, knowing that he was too thin and he needed the calories to help his body heal, but he just felt too nauseated to have an appetite. Once he took the narcotics, he felt good and could eat large portions of food with no trouble. That lead to his next challenge: coming off the narcotics. His body had become addicted to them and he didn't feel well unless he had them.

Zach knew he had to eventually buck up to his body's reliance on those pills, and that's just what he did. He made himself suffer until he no longer depended on them for relief. Chris and I were absolutely amazed and extremely proud of Zach's ability to utilize his willpower and determination. Those were astonishingly strong character values he exhibited throughout the entire journey of his healing process. Giving up the pills was yet another testimony of his strength. Maybe it was all the prayers that gave him the strength, but he kept pushing himself to get back to life as it was, as if he would accept nothing less for himself than having things the way he remembered them to be.

Something that had better medicinal value than any of those pills was the day that Zach got out and drove his pickup. It was the first new vehicle he'd ever owned and he was so proud of it. It was like punishment for him to sit inside the house and look out the window at that pretty grey Ford parked in the drive way. He had not even had the chance to drive it much before his accident and wasn't sure he ever would again until Matthew challenged him to try it.

Reality Sets In

Matt believed that Zach could drive, and he offered to sit beside Zach to help. Zach's right leg, in a temporary prosthetic, could reach the pedals, so technically (other than not being able to feel his foot on the gas and brake) he was capable of driving. He wouldn't need his left leg, so it didn't matter that he didn't yet have it in a prosthetic.

Zach thought about it and decided he wanted to do it, so Matt wheeled him out and lifted him into the driver's seat, having to be extra cautious in the way he handled him so he wouldn't tear open Zach's fragile wounds. Zach slowly took a trial run through the barn yard, then headed out onto the dirt roads with Matt seated next to him...who later admitted feeling a little uneasy riding with a guy who had no legs! They drove off together to check Zach's fields, something that put a smile on Zach's face and helped him feel like maybe life was going to get better after all.

Once Zach started getting out more, he felt ready to visit church. It was nearly Easter, the time of year when our Methodist church puts on an Easter Cantata—a beautiful arrangement of songs that are sung by a large choir, accompanied by a full orchestra—like the Christmas Cantata. It's an event that draws a large crowd to each of the three different services Sunday morning, so instead of holding it in the sanctuary, it's moved to the life center where more people can be seated.

Chris and I watched for Zach and Jodi's car so Chris could unload Zach's wheelchair and I could help Jodi with Brynlee. We were nearly late getting inside the church which was already full, but there were a few folding chairs in the back row still available, so we wheeled Zach toward their direction. We hadn't even sat down yet when we heard a choir member from up on the stage yell out, "ZACH!...... ZACH'S HERE!" The woman pointed in our direction and then heads started turning to look toward us in the back of the room. Immediately, people's faces lit up and they began to clap. The clapping grew louder and louder as more joined in, and before long, the whole room was standing and facing us while applauding, which went on and on for quite some time.

Needless to say, we were overwhelmed. Tears filled our eyes. Actually, I was bawling just like the day our town of Assaria welcomed us home. We knew people would be happy to see Zach at church again, but we had no idea they would respond as they did. We all felt so loved and cared for. Zach was bombarded with people after the service who wanted to shake his hand and tell him how much they admired his strength. That's another day we'll always remember.

21

GOTTA KEEP YOUR HEAD UP

The month of April arrived and Zach received his first permanent prosthetic for his right leg. That made him more than anxious to get the left leg as well, but he still couldn't be fitted for it until his wounds were healed. Healing was such a slow process, especially since he had made another trip back to St. Louis in March to have the rest of the biomembrane removed from his back and left leg, causing new places to be raw and sore. At least he was put under anesthesia to have it done this time, but it caused him to go backwards with his healing.

Discouragement was really beginning to set in for Zach. He was sick of being covered in bandages and so fatigued from the pain of his wounds, which after weeks and even months weren't making any improvement. His back, left leg, and also his head were bright red and either bleeding, blistering, or weeping, and looked as red and inflamed as they had in the beginning—they just wouldn't heal! He visited with wound doctors and dermatologists in several different cities, hoping when one couldn't find the cure, another one would.

So many different compounds and methods were used, each seemingly showing signs of working only to fail after time, and the wounds that looked as if they were healing would reopen or new ones would form nearby. Wound doctors used antibiotics and various ointments, then tried bleach solutions that seemed promising at first but eventually proved useless as well. They even tried slathering on honey, an old method based on the belief that the honey had natural healing properties that worked for hard-to-heal wounds. Maybe it worked for some people, but it didn't work for Zach. It just left him sticky.

Time was going too slow for the guy who used to be busy every minute that he wasn't sleeping. He needed pep talks every now and then to boost his morale. All of us did our best to feed him with reassurance. It was hard to muster up positive reinforcement some days when we felt the same way he did, but we kept reminding him that he was eventually going to get well, and all of the pain and waiting to heal was going to turn into merely a bad memory.

If only I could live what I preached. I remember driving to town one day when I began to feel angry and defeated. I had just watched Zach suffer the burning pain of yet another shower and dressing change at our house, and it killed me to see him hurting so much. It had been nearly four months of the same routine and he still wasn't healing. I was starting to wonder if he would ever heal! As I drove down the road, I began crying and pleading to God for a break-through for Zach. I needed renewed hope to deal with it all. I was headed to the mall where I went to pick up a blouse that I had ordered from one of the stores there. My eyes were swollen and red from crying and I was in no mood for putting on a happy face or making friendly conversation if I ran into anyone I knew. I just wanted to go in as quickly as possible, get my blouse, and head back home.

After making a beeline straight to the store, I remember standing at the counter where a shirt hanging on a rack nearby caught my attention. The word "Believe" was printed on its front. I finished paying and took off down the mall to go back to my car, passing by a display of women's handbags. There, in the foyer of the mall as I walked by, was a purse with sparkling jewels across its front spelling out "Through God all things are possible." I stared at it for a moment as I walked onward to the mall exit, thinking that it was interesting that two times, one right after the other, inspiring messages caught my eye, practically jumping out at me. "Was this God already working to lift me up?" I thought to myself. "It's hard to imagine that He'd work that quickly." But then, my negative attitude caused me to doubt: "No, these things were just my wishful thinking." I dismissed the idea, got into my car, still feeling distraught, and turned on my radio for distraction when the words of a song playing at that moment commanded my attention. As I listened, my heart began to open. It was as if the song was playing especially for me. The cheerful lyrics to the Andy Grammer song told me that this is "just a journey—I can drop my worries." He reminded me that it's hard sometimes, but to remember to keep my head up—I could "let my hair down," because "...only rainbows (come) after rain, and the sun will always come 'round again."

My eyes welled up with tears. The song spoke straight to my heart. It took three attempts to make me see, but I finally got the message. I knew and felt that God was again letting me know everything was going to be okay. He was telling me not to give up or to have doubt. He hadn't deserted us. I immediately felt a weight lift off of me, and my faith and mood were restored.

I realize that not everyone will believe that God speaks to us through these subtle messages that I believe He uses. I'm sure that many would say I'm twisting things to make them into whatever I want them to be. They have a right to their opinion, but I think that if people close their minds to the opportunities to tune in to what God or the Universe is trying to tell them, they are going to miss out on important messages that could make great differences in their lives.

I believe that God uses anything around us to get our attention and send us messages. He does it every day, but either our minds are closed, we are too busy, or we're not quieting our minds so that we can hear these messages. When you start paying attention to the small details, you learn that there is no such thing as coincidence, and you begin to know that God, and even your loved ones who have passed on, are really not so far away as one might imagine they are.

I watch Joyce Meyers on TV, a renowned Christian speaker from St. Louis, who says, "Sometimes you just know, that you know, that you know, when you feel God speaking to you." Well, it's like that for me. I don't have to prove it to anyone—I just know. That time I turned on the radio, the message came in a way that lifted my spirits and spoke right to my heart, saying "Relax...I've got this!" And how amazing that rainbows were referenced again: "...only rainbows after rain, the sun will always come again."

Zach's healing did eventually get better. Once Jodi and Zach followed up on something that we all had remembered reading about, back at Barnes Hospital, things did begin to finally turn around.

There were posters on walls in the hospital that we saw many times as we would walk down the halls that advertised the use of hyperbaric oxygen therapy. The posters said that HBOT was used for wounds that were hard to heal. We had wondered why nobody had mentioned this or offered it as an option when Zach wasn't making progress with his wounds. Whenever we'd ask the doctors, they didn't seem to know much about it or act very fired up about looking into it. So, Jodi took it upon herself to do some research.

She found a clinic in Hutchinson that offered HBOT and dug right in to getting Zach set up with an appointment. The wound doctor there looked at Zach and believed HBOT was possibly a good method to try, but it was expensive and required authorization from insurance before it could be considered. He felt confident that he could heal Zach with alternative methods that he wanted to try first but had no luck, so he began the process of hyperbaric therapy. That was exciting but very short-lived because in order for the hyperbaric treatments to be successful, Zach needed to receive them on consecutive days every week, and the clinic did not have appointment times available for him to do that. Jodi and Zach became frustrated and set out to find another clinic offering HBOT. Fortunately, they soon found a place in Newton, Kansas, that was recommended to them by certain followers of Zach's Facebook page. The Newton clinic jumped right on the ball to get authorization for use of the hyperbaric oxygen therapy for Zach. It took some time, but Zach's insurance allowed a certain number of treatments, and therapy began.

HBOT was like something right out of a space age movie. Zach was made to lie flat on his back on a table where he was slowly inserted into a completely enclosed, clear chamber. The pressure inside the chamber was slowly increased, causing his lungs to gather up to three times more oxygen than would be possible for him to breathe at normal air pressure.

Body tissues need an adequate supply of oxygen to function, so when tissue is as injured as Zach's was, it can require more oxygen to heal. Hyperbaric oxygen therapy increases the amount of oxygen dissolved in the blood, which can improve oxygen delivery for vital tissue function to help fight infection.

Signs began to show after a few treatments that the method was working for Zach! The process was even relaxing for him (although Zach felt somewhat uneasy when information was disclosed to him that the chamber was considered highly flammable and could ignite from something as small as a spark of static electricity—the reason why he had to wear a grounding wire before entering the chamber). The only side effect was a bit of ear pressure which caused a popping sensation, something like when you travel to higher elevations or dive into deep water. The whole procedure was simple for Zach as he laid on his back and watched tv from inside the tube.

Jodi, on the other hand, didn't have things quite so simple. She was Zach's driver for the forty-five-minute trip to Newton, four times a week, carting Brynlee along and chasing her around the clinic for the two hours each time that Zach laid in the tube. The staff at the clinic became attached to our little monkey and gifted her with stickers and even toys from time to time. They enjoyed spending time with her and were entertained by her presence.

Just as it had been since the beginning of Zach's accident, schedules continued to be nonexistent for Brynlee. Naptime and meals were frequently on the go, but she adapted well. After eight months of irregularity, she had gotten used to being away from home and on the run to appointments. It was fortunate that Jodi had quit her job at the bank to stay home with Brynlee when she was born. There would have been no way to take care of all she needed to do and maintain a job outside the home.

From the end of June until nearly the end of September, Zach went through 50 hyperbaric treatments at the Newton wound clinic. His insurance company only approved a few in the beginning, but the clinic convinced them that Zach's wounds were making real progress as a result of the treatments but would need more to accomplish complete healing. Thank goodness somebody in the insurance company had the foresight to approve additional treatments! Slowly but surely, the skin on his leg, back, and chest healed! His head wound took longer but was much improved. For the first time in months, Zach was free of the pain that had plagued him for so long! No more bandages on his body. No more tortuous showers or dressing changes. No more pain-wracked nights, greasy ointments, or trips to the ER for infections. He was finally healed! Now he would begin the process of getting his left leg fitted for a prosthetic so he could rise out of that wheelchair and walk again!

There was so much to be thankful for—the compassionate, caring staff at the wound clinic who went beyond their duties to show kindness to Zach, Jodi and Brynlee; the insurance company that allowed and covered extra HBOT treatments; and our community for their fund raisers which helped cover the cost of traveling to and from the clinic. How fortunate we were! We had prayed for God to put the right people in Zach's path, and He came through again!

The day that Zach met Steve Peeples, a prosthetist in Wichita, was the day that Zach found another one of those "right people." A follower of Zach on Facebook, whose dad was an amputee, read that Zach was having problems with his right prosthetic leg and highly recommended Steve, who had been extremely helpful in getting his dad up and walking. With Steve's help, Zach once again moved forward in attaining the goals of his life.

Zach had been enduring discomfort with his right leg since the day he first received a prosthetic, putting up with it because he thought that was just the way a prosthetic was supposed to feel, but his first appointment with Steve made him realize what a difference a good prosthetist can make in an amputee's life. Steve took one look at Zach's right leg and saw that it was fitted wrong to the extent that it potentially could cause damage to the leg. Steve made an assessment, cast him for a new socket (the part of the prosthetic that holds it on to the leg), and created a new and improved leg that fit Zach so much better. The change made a world of difference and was a great relief.

Zach was thankful to have the right leg feeling and functioning better and was impatient to start the process to get his left leg. Steve and Zach had first met in May, which was before the hyperbaric treatments and also before Steve could do anything for Zach's left leg until it was healed enough to withstand the pressure of a tight-fitting socket. But Steve gave Zach hope and goals to look forward to.

After Zach had been to Wichita for his prosthetic appointment, he stopped by our farm office where I was working. I still remember what he said as he visited with me. He sounded a little uncertain but had hope in his voice when he told me, "Steve said he's going to get me back to doing everything I was able to do before my accident. He talked like he really thinks he can do it. He's worked with a lot of amputees and said he'll get me back to hunting and farming and anything else I want to do." I could tell that Zach wanted to believe it so badly, but that he was afraid to get his hopes up too high. I wasn't sure what to expect either. We didn't know anyone who was an amputee and it was all so unfamiliar to us.

I wanted to stay positive and believe that good things were around the bend. "Well, that sounds exciting!" I replied. "The way he talks, I'm sure he knows what he's doing. I'm anxious to see what he can do with you."

"Yeah, I wish my left leg would heal up so I can get fitted." Zach paused a moment and then added, "Steve says he's going to work with the insurance company to try to get me a microprocessor knee. He said that's definitely what I'll need to be able to farm and do all the things I want to do, but it's really expensive and insurance may not cover it."

I was somewhat familiar with what a microprocessor knee was because of all the research Zach had done and shared with us. In general, there are two kinds of prosthetic knees: microprocessor and mechanical. Mechanical knees use a hinge to replace the knee joint. Zach's insurance was willing to pay for that type of knee.

The microprocessor knee is much more complex. The one that Steve was recommending for Zach was called the Ottobock X3 and was considered one of the most technologically advanced microprocessor prosthetic legs available. The technology was designed by the military after Operation Desert Storm to help military men and women return to service. The knee can sense in real time the resistance Zach would need to support himself while walking the terrain on the farm. If Zach tripped on a clump of grass or dirt in the field, the knee's sensors would activate a stumble recovery mode which would help prevent him from falling. Prevention from falls was a critical necessity in Zach's case. If the left side prosthetic gave way, he would fall on his delicate left arm and shoulder, which might damage everything that had been so complicated to repair.

The Ottobock X3 was Zach's best chance to return to work on the farm and provide for his family, the closest replacement to a natural knee that existed. The sad thing was that Zach's insurance would only commit to pay for two percent of the six-figure cost because it considered the microprocessor knee to be a luxury. Their refusal to fund the Ottobock X3 was extremely frustrating for Steve and Zach—even the most advanced prosthetic is not as good as a human's natural knee, and to call it a luxury was adding insult to injury. The Ottobock X3 would be such an asset to Zach's active way of life. Zach didn't want to rely on disability payments. He didn't want to change his career. He wanted to farm, and he was determined to do whatever he had to do to get back to his farming operation.

Our generous community offered several times to raise more money to buy Zach the Ottobock X3, but Zach adamantly refused the offer. They had already done so much to help with so many expenses, and he was not comfortable with accepting more. Besides, it was going to be an ongoing expense throughout his life because the life span of a microprocessor knee is approximately seven to ten years. After that long, it most likely would be worn out or need to be rebuilt. No, the community fundraiser was a very generous offer, but Zach wanted a better way to take care of his future mobility. He was determined to prove to his insurance company that he needed the microprocessor prosthetic to be able to work on the farm and make an independent living—that the Ottobock X3 was a necessity, not a luxury.

22

WALKING ON

I was caught completely by surprise one day in August when a friend approached me and said, "I was so excited to see Zach walking today!"

"What?" I asked, bewildered.

"Haven't you seen Jodi's video on Facebook today? It shows Zach walking!" I could hear delight in my friend's voice. I could tell she was enjoying getting to be the one to share the news with me. I quickly grabbed my phone and began searching to find Jodi's post. I knew Zach was at the prosthetic clinic, but I didn't realize that it was the day he would get his left leg and would walk!

Sure enough, there it was, a video that Jodi had posted of Zach up on two legs! Holding the phone in my hand, I watched Zach shakily taking his first steps. He was between two parallel hand bars, holding on to steady himself. My heart pounded as my eyes focused intently on the screen; I didn't want to miss a single detail. I was so happy—inside I was shrieking with joy! We had dreamed of this day for so long and it was finally happening! He was walking again!

Channel 12 news was on top of the moment again. They caught word that Zach was taking his first steps at his prosthetic appointment and set out to do a follow-up story at Peeples' Clinic. That evening, Chris and I excitedly witnessed the extensive TV coverage that showed Steve coaching Zach through the process of walking on prosthetics. We could see the concentration on Zach's face as he took slow steps, one after the other, endeavoring to follow Steve's directions. Afterward, Steve congratulated Zach on his efforts and then, grinning enthusiastically, high-fived him. Zach had caught on so quickly! In the TV interview, Steve commented that Zach was already accomplishing on his first tries what took most amputees several weeks to learn. After allowing Zach to get a good feel for balance with the parallel bars, Steve had Zach walk up and down a hallway with just the use of a cane. The Channel 12 news cameras followed behind, filming Jodi and Zach walking slowly side by side with their arms around each other and little Brynlee running up to grab Jodi's hand so that she could be a part of the procession. The scene almost seemed too good to be true. Zach was walking! Chris and I watched it over again and again on our DVR that evening.

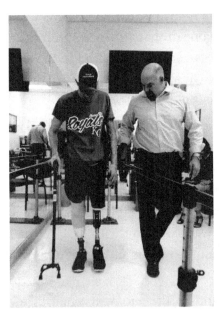 

Photos by Lindsey Bauman, The Hutchinson News.

Even though Peeples' clinic was an hour drive away, making the trip there was worth it for Zach. He needed his prosthetics tweaked for fit and function on a regular basis, and he was also getting instructions from Steve for improving his gait, learning how to get up and down from the floor, and practicing going up and down stairs. Zach's enthusiasm for the commute and the workout ran high. Each time Zach made the trip, Steve was excited and pumped to work with him. Steve wasn't only a prosthetist—he was Zach's coach and a cheerleader as well. Steve also worked with a man who became another great motivator for Zach—Matt Amos, the director of patient relations at Peeples'. Matt, an athletically built Marine who did three tours of duty in Iraq and Afghanistan, was a double amputee as well. He lost his legs in an IED explosion. His strength, determination, and positive attitude were all attributes that Zach highly respected. Zach also found it helpful to have someone he could relate to, someone who had experienced firsthand the struggle of daily living with prosthetics. Through the inspiration of both Steve and Matt, Zach made enormous strides with his physical achievements and his confidence. He was fortunate to find these strong, caring men who have a passion for helping amputees get their lives back. Their connection was so strong that often when Zach went for his appointments, the three of them would visit way past closing time. They talked about hunting and their love of the outdoors, which empowered Zach more than ever to master his disabilities and motivated him to work even harder.

In September, not quite a year from the anniversary of Zach's accident, our family gathered to witness something we had feared would never happen again. It was a cloudy evening and the sun was about to set. The corn harvest was in progress. Chris called to tell me that Zach was planning to drive a combine, and he knew that I would want to be there.

I dropped what I was doing, jumped in my car, and headed the short distance to the field located across the road from the farm. There were several people, most of them family, standing in a group, including Brynlee and her cousin Liam, who were running around together and playing in the dirt. Others in the crowd were our good friend Jim, who farms nearby; Les, our shop/farm employee; and a camera crew from the Salina Journal, who was covering the story.

I parked my car along the edge of the field and ran out to where everyone was gathered. They were all excited to watch Zach take the next step in his road to recovery—proving to himself that he was capable of driving a combine again.

Dressed in shorts and resembling the bionic man because of his titanium legs, Zach carefully made his way through the loosely tilled soil, Chris by his side, toward the large red combine parked in the field with its diesel engine idling. The two of them approached the ladder.

Each of us out there in the field stood watching intently, practically holding our breaths as we saw Zach climb each rung higher and higher. Considering that his right hand was still not very strong, his left hand had no ability to grip or feel, and he had just learned to walk on prosthetics, we were awestruck to see him accomplishing this effort—it was surreal to watch!

Chris closely followed his son up each step, spotting from behind, ready to catch him if he were to falter or fall. When he reached the cab, I could sense a collective sigh of relief. Zach opened the cab door and slipped inside, then sat down in the operator's chair. Chris positioned himself in the passenger seat next to Zach, then pulled the heavy glass door shut. Zach placed one hand on the steering wheel and the other on the control knobs. The engine roared as he opened the throttle, and off they went. As they approached the corn rows, Zach pressed the control that lowered the massive header to the ground, and the giant machine gobbled up the standing stalks of corn. Zach was operating the combine as if he had never missed a day! I don't think there was a dry eye in the field that evening as we stood silently, absorbed in the moment. Even Brynlee and Liam paused from kicking the dirt to watch the combine growl off in the distance.

I watched the photojournalist snap several shots and then my attention shifted to another picturesque sight—the silhouette of Les standing alone against the setting sun, smoke curling from the cigarette in his hand. He was watching the combine like the rest of us, but a powerful feeling came over me while I observed the scene in front of me. Because Les was the one who saved Zach's life, I felt like seeing him standing out there at that moment watching Zach reclaim his life, was like seeing a guardian angel watching over Zach.

Our friend Jim wanted to ride a round with Zach, and then I took my turn. I was so happy to be sitting next to him, watching him drive just as he had done hundreds of times before. Although his thin left arm still had skin with the texture of cheesecloth due to the grafts, I couldn't stop thinking how blessed he was to have that arm and hand to steer the wheel—he was so close to losing them. I recalled how Dr. Moore said that his left arm would only lift from the elbow and that there would be no working muscle in the shoulder, yet here he was, using the strength of his shoulder to allow his arm to steer the combine.

"Does this make your shoulder hurt?" I asked.

"No", he replied. "I can tell that the muscle in my arm will get tired pretty fast, but it doesn't hurt. My back is what bothers me some."

"You'll probably have to just a do little at a time so you don't strain it," I said, giving voice to a mother's concern.

Zach was focusing on the header and the rows of grain ahead of him, paying close attention to the position of the combine relative to the stalks of corn. When he turned the giant machine at the end of the row to head back in the opposite direction, rain sprinkles dotted the windows of the cab. Zach looked up and pointed his finger to something that he wanted me to see. Looking for what had caught his attention, I glanced at the cloudy sky and saw a streak of radiant color shimmering in the distance. The partial rainbow sparked an immediate sense of awe and reverence in my soul, and I smiled knowing that God was reminding me yet again that He was the supreme architect of Zach's recovery.

Zach didn't know the significance of the rainbow and what it meant to me. I wanted to tell him right then at that moment but decided to wait until a later time. When we reached the end of the row, I climbed out of the combine and let Zach return to the field where he continued to cut corn for nearly an hour, using the good sense to quit while he was ahead. His goal had been accomplished—he had proven to himself what he could do. He parked the combine and let his brother Matthew assist him in getting down the ladder. I pulled out my camera and took photos of Matt's upward stretched arms reaching for Zach as he stepped backwards down each step. As Zach tenuously navigated the ladder, Matthew kept ahold of Zach's waist and assisted him in getting back to the ground. He had his brother's back—a very moving moment.

Fall harvest ended. A full year had passed since Zach's accident, and winter was approaching with the usual routine of machinery repair and maintenance. Staying in the house drove Zach crazy—he felt useless when he knew there was so much work to do, so he made a point to go out in the shop every day and work at whatever he could manage. Even though he wasn't always successful, he tried hard to use the wrenches and other tools, but most required more strength than he had in his hands. He quickly found out that the tight places inside and under the equipment were a challenge to maneuver with prosthetics, but his determination made him keep trying.

Chris's heart ached the times that he sensed Zach's frustration for failed attempts of working on equipment, and had to ask for help. Even little tasks required so much more effort from him than they used to. Chris reassured Zach that things might take more time, but that it was okay—there was no hurry, and the fact that Zach was even able to do what he could do was more than enough.

Chris and I were so pleased that Zach never quit trying. He was determined to function the way he used to and would accept nothing less. Knowing that he would have surgery in the future to install new tendons which would allow him a better grip and more strength were motivation, giving him hope and incentive to keep pushing. He also knew that it probably was just a matter of time before the nerves in his hands would grow back, and that would certainly make a world of difference in his hand motor skills.

In mid-November, Dr. Moore initiated the process of repairing Zach's left hand. Nine months had gone by since he'd last been to St. Louis, so it was a great pleasure for Zach and Jodi to see Dr. Moore and her medical team after so much time had passed. When Zach walked into their office, faces lit up. Zach looked like a whole new man. Standing tall and strong, he was upright and walking. He had put on weight and gained muscle, the bandages were gone, and his hair had grown back. Neither Dr. Moore nor Dr. Snyder-Warwick had ever known him as this good-looking guy standing before them. They'd only seen him frail and sick, covered in sores and bandages, weighing less than one hundred pounds, lying in bed or sitting in a wheelchair. They were so excited and amazed to see how far he'd come. It was a joyful reunion as they reminisced about the darker days and celebrated the light of his recovery and successful outcome.

Dr. Moore mentioned that she saw the YouTube video Jodi had made about Zach's first year after the accident. She said it made her cry to watch what he had gone through before he came to be her patient. She then specifically addressed the part of the video where Zach was doing pushups. Zach was aware of what she was referencing and beamed with pride, sure that Dr. Moore would be impressed with what he could do with his rebuilt shoulder, but he didn't get the reaction he expected. Instead, Dr. Moore reprimanded him, explaining that he would not gain much muscle and strength from that activity, but instead would wear his shoulder out faster. She told him that it was not a good idea for him to continue doing pushups. That was disappointing news to Zach. He didn't feel any strain or pain in his efforts to strengthen his shoulder. Doing pushups gave him the mental satisfaction that his shoulder was functional and getting stronger. Dr. Moore hadn't intended to crush Zach's enthusiasm. She merely wanted him to be aware of her concerns so that he wouldn't harm himself.

Getting down to business, Dr. Moore told Zach she was having a difficult time making a decision. She couldn't decide which procedure would give Zach a hand that would best suit his needs in post recovery life. She was weighing two options and wanted his input. She explained that inserting long tendons that would enable him to flatten his hand, making transfers from one surface to another easier when his prosthetics were removed, might also mean he wouldn't be able to make a tight gripping fist. Her other thought was that using shorter tendons that allowed him to make a tighter fist might also cause his hand to cup, making it almost impossible to lay his hand flat when he'd need to transfer himself. Dr. Moore then expressed another concern that could be a threat. She explained that the cadaver tendons could possibly adhere to the insides of Zach's fingers as they healed, which would inhibit him from opening and closing his hand. Natural tendons exist within sheaths, which are tunnel-like spaces that allow the tendons to slide back and forth. Zach no longer possessed these sheaths—his had been burned away.

After visiting with Zach, discussions with her colleagues, and much contemplation, Dr. Moore decided to put off installing the tendons and instead came up with a plan that she felt would hopefully have a better outcome. She explained that she could install silicone rods through his hand, to the end of each finger, to create passageways (sheaths) for the tendons. The rods would also blaze paths through the scar tissue making it easier for cadaver tendons to be inserted. That was the plan Dr. Moore felt most confident with. Zach agreed and surgery was conducted to insert a rod into each of Zach's four fingers. The tendon surgery would take place later down the road.

It was a good thing for Zach that he didn't have much feeling in his fingers, because after the surgery was done to install the rods, his hand would have given him a lot of pain if he did. It turned my stomach to see that each finger had a zig zag pattern of stitched incisions down its entire length where Dr. Moore fileted the skin open. Zach would have to wait several months for complete healing before the rods could be removed and replaced with the cadaver tendons. That meant he would have to keep his hand extra clean to prevent infection, so getting it dirty in the shop was not a risk worth taking.

As careful as Zach tried to be, he was not ultimately successful in keeping infection out. Three months went by with only one more week to wait until the rods would be removed when redness and swelling showed up in his finger and thumb. Zach and Jodi went to the emergency room in Salina, which led to a call to Dr. Moore in St. Louis. The Salina doctor gave Zach the startling news that Dr. Moore insisted they make a fast trip to St. Louis—not the next day, but right that moment!

Jodi sent out a request for prayers as the two of them hit the road and traveled to St. Louis. They checked in for the night and surgery was performed the following morning. A rod had to be pulled out of the infected finger. The doctors didn't know if the tunnel it had created would stay open until the rest of the rods healed, but the prognosis was doubtful. This was tragic news for Zach as it would set back his tendon surgery and even possibly change the overall outcome. At least it was only one finger. The other three looked healthy. He had that to be thankful for.

The infectious disease doctor remembered Zach well because of how sick he was when he first came to St. Louis. After examining the hand, he told Jodi that Zach needed to be put on a high-powered antibiotic for at least a week. After monitoring him for seventy-two hours, the doctor sent him home, but before Zach was released, Jodi had to be taught how to administer the antibiotics through a pic line.

By April, Zach was getting close to the projected window when the remaining rods would be removed, but unfortunately another infection showed its ugly head and another rod had to be removed ahead of schedule. With only two rods left in his hand, Zach grew fearful that Dr. Moore might not be able to engineer a complete use of his hand because of the complications. She put him back on high-powered antibiotics for two weeks and told him that if he stayed infection free, she would perform the tendon surgery the next month. But would the tendons be able to do their job without the proper tunnel space provided? Could she insert them successfully? At that point, there was no guarantee.

Dr. Moore was disappointed that she was forced to pull the second rod out early. "Things had looked beautiful on the inside of his finger," she told us. On the brighter side, his other hand, the right one, had healed nicely. The nerves had grown back and he could make a tight fist again. Since he was right-handed, that was a gift.

We had wished for another gift we so wanted to have happen—the good news from Zach's insurance company that they would cover the expense of a microprocessor knee. But In spite of Zach's logical request they refused, even with the prodding of an attorney who heard about Zach's story through a magazine article and offered to help, pro-bono. The insurance company granted Zach a mechanical knee and that was the most they would do. But Steve, Zach's prosthetist, came through for Zach in the long run. One of his patients, a veteran, had a microprocessor knee that he no longer needed because he had updated to a newer version. He graciously offered to loan his outdated knee to any patient whom Steve felt could use it, and Zach was the one Steve chose.

The microprocessor knee changed everything for Zach. His mobility improved so much that he became like a kid with a new toy. There was no stopping him after acquiring that knee. His confidence bloomed and so did his disposition. He was so happy that he literally had a skip in his step. Jodi posted videos of him racing Brynlee in the shop, doing pullups, pushups (yes, he still did pushups), hunting, driving his four-wheeler fast down the road, and even jumping on Brynlee's trampoline! He was back again—back to the kid-like, playful Zach we all knew and loved.

23

BLINDED BY THE LIMELIGHT

Zach's story was such an inspiration to so many. People on Facebook and everywhere we went were constantly telling us that. He was sought out again and again by organizations to speak of his miraculous journey and to share the story of his experience. Newspaper and magazine journalists wrote numerous articles on him and Jodi, including the popular *Guideposts Magazine*. Television news stations followed up all along the way. Our family was even contacted by the evangelical television show, *The 700 Club*, and Zach's story ended up being one of the show's most popular episodes that year. Zach and Jodi had become faces that people from all over recognized.

I understood their story's appeal and their popularity with the public, but the constant requests for so many personal appearances and speaking engagements added tremendous stress to Zach and Jodi's life. While they both felt humbled and honored to be asked, public speaking was not something that either one of them felt ready for or even called to do at that time in their lives.

The two of them had just been through an excruciating struggle to realign their future to a new normal. What they most wanted was to move forward and put the pain they had endured in the past so they could focus on rebuilding their lives together.

I completely understood how the two of them felt. As much as I wanted to write this book, I had no desire to revisit the emotional roller coaster we had ridden for so long. I wanted our lives to get back to the way they had been before the accident, to keep our focus on the happy days ahead. As a family, we were just beginning to heal. Circumstances had turned around for the better, and I would have to relive painful memories if I wanted to tell our story truthfully, just as Zach and Jodi would have to revisit and keep fresh in their minds the agony of their experience if they chose to speak publicly about their journey.

The Bible tells us, "To every thing there is a season," and that events will naturally come about when the time is right. God has a way of grooming us for what He has planned. If it is His will to use someone, things will eventually lead them to the way. Every journey starts with a single step. Although Zach was reluctant to speak to large groups of adults, he was willing to help however he could on a much smaller and more personal scale. He felt good about, and hoped he could make a difference, when he was asked by a local organization to talk to grade school students about farm safety.

Sometime after that he felt compelled to go to Via Christi hospital in Wichita to visit a twenty-one-year-old burn victim who occupied the very room that Zach laid in when he was hurt. The young man was in serious condition and was undergoing surgical procedures and skin grafts. His mother found comfort in talking to Zach and in reading Jodi's texts that reassured her there would be an end to her son's painful ordeal.

That trip to Wichita was the start of several one-on-one visits that Zach made when he thought he could help people who had disrupted lives. Another young patient in Wichita was so upset after he lost his leg in an accident, that his mother sought out Zach in hopes that he could bring her son out of his depression. Zach's visit did help. Her son later wrote on Zach's Facebook page to express his gratitude:

> Hey man. Just wanted to share with you that when I lost my leg a couple years ago and you came to visit me at the hospital, a complete stranger at the time, and told me your story, it changed my whole perception of my situation for the better. I tell a lot of people about that day, and I still remember it often. You let me know things were going to be alright, and you gave me hope and in a situation like that, there is no greater gift. So, thank you again man, and I'm truly glad you made it.

When I read that post, the message really touched my heart. I felt so proud of my son. He had been through hell, yet it didn't change him or make him bitter. He didn't allow his misfortune to leave him weak and dependent. Instead, he was picking right up where he left off as if his circumstances were a mere bump in the road. He was even reaching out to others, instilling hope and sharing his strength along the way. Without even realizing it, Zach had become a role model for others. People admired him not only for his will to survive, but also for how he set his mind on not letting the accident define him or take over his life and keep him from doing what he desired.

In the spring of 2016, Zach was asked by his former high school counselor, Judy White, if she could use his story in her address for the local high school graduation ceremony at which she was the featured speaker. Even though it had been seven years since Zach had attended classes there, she wanted to use Zach's character as an example of how to carry on when life offers severe challenges. Mrs. White told the class of fifty-four seniors, all dressed alike in purple hats and gowns, that Zach's attitude was the epitome of the adage, "Never give up." She spoke eloquently about how Zach had weathered his personal storm, and in so doing, had become an inspiration to his community. Projecting photos from his accident and recovery on a large screen at the front of the gymnasium, Mrs. White shared the story of his determination and healing. She emphasized that Zach had looked forward, not back, when he was suffering his deepest pain. She summarized Zach's experience with her own favorite saying, "Life isn't about waiting for the storm to pass; it's about learning to dance in the rain."

Next, she read an essay that Zach had written for a college scholarship application when he was a senior in high school. I don't think I ever saw that essay back then, but after she read it, I thought to myself how ironic it was that his own words would come to mean so much in his future. He had written, "It's important to be involved in your community—to know what's happening and be willing to volunteer time for people in need."

A memory came to my mind of Zach taking our loader tractor with the scoop attached, to clean the snow from a winter storm off driveways and streets of elderly people in and around our little rural town. He loved doing that type of activity and didn't actually consider it work because it made him feel good to help someone.

Most of what he learned about helping friends and neighbors came from his dad, Chris, who has shared much of his time and resources with almost every farmer or friend he knows. There's almost nothing that Chris can't repair, and both Zach and Matt grew up in their dad's shadow learning to do the same. Sometimes I felt that Chris was *too* generous and that some whom he helped had taken advantage of him. Also, many times when recipients of his aid offered to pay him for whatever he'd done, he would say, "Don't worry about it. Maybe someday I'll need something from you." Well, that is exactly how it turned out. Giving to others came back ten-fold when his son was in need.

In her address, Mrs. White told the class, "Because that is how Zach lived, that is how his community responded when he needed help. Thousands of dollars were made available through fund raisers to help his family with expenses. His determination to get back to farming has inspired the entire community." She concluded with, "Working on the farm, shadowing his father—those experiences provided Zach with his fondest childhood memories, and now his daughter will be following him. That's the value of doing things the right way and giving back to your community."

At the end of her speech, Zach walked gracefully into the gym, Jodi by his side with Brynlee in her arms. Seeing him stroll across the gym floor on prosthetic legs was a powerful reminder of what he had been through and overcome. Mrs. White acknowledged the three of them with a formal introduction, and the audience rose in response with a thundering ovation.

Chris and I knew ahead of time that Zach was going to be mentioned in Mrs. White's speech, but we had no idea she was going to go into such detail and make his story the head topic! Tears flooded our eyes and wet our faces as we rose with the crowd, saluting the young family as the blanket of applause wrapped round them.

How did something so tragic and painful as Zach's accident turn into something so inspiring and heartwarming? It was hard to wrap my head around the fact that so much good could come from so much hurt, but more and more, circumstances revealed to us that God had his hand in all that occurred. There was just no other way to look at it.

Zach's story compelled people to provide love and support again and again. Every time we turned around, someone was doing something to contribute in one way or another. Our neighbor and good friend Jim worked long hours remodeling Zach and Jodi's house to make it more accessible for Zach's wheelchair whenever his prosthetics are removed. He widened doorways, built ramps where needed, and added a bathroom with a lower sink and large wheel-in shower. He redesigned a bedroom to include a walk-in closet that had low hanging racks so Zach could reach his clothes from the wheelchair.

A few of the other examples:

- A local Ambucs Club came out to Zach's house and built a well-designed wheelchair ramp for the backdoor, and friends gave their labor to add onto the expansion of Zach's roof to allow for a room addition.
- A poker run for motorcycle enthusiasts which concluded with another auction was arranged by friends, who with many caring individuals and businesses raised more funds for Zach. People donated and purchased a variety of items, just as they had done at the first auction held at the school.
- A 5K color run was held at the fairgrounds, and a second color run was arranged at the school where burn victims Alex and Scott (along with Sally) came to participate!
- People donated money to a Go Fund Me account and a local bank account that volunteers set up for Zach.

Another donation of pure love was given by a farmer, Tim, who lived in faraway Pennsylvania. He saw a video of Zach's story that Jodi created on YouTube and felt a connection. Tim had been burned in an accident, only not as severely. He and Zach started corresponding on Facebook about a fundraiser for Zach that was going to be facilitated through Wendy's Restaurant. Joking that 1200 miles was too far to go for a hamburger, Tim decided he would do something for Zach from home. He raised $2,000 when he sold his late wife's collection of about one-hundred handcrafted Longaberger Maplewood baskets at an auction in his hometown and gave all the money to Zach. Tim even flew out to meet Zach in person when wheat harvest came in June. He spent a few days visiting and observing our harvest crew and he continues to keep in touch.

Sometimes I can hardly believe how fortunate our family has been when I think of all the people, including complete strangers, who wanted to get involved or show they cared. God was working through them, and our entire family still feels humbled and blessed.

24

TIME HELPS HEAL THE WOUNDS

Zach had his final surgery—somewhere around number thirty in all—in June of 2016. It was time to remove the silicone rods in his hand and fingers and replace them with tendons. Up until then, he couldn't open or close his fingers to make a fist, and other than using it to support himself for balance, his hand had no function or even feeling. To me, his hand resembled that of a doll—lifeless and rubbery. In a surgery that took all day long, Dr. Moore sutured in thigh tendons from a cadaver, something she'd never utilized for hand surgery before, but she needed the tendons to be long enough to reach from his forearm to the ends of his long fingers.

After she removed the remaining rods and attached the tendons, Dr. Moore brought Zach up out of sedation just enough to see if he could open and close his hand. Still in a foggy state of consciousness, he cooperated as requested, but when he opened his hand, he popped one of the tendons loose. This is just one more example of why Dr. Moore is great at what she does. She was perceptive enough to anticipate problems and repair them before she finished surgery and closed Zach up.

Time Helps Heal the Wounds

Just like the others, the surgery was a qualified success! Our Dr. Moore is a miracle worker, and again, we felt so fortunate and blessed to have found her. Zach's body accepted the tendons with no complications. He could open and close his left hand again, and with time it got stronger and many of the nerves grew back, giving him feeling in the majority of his hand and fingers. As it turned out, his thumb was perfectly healthy on the inside once some of the scar tissue was removed in surgery, which was all he needed to make it useful again.

Electricity does such unpredictable damage to the human body. I find it odd that the end of his thumb had to be removed early on because it was burned so severely, yet according to Dr. Moore, the middle of his thumb still had its tendon and was functional. And why hadn't things happened that way to all the other fingers? Thank goodness he still had his thumb—what little there was left of it. Having a thumb makes all the difference in the world in terms of the ability to grasp. I'm also thankful that Zach inherited Chris's and my genetics towards long fingers and legs. Zach had longer appendages to work with even after parts of them were destroyed or removed.

Something I thought rather funny and ironic happened a few months after Zach's final surgery. Jodi received a message from Dr. Moore, who told Jodi she had viewed Jodi's online videos of Zach getting stronger. Dr. Moore observed that Zach was still using his left arm to perform activities that initially she predicted he wouldn't be able to do. Zach knew that she didn't think it was a good idea for him to do pushups—she had made that clear—but that didn't stop him from living the way he wanted. He continued to use his arm for exercises he felt comfortable doing, and it continued to get stronger. The ironic twist is that Dr. Moore asked if Jodi would make a video of Zach doing pullups, and also pushups! She explained that she travels to conferences far and wide to speak to other surgeons about her work, and she wanted to share the incredible progress Zach had made with his shoulder, arm, and hand. I was not sure if that meant Dr. Moore had changed her mind about Zach working out that shoulder, but we knew for sure that he was far exceeding her expectations. Even now she shakes her head in disbelief each time she sees Zach and even admits that she doesn't know how or why the grafted muscle on his shoulder morphed into a working muscle.

The entire staff and medical personnel who worked with Zach are amazed with his recovery and progress. They remember him vividly because of the extensive damage to his body and know what a miracle he represents. Zach's hand still is not what it was before the accident by any measure, but after no appreciable use at all, he is thankful to have a hand that functions as well as it does. Because of God's grace and Dr. Moore's skill, Zach is fortunate to even *have* a hand! That blessing is something none of us take for granted.

Zach knows that he is blessed to have his health and the multiple functions that have been restored in his body. Often reflecting on his journey, he is quite aware of how differently his life could have turned out. In a way, one could say he is a new man—literally! Nearly every part of his body had been affected in some way or another by the electrical shock and was either healed, repaired, or replaced. The wonderful gift to everyone who knows him through the changes is that even though he's rebuilt physically, he hasn't lost the admirable character that was the basis of his being. He is still the same guy we all loved and continue to love.

While everything I've mentioned sounds wonderful—and it is—I don't want to belittle the hardships that Zach deserves credit for dealing with so gracefully. Everyday life for Zach is not easy or without complication. Most people assume that Zach's life is back to the way it was before the accident. Without meaning to sound negative or unappreciative (I think I've made myself clear how grateful I am for Zach's continued existence), the reality is that Zach is *not* back to what he was and never will be. His life has been altered in so many ways, but he's learned to let go of what he'll never do again and he has accepted his new normal. It took an incredible amount of determination and perseverance for him to get to that place. Back when he first arrived home and he had to face the reality of his circumstances, there were times he didn't think he could go on. The *emotional* anguish hurt just as much as the physical pain—especially each time he caught a glimpse of himself in the mirror. Those were the times he'd sit in his wheelchair staring at the reflection of a frail, withered man, missing most of his legs, covered in reddened sores and scars, not recognizing who was staring back. The vision caused him to break down in uncontrollable tears every time; all while fearing that his life as he knew it was over, with no future in sight. I thank God that he was able to get past those dark days.

Today he makes his life look easy and he doesn't complain, so I can understand why most people don't realize the struggles he endures on a daily basis. How many would completely comprehend the difficulty of transferring to a wheelchair from bed in the middle of the night, then maneuvering into the bathroom to transfer to a toilet seat, and finally reversing the process to return to bed? What about trying to shower with no legs? The general population doesn't know that wearing prosthetic legs is more uncomfortable than walking in stiff dress shoes, or that every time Zach's weight fluctuates or even changes because of fluid retention, he has to make an appointment with a prosthetist who is an hour away to have new sockets made and fitted. The summer heat makes him miserable. Every hour or so he's frustrated that he has to stop what he's doing, to pour a pocket of sweat from the rubber socket because his leg will slip off if he neglects to do so. When the socket gets slippery, he has to take the leg off to carefully clean and sanitize the socket, then thoroughly dry it out before putting it back on. The process is necessary to keep him from getting fungus and infections, and even with the most fastidious procedures, sores still pop up on his leg from time to time.

Then there are the excruciating phantom pains that come without warning and hurt so badly that they take Zach's breath away. Phantom pains are such a mystery. It just doesn't make sense how a person can experience painful sensations in a limb that is no longer there, but phantom pain is very real and also quite common in amputees.

What hurts Chris and me to the core is when an unexpected activity comes up for Zach, and he and the rest of us again realize that he can no longer physically participate in that activity. Nobody has ever heard Zach whine or complain when this happens, but his face subconsciously reveals the disappointment. This is when I immensely admire the mature, humble man he has become. His strength and humility are exceptional. It hasn't been easy, but Zach has adapted. I firmly hold to the belief that because of his determination and character, those occasions that now look like limitations will someday become challenges that he will take on and overcome.

When I think of how Zach has handled the changes in his life, I actually think he adapted quicker to his situation than his dad did. Chris had a hard time accepting Zach's new normal. Seeing his son go through the ordeals and trials practically broke Chris. It left a deep wound in his heart that was slow to heal.

From the perspective of hindsight, I see that Chris and I would have undoubtedly benefited from grief counseling in that period of time when we felt disconnected from one another. I didn't understand then, but I eventually figured out that Chris's pain caused him to harbor a huge amount of anger inside. Because of that burning frustration, he wasn't acting like his usual self, so I didn't recognize him as the man I knew in the happy years of our marriage. I saw his harsh behavior as personal attacks—misplaced blame which pushed me further and further away. It took a lot of prayer and insight to overcome such painful emotions, but eventually God showed me how to look at Chris with compassion instead of judgment. When I began to view Chris's behavior with understanding eyes, our strained relationship started to turn around. It didn't happen overnight and it definitely wasn't easy. There were times when I felt he was not deserving of the kindness and patience that I tried to make myself display. Sometimes I had to go punch a pillow when I really just wanted to lash out at his unappreciative demeanor.

In retrospect, the situation makes more sense to me now. Chris has suffered several tragic losses in his life, and when Zach's accident topped the list, I think he simply broke apart. He dealt with his pain in a reckless way, justifying his actions because he felt unfairly impinged upon. He felt he had been dealt more than his justifiable share of loss and tragedy. That made him angry. I know that's why he turned to alcohol when his emotions were still so raw. I thank God that my prayers were answered and he eventually got a handle on the way he dealt with his pain.

Trying to overcome that deep hurt was a process that took Chris a lot of time. Dealing daily with the reminders undermined the healing for Chris. Something as simple as people commenting on how Zach was doing would test his resolve. When people would say to him, "It's so good to see that Zach is back to normal again," he knew they meant well and were expressing their joy over seeing Zach return to the farm, but inside, those comments triggered negative feelings for Chris. In his eyes, Zach's life was not normal—it was harder than it had ever been—and certainly not the way it used to be. Because Chris worked with Zach daily, he saw the struggles Zach wrestled with that other people didn't. Chris was grieving for Zach, not as much because he missed the capable young man Zach used to be, but because he knew that *Zach* missed the guy he would never be again.

Zach's athletic coordination and strength before the accident allowed him to shimmy up pivot irrigation towers where he'd straddle the long steel pipes to do repairs. He would pick up large rocks and lug them out of the fields or crawl into tight places on his hands and knees. Because we sometimes irrigate out of the river, Zach would wade into the swirling water to pull out the pumps when the river flooded, and he would drag heavy limbs away from the intake pipes. The list goes on and on of the many tasks that required his strength and agility. Farming is such a physical occupation, and Zach loved that aspect of it. He was always the first to dive right in to a tough and/or dirty job. After the accident while he was regaining his mobility, Chris and he encountered almost daily yet another job that reminded them of Zach's new limitations. Chris felt a stab in his heart each time he'd see Zach want to help but instead step aside and regretfully allow someone else to take over the task for him.

I eventually understood where Chris was coming from and why it was harder for him to get used to the new normal, but my perspective on Zach's life was completely different than Chris's. To me, Zach died—I thought I had lost him forever—but then God returned him! Not only did God spare Zach's life, but He gave Zach back to us to love and live with, hopefully for years to come. And Zach could have ended up in such worse shape both physically and mentally, but now he is thriving again in spite of his struggles. He has learned to adjust his life around his limitations. Above all else, he is happy. For my own part, I just feel so full of gratitude that there is no room in my heart for disappointment. Zach's scars are thankful reminders of God's great mercy and when I look at Zach today, I don't see a man with handicaps—I see a warrior!

Time Helps Heal the Wounds

I wanted to help Chris focus on the positive side of Zach's situation and feel the same joy in his heart that I felt. This was a role reversal, because he is usually the positive one between the two of us. During those trying times when he would vent his sorrows I listened, and then I would point out the good and remind him how much we are blessed. He already knew that in his heart, but his mind still wept. I reminded him that there are so many parents in the world who have lost children and would give anything to have them back, even for one last time to say goodbye. We are so blessed that we aren't in that position. Chris would protest that he does feel blessed and is of course grateful for Zach's life, but he can't help it—he still is sad. He doesn't mean to come across any different, but humans process grief in different ways. What we were going through *was* grief. We lost our son as he was and we hurt for him, even more than for ourselves. It's a painful process that hopefully improves with time.

Time has been a benefactor in Jodi's healing as well. She went through a tremendous amount of stress that tested her strength, but she endured the horror of uncertainty and fought back one day at a time. It's been a big adjustment for her to give up some of what Zach and she used to do, but I never hear her complain. She is so grateful to God for sparing her husband's life—that gift of grace outweighs the changes and sacrifices she has had to deal with. She's proven her love for Zach and has been an inspiration to her peers—she is what a loving, supportive wife looks like. To this day I can't listen to Rachel Platten's *Fight Song* without thinking of Jodi. It was popular when Zach was fighting for his life in Wichita. I think of Jodi whenever I hear that song because it reminds me that she was a fighter who never gave up on Zach. In all the turmoil of the storm she and Zach went through, sometimes she wanted to scream and fall apart, but her strong will and faith held her up and kept her believing that Zach was going to fully recover and she wasn't going to let anyone tell her differently. That doesn't mean she was never fearful—she just chose to focus on the positive.

Matthew is another in our family who has had to make adjustments after Zach's accident. He has had to take on more of the farm work that requires elbow grease in our family operation. He and Zach had been doing farm duties together ever since they were old enough to be helpful, but that's changed somewhat. Every now and then when Matt's grunting and sweating over something that's labor intensive, while Zach's standing by to assist the best that he can, Matt likes to tease him about how he's not doing his fair share to pitch in. Zach knows it's all in fun and they both continue to enjoy working together. Back when we thought we were going to lose Zach, Matt posted a message on Facebook. He said, "If I'm given one miracle in my lifetime, now is when I want to use it. My baby brother needs it." His miracle was answered—"Hallelujah!"

Wheat harvest 2016 began just a couple of weeks after Zach's hand surgery. It was like God had hit the reset button and life on the farm was back in high gear, just like the way it had been before the accident. The combines were in full swing, gobbling up the golden wheat, and inside one of them was Zach. He was sitting proudly in the driver's seat, operating the large machine just as he had done so many times in harvests past. Healed and strong, he managed the complex piece of machinery for nearly two weeks solid, from morning until late at night, never missing a day. I could not look at him without knowing that he was the embodiment of answered prayers! There simply are no words to describe how full my heart felt to see Zach out there doing what he loved and what he had worked so incredibly hard to get back to. Our family all felt that joy. Even people we didn't know felt that joy. It seemed that we couldn't go anywhere without having somebody acknowledge how happy they were to see Zach back in the saddle again.

With Zach able to return to work, his and Jodi's future looked bright again, and the two of them were ready to expand their family. Brynlee had already turned three years old, and before the accident, a three-year span was the amount of time they had hoped to have between children.

Sadly, Jodi miscarried while trying for child number two. The first miscarriage was followed by a second. Jodi suffered a deepening depression. She had been so excited to be expecting again but then plunged into the depths of despair with each loss. It was hard for me to see her so upset. It crossed my mind that maybe she was losing the pregnancies because something was not right with Zach's health. After all, his body had been through tremendous trauma, and he had taken so many powerful drugs for such a long period of time. I worried that those two factors might have affected his ability to conceive healthy children. Thank goodness the worries were unfounded! Jodi's doctor reassured them that Zach's health had nothing to do with the miscarriages. That was comforting news, and there was at least the fact that Jodi had been able to get pregnant, but those encouraging bits of information sure didn't do much to mend her broken heart over the losses.

Before long, fall rolled around and the two-year anniversary of Zach's accident came and went. On another beautiful, sunny October day that reminded me of that fateful day two years ago, our family was headed to a Kansas State University football game instead of the Fall harvest field. As we were driving east down the highway towards Manhattan and anticipating the excitement of game day, I was thinking about what a difference two years makes. So much had taken place, that the time seemed to pass in a blur—the aftermath of that tragic day had consumed much of our lives.

But we were finally picking up from where we left off, and joy was a part of our world again.

Normally we would be too overloaded with farm work in October to schedule time for a football game, but that particular day was special. It was an exciting day for our family because Zach and Jodi were going to be recognized as the winners of *The Farm Family of the Year* photo contest, an event sponsored by an energy, grain, and food company called CHS, North America's leading farmer-owned cooperative. The photo contest was designed as a way to help build pride in the cooperative system. CHS teamed up with Kansas State University to recognize a family whose agricultural impact affected others in a positive way, and apparently Zach and Jodi's family photo generated the most votes. Again, our community and others came through to lift us up!

Our family received a VIP experience at the K-State football game, which included game tickets and hospitality passes with box seats. Zach and Jodi were ushered out on the field between quarters of the game and introduced to thunderous applause. They shook hands with the official presenters, accepted a plaque, and best of all, were awarded a football autographed by the famous KSU coach, Bill Snyder!

K-State's mascot, Willie the Wildcat, sauntered over to greet them, making Brynlee feel a bit uneasy. She ducked behind Jodi's legs and clung on tightly, peering out at him with wide eyes, afraid he might scoop her up and run off. To her, he looked like a fun guy when he was at a distance, but up close—well, not so much. When Willie backed off, Brynlee regained her confidence and won the hearts of the crowd by waving to them. She looked like a little Miss America standing out on the field offering her tiny hand to the cheerleaders and the vivacious assemblage of students who cheered and waved back to her from the bleachers. It was quite the big day for the three of them.

Time Helps Heal the Wounds

Life is such a gift. Our family has come to appreciate that realization more and more every day we are together. We are back to chasing our tails during the busy farm seasons, but we no longer take a day or each other for granted. We know only too well how circumstances can change in a heartbeat.

Speaking of heartbeats and changes—a few months went by, and Jodi was blessed by a positive change. A sonogram confirmed that Jodi and Zach had created a new little heartbeat! The pregnancy was successful, and although it was cut short by a month for an early arrival, baby Brycen Zachary Short was born on November 9, 2017, as healthy and precious as he could be.

A son—the sixth generation to come home to the Short family farm—a rainbow baby. That was a new term to me, *rainbow baby*. I was told that it's coined as such when it's the surviving baby after a miscarriage—Aaahhh, of course! That makes perfect sence—God sent another rainbow!

EPILOGUE

Zach has come such a long way since that awful day of his accident. Many people have told us that they believe he must've been spared for some great purpose that he'll fulfill in his future. That may be, but I tend to believe that he has already fulfilled a great purpose. I believe that God used him and his tragedy to bring people together in a loving way—to strengthen their faiths by showing them how ever-present He is in our lives today. We witnessed miracles seeing Zach raised from out of the ashes and into a productive life. We all saw and felt God's grace, spirit, and love through people who supported Zach with their caring acts of love and kindness. That's the part of Zach's whole journey that never made sense to me. Horrible things happen to many people every day. I never understood what made so many people care about Zach and get involved as much as they did, especially strangers who didn't even know him! What made them want to follow his story or care enough to pray for him and support him with generous donations? When I put that question out to the public, I was given the same answer from all who replied. People told me that they were so inspired and moved by Zach's story that they became connected to it. His story restored their faith in God and humanity—it gave them hope. I can't help but think that was a God thing. As my pastor at church once said, "Generosity defines the grace within us. Grace transforms people to be more God-like every day." Maybe that was God's plan throughout this journey—to teach us to love, care and be more like Him.

NEWS AND PUBLICATIONS

Salina Journal (newspaper): 10/26/2014, 10/27/2014, 10/28/2014, 10/31/2014, 11/07/2014, 11/19/2014, 11/26/2014, 12/16/2014, 2/15/2015, 9/13/2015, 10/25/2015, 10/26/2015, 1/17/2016, 5/16/2016, 6/18/2016, 10/17/2016, 1/17/2017, 2/26/2017, 11/23/2017

Kansas Farm Bureau: Kansas Farmer Book by Scott Stebner

The Hutchinson News (newspaper): 9/06/2015, 5/07/2016

Philips Seed Magazine cover 2016

High Plains Journal cover/story 12/14/2015

The Spotlight (newspaper): 9/17/2015, 10/15/2015

Kansas Agland (newspaper): Fall 2015 /story

Guideposts Magazine cover/story June 2015

Christian Broadcasting Network: The 700 Club (TV program) 9/05/2017

KWCH Channel 12 (Wichita Kansas news station)

You Tube: Nothing Short of a Miracle #1, #2, #3 created by Jodi Short

You Tube: Say I Won't Stories: Zach Short's Story-Thrive. Don't just Survive

You Tube: Salty Roan Productions (saltyroan.com): Zach Short Farm Accident

Made in the USA
Coppell, TX
14 April 2020